THE HARMONY GUIDES

300 Crochet STITCHES

VOLUME 6

includes basic stitches, lace patterns, motifs, filet, clusters, shells, bobbles, loops

COLLINS & BROWN

First published by Lyric Books in 1986 as
The Harmony Guide to Crochet Stitches

Re-issued in 1998
by Collins & Brown Limited
London House
Great Eastern Wharf
Parkgate Road
London SW11 4NQ

ISBN 1 85585 638 7

5 7 9 8 6

British Library Cataloguing-in-Publication Data:
A catalogue record for this book
is available from the British Library.

Printed and bound in Spain

Contents

Introduction

Holding the Hook and Yarn

Everyone has their own personal way of holding the hook and controlling the yarn in crochet. Righthanders hold the hook in their right hand, usually **a** as though it were a pencil; or **b** in a firmer, overhand grip.

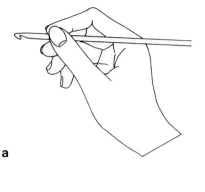

a

b

c The left hand holds the work and at the same time controls the yarn supply. If you prefer, the left hand index finger can be used to manipulate the yarn, while the middle finger holds onto the work.

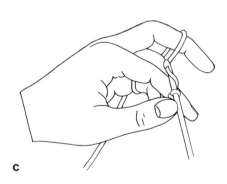

c

d To maintain the slight tension in the yarn necessary for easy, even working, it can help to arrange the yarn around the fingers of the left hand in this way.

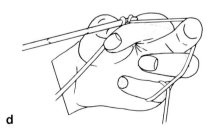

d

Hint for lefthanders: Prop the book up next to a mirror, so you can see the illustrations in 'mirror image', while still being able to read the text from the original page.

The Base Chain

Almost all crochet starts with a base (or foundation) chain. This is the equivalent of 'casting on' in knitting. The base chain is a series of chain stitches, which normally begin with a loop secured by a slip knot.

Slip Knot

a Make a loop; hook another loop through it. **b** Tighten gently and slide the knot up to the hook.

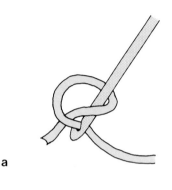

a

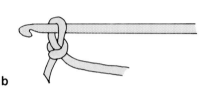

b

Chain Stitch (ch)

a Wrap the yarn over the hook in an anticlockwise direction (or hold the yarn still and manoeuvre the hook); **b** draw the yarn through to form a new loop without tightening up the previous one.

Note: Unless otherwise specified, always wrap the yarn this way round.

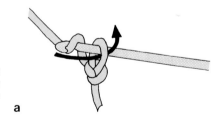

a

b

To make a length of base chain, make as many chains as required.

Hint: Keep shifting your left hand position up close to the hook every couple of stitches or so; this is easy, if you use a right hand finger tip to hold down the loop on the hook, while you do so.

To count chains correctly as you make them, do not count the initial slip loop as a chain. To count them afterwards, first make sure that they are not twisted and that you are looking at the 'front' **c**; then count back, but ignore the loop still on the hook.

Front

c

Back

Double Base Chain

Hint: You may find that a base chain of double chain is not only more flexible than one made of single chain, but also easier to make, to count afterwards and to work back into.

a Make 2 single chains; **b** insert the hook into the 2nd chain from the hook (i.e. the first chain made) and work one single crochet (see Single Crochet); **c** insert the hook into the single vertical thread which forms the lefthand side of the previous single crochet and work another single crochet; repeat this last step.

a

b

c

Slip Stitch (sl st)

a Insert the hook into the work (into the 2nd chain from the hook), wrap the yarn over the hook, draw the yarn through the work and the loop on the hook in one movement — that is one slip stitch completed; repeat this last step, **b**.

a

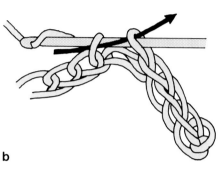

b

Single Crochet (sc)

a Insert the hook into the work (into the 2nd chain from the hook), wrap the yarn over the hook and draw the yarn through the work only, **b** wrap the yarn again and draw the yarn through both loops on the hook **c** 1 sc made.

a

b

c

Half Double Crochet (hdc)

a Wrap the yarn over the hook and insert the hook into the work (into the 3rd chain from

the hook), **b** wrap the yarn over the hook, draw through the work only and wrap the yarn again; **c** draw through all 3 loops on the hook.

a

b

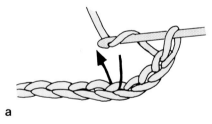

c

Double Crochet (dc)

a Wrap the yarn over the hook and insert the hook into the work (into the 4th chain from the hook); **b** wrap the yarn over the hook, draw through the work only and wrap the yarn again; **c** draw through the first 2 loops only and wrap the yarn again; **d** draw through the last 2 loops on the hook.

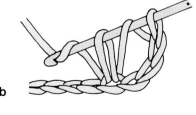

a

b

c

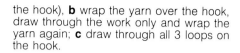

d

Treble (tr)

a Wrap the yarn over the hook twice and insert the hook into the work (into the 5th chain from the hook); **b** wrap the yarn over the hook, draw through the work only and wrap the yarn again; **c** draw through the first 2 loops only and wrap the yarn again; **d** draw through the next 2 loops only and wrap the yarn again; **e** draw through the last 2 loops on the hook.

a

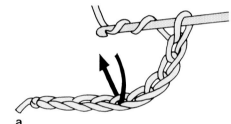

b

c

d

e

Making Crochet Fabric

Double Treble (dtr)

a Wrap the yarn over hook 3 times and insert the hook into the work (into the 6th chain from the hook); **b** wrap the yarn over the hook, draw through the work only and wrap the yarn again; **c and d** draw through the first 2 loops only and wrap the yarn again; repeat this last step twice; **e** draw through the last 2 loops on the hook.

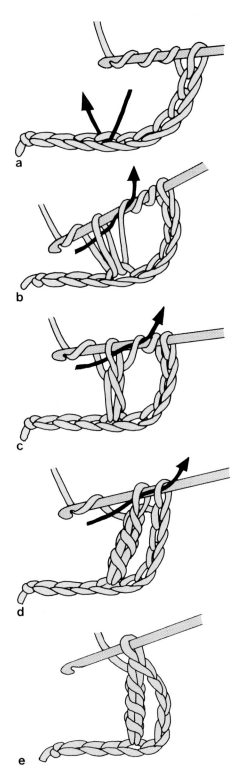

Longer Basic Stitches

Longer basic stitches — usually called Triple Treble (ttr), Quadruple Treble (quad tr),

Quintuple Treble (quin tr), etc — are made by wrapping the yarn 4, 5, 6, etc, times over the hook at the beginning and by wrapping and drawing through 2 loops more times to complete the stitch.

Making Crochet Fabric

These are the basic procedures for making crochet fabric — the things pattern instructions assume you know.

Working in rows

To work to and fro in rows make a base chain (see page 4) to begin.
Hint: It can be very frustrating to be approaching the end of a long first row only to discover that you have miscounted and there are too few chains in the base chain to complete it. Leave a generous end of yarn when making your initial slip knot; then it is simple to remove your hook temporarily from the working loop, insert it through the end of the base chain and, using the spare end of yarn, to add the necessary chains.

a The first row of the fabric is made by working across the base chain as shown in 'The Basic Stitches' (Righthanders work from right to left; lefthanders work from left to right.) Insert the hook under either one or two of the three threads, which make up each individual chain. **Hint:** Choose which you find suits you best and then be consistent.

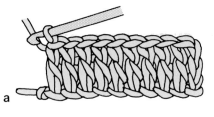

At the very beginning of the first row, in order to give the first stitch room to stand up to its proper height, one or more of the base chains is 'skipped'. These then bend and stand up alongside the stitches. Together they look like and may often 'count' as the first stitch in the row. The number of chains skipped depends upon the height of the stitch they are to match as follows: single crochet = 1 or 2 chains skipped; half double crochet = 2 chains skipped; double crochet = 3 chains skipped; treble = 4 chains skipped; double treble = 5 chains skipped. For this and other reasons you must expect to make a larger number of chains for the base chain than there are stitches required in the base row.

b At the end of each row 'turn' the work, so that another row can be worked across the top of the previous one again from right to left (lefthanders from left to right). **Hint:** It does not matter which way you turn, but it helps to be consistent.

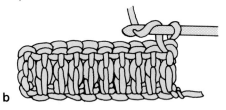

Before the new row can begin a 'turning chain' (one or more single chains) must be worked to bring the hook up to the height the row will be. The number of chains for turning depends upon the height of the stitch they are to match as follows: single crochet = 1 chain; half double crochet = 2 chains; double crochet = 3 chains; treble = 4 chains; double treble = 5 chains. **Hint:** These numbers are guidelines only. Depending on your personal technique, the type of work you are doing, the thickness of yarn and size of hook you are using, you may find from time to time a larger or smaller number of chains gives better results.

c The turning chain may also count as the first stitch in the new row. In this case skip the first stitch in the previous row, but (**d** and **e**) remember to work a stitch into the top of the previous turning chain when you reach the end of the row. If the turning chain does not count as a stitch, work into the first stitch at the beginning of the row, but not into the top of the previous turning chain at the end.

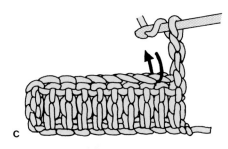

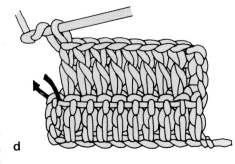

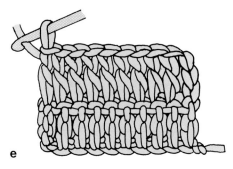

To make each stitch insert the hook under the two loops lying on top of each stitch in the previous row. (Instructions always specify if you are to insert the hook in any other place.)

Note: All the pattern instructions in this book indicate how many stitches are required in the base row, how many chains to allow for the base chain, how many chains to work for turning, whether the turning chain counts as a stitch and if the first stitch is to be skipped.

Joining in new yarn

To 'join in' new yarn, because the pattern has involved fastening off in one place and rejoining in another, or to begin an edging, insert the hook into the appropriate place, **a** loop the yarn over it, draw through and make 1 chain. (**Hint:** If you feel it would be more secure, make the first loop with a slip knot as though for starting a base chain.)

You will often need to join a new ball in the middle of the work, when the old ball runs out. Then just as you make the final 'yarn over' to complete a stitch, simply drop the old yarn, make a loop with the new one, pick this up and draw through to complete. Hold down both short ends temporarily until you have worked the next stitch. A knot or splice is unnecessary.

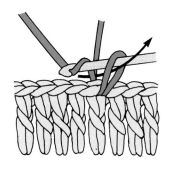

a

If you are making a solid fabric (single crochet shown here), **b** lay the new yarn in advance across the tops of the stitches ahead and work over it **c**; and, after the change, work over the end of the old yarn. This saves later 'darning in' time.

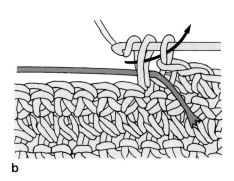

b

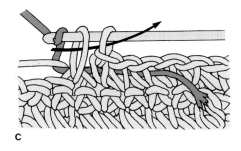

c

Fastening off

To fasten off the working yarn permanently, make one chain, cut the yarn about 5cm away (**Hint:** Longer if you need to sew pieces together), draw the end through the chain and tighten gently.

Changing color

When you are joining in, or changing from one yarn to another for reasons of color (Double crochet shown here), you drop the old color and pick up the new before you complete the last stitch in the old color **d**, so that the loop on the hook afterwards is already in the new color, **e** and **f.**

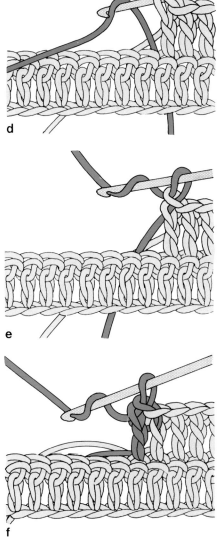

d

e

f

When you are working whole rows in different colors, make the change during the last stitch in the row, so the new color for the next row is ready to work the turning chain.

Do not cut off any yarns which will be needed again later at the same edge, but rejoin them as required, leaving an unbroken 'float' thread up the side of the fabric.

If, at the end of a row, the pattern requires you to return to the beginning of the same row without turning and to work another row in another color in the same direction, complete the first row in the old color and fasten off by lengthening the final loop on the hook, passing the whole ball through it and gently tightening again. That yarn is now available if you need to rejoin it later at this edge (if not, cut it).

When you are changing color during a row, for instance, when following a chart or other multi-color pattern, it is important not only to change color just before you complete the previous stitch, but also to be very aware which is the right and wrong side of your fabric at all times. After every color change and before continuing, make sure all yarns which are not for the time being in use are taken to the wrong side. When they are rejoined later, allow them to form loose 'float' threads on the wrong side. (**Hint:** In some circumstances, notably with solid stitch patterns on right side rows, you can avoid 'floats' by working **over** any yarns you need to carry along, or by winding off short lengths of yarn into separate balls. These can then be introduced at different points along the row and picked up as required. Your precise treatment will depend upon the stitch pattern, the nature of the article, the character of the yarn and your personal preferences.)

Working in rounds

a To work in rounds make 3 or more chains (the exact number depends on the design) and join them into a ring by inserting the hook into the first of them and making a slip stitch.

b To begin each round make a 'starting chain' (the equivalent of a 'turning chain' — see above) to match the height of the stitches of the round. Insert the hook always into the center of the base chain ring to work the stitches of the first round; **c** from the second round insert the hook under the top 2 loops of the stitches in the previous round, unless otherwise directed.

d When each round is complete insert the hook into the top of the starting chain and make a slip stitch to join the round.

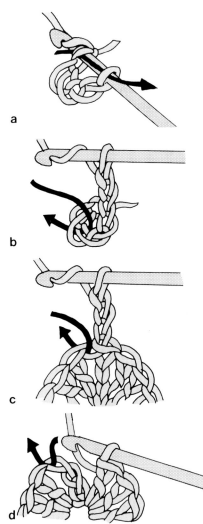

a

b

c

d

Making Crochet Fabric

Note: Unless otherwise specified, do not turn the work between rounds, but continue with the same side facing and treat this as the 'right side' of the fabric.

To make an alternative base ring — particularly suitable when it is desirable to leave no hole in the center of the fabric — **e, f, g, h** and **i** simply loop the yarn once (or two or three times) round a finger. Afterwards you can draw up the loose end and tighten the center of the fabric, if necessary.

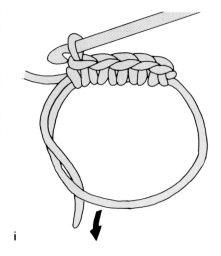

i

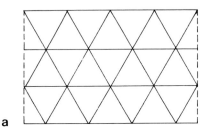

a

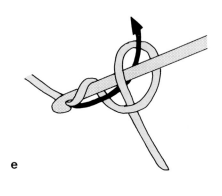

e

To fasten off after making the slip stitch which completes a round, do not make another chain, but **a** cut the yarn and draw the end through to the front; then **b** insert the hook again from the back through the place in the fabric where the slip stitch was worked (but not through the slip stitch loop itself) and draw the end of the yarn once again through to the back. Tighten gently.

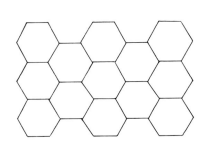

a

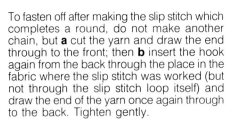

a

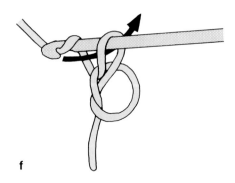

f

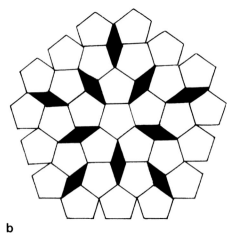

b

b

Joining motifs

Depending upon their shape some motifs, such as squares, hexagons, etc, fit together exactly **a. b** Others leave interesting spaces which may be joined along the edges that touch by sewing or crochet.

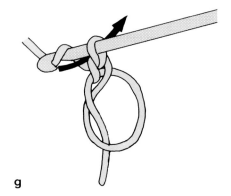

g

a

The actual techniques of joining may be a whipped **d,** or flat seam **e** woven with a needle. Slip stitch **f,** or single crochet **g** through both edges at once worked with a hook. To be invisible the crochet joins should be done on the wrong side of the work, ie with the right sides of the motifs together. Both stitches create a certain bulk and it may be more suitable to pick up just the single outer **h,** or inner **i** loop of each pair of stitches. Single crochet — particularly Corded Single Crochet **j** — makes a ridge which can be used as a positive, decorative feature when worked on the right side.

Fancy or openwork motifs, or those which leave space between them, may be joined indirectly with a suitable series of chain arches and bridges anchored with slip stitches or single crochets **k.**

Some designs, particularly those with picots or chain arches round their edges, can be joined to previous motifs during the course of their final rounds. This is done by interrupting the picots or arches at half way and slip stitching to the corresponding places on the adjacent motifs **l.**

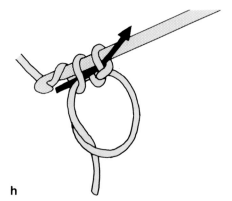

h

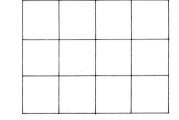

a

Spaces between motifs are sometimes filled with small single round motifs, made and joined in at the same time as they are worked.

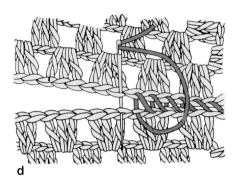

d

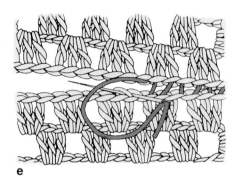

e

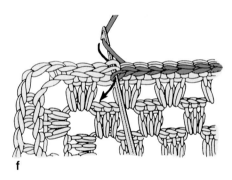

f

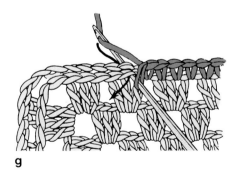

g

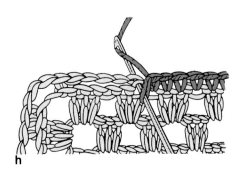

h

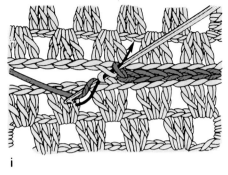

i

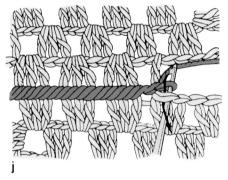

j

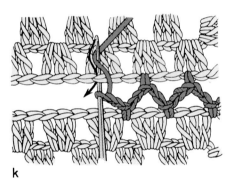

k

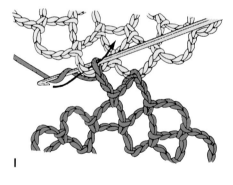

l

Stitch Variations

Most crochet stitch patterns, however elaborate, are made out of basic stitches. Excitingly different effects can be created by varying slightly just one stage in the standard stitch-making procedure, for example, the position and manner of inserting the hook into the fabric.

Groups

For decoration

A 'group' — several complete stitches worked into the same place — may consist of more than one kind of stitch. **a** A group of 5 double crochet stitches is sometimes called a 'shell'.

a

Hint: Always check exactly what is meant by the terms 'group', 'shell', etc, at the beginning of each set of pattern instructions.

For increasing

In a fabric made of solid, basic stitches, such as **b** single crochet, or **c** double crochet, working 2 or more stitches into one stitch at the ends of the rows is usually the best way of 'increasing' smoothly (making the fabric wider by adding stitches on).

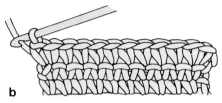

b

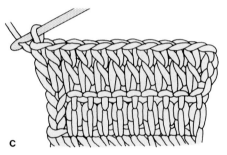

c

Clusters

For decoration

A 'cluster' — 2 or more stitches joined together at the top — may consist of more than one kind of basic, or special, stitch. Any combination of stitches may be joined into a cluster by leaving the last loop of each temporarily on the hook until they are all worked off together at the end.

For decreasing

Clusters of single crochet and double crochet stitches in simple arrangements, as

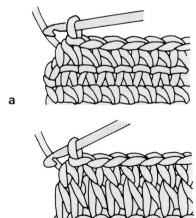

a

b

Stitch Variations

shown here **a** and **b**, are used for 'decreasing' (making the fabric narrower by reducing the number of stitches) as well as for pattern interest.

To work 2 single crochet stitches together (sc2tog)
a Insert the hook into the next stitch (or as required), wrap the yarn round the hook, draw a loop through; **b** repeat this step into the next stitch, (3 loops on the hook); **c** wrap the yarn and draw through all the loops on the hook to complete.

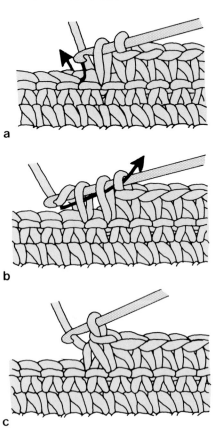

a

b

c

To work 3 single crochet stitches together (sc3tog)
Work as for sc2tog until there are 3 loops on the hook; **a** insert the hook into a third stitch, wrap the yarn and draw through a loop, (4 loops on the hook); **b** wrap the yarn and draw through all the loops on the hook to complete.

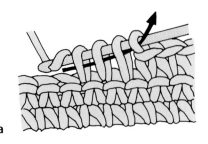

a

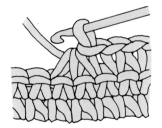

b

To work 2 or 3 double crochet stitches together (dc2tog, or dc3tog)
a Wrap the yarn round the hook, insert the hook into the next stitch (or as required), wrap the yarn, draw a loop through, wrap the yarn and draw through 2 of the loops on the hook (2 loops left on the hook); **b** repeat this step into the next stitch (3 loops on the hook); **c** for dc3tog repeat it once more into the next stitch (4 loops on the hook); **d** wrap the yarn and draw through all the loops on the hook to complete.

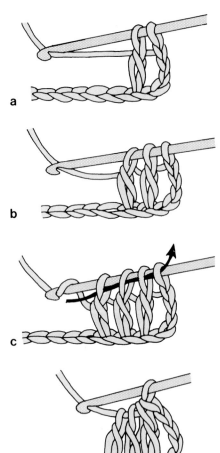

a

b

c

d

Hint: It is important to be sure exactly how and where the hook is to be inserted for each 'leg' of a cluster. The 'legs' may be worked over adjacent stitches, or stitches may be skipped between 'legs'. To make Bobbles or Puff Stitches (see below) all 'legs' are worked into the same stitch. Clusters, like single stitches, are sometimes worked round the stems of previous stitches, for example dc/rf3tog, (see Raised Stitches below).

Summary of Basic Clusters

For decoration and decreasing
In each case repeat from * to * for each 'leg' of the cluster, ending yo, draw through all loops on hook.

sc2(3)tog
insert hook as indicated, yo, draw loop through = 3(4) loops on hook.

hdc2(3/4)tog
yo, insert hook as indicated, yo, draw loop through = 5(7/9) loops on hook.

dc2(3/4/5)tog
yo, insert hook as indicated, yo, draw loop through, yo, draw through 2 loops = 3(4/5/6) loops on hook.

tr2(3/4/5)tog
yo twice, insert hook as indicated, yo, draw loop through, (yo, draw through 2 loops) twice = 3(4/5/6) loops on hook.

dtr2(3/4/5/etc)tog
yo 3 times, insert hook as indicated, yo, draw loop through, (yo, draw through 2 loops) 3 times = 3(4/5/6/etc) loops on hook.

Between Stitches

Inserting the hook between the stems of stitches and beneath the bundle of threads which joins them at the top opens up a solid fabric (see 'Wide Double Crochets' stitch pattern, page 22).

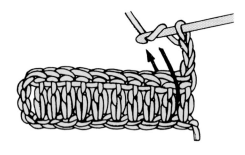

Under One Loop Only

Inserting the hook under one top loop only (either the back loop, or the front loop), leaves the other loop exposed as a horizontal bar. Depending upon which stitches are picked out in this way, horizontal ridges or 'woven' effects can be created. The fabric also tends to become more elastic.

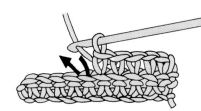

under back loop

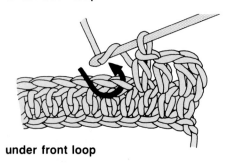

under front loop

Spikes

'Spikes' are made by inserting the hook further down into the fabric than usual, either below the next stitch, or to one side of it. **a** A loop is drawn through and up to the height of the current row; **b** the stitch is then completed normally.

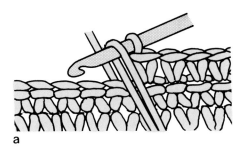

a

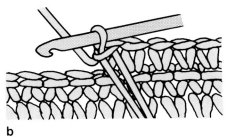

b

Spikes can be worked singly, in sequences, or **c** in clusters by inserting the hook in different places, drawing a loop through each and finishing by drawing a loop through all the loops so collected. They add interest to fabric texture, but are most dramatic when worked in contrasting colors.

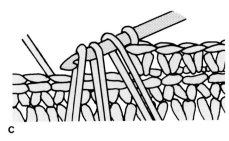

c

Hint: It is important to work 'spike' loops loosely enough to avoid squashing the fabric, but with sufficient gauge to maintain the stability of the fabric. When a whole sequence of stitches is 'spiked', it may help to work each one as a 'twin' cluster together with a stitch worked normally under the top 2 loops of the stitch above as follows:

d Insert the hook as indicated for the 'Spike', wrap the yarn round the hook and draw a loop through and up to the height of the current row; insert the hook under the top 2 loops of the next stitch, wrap the yarn and draw a loop through, (3 loops on the hook); **e** wrap the yarn and draw through all the loops on the hook to complete.

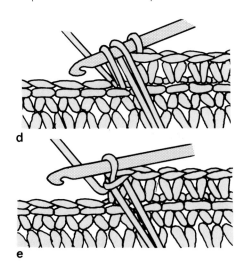

d

e

Marguerites (Stars)

A popular form of 'spiked' cluster — often called a 'Marguerite' or 'Star' — is formed by inserting the hook 3, 4, 5, or perhaps even more times, partly into the side of the previous stitch and partly into the next few stitches in the previous row.

To work a Marguerite with 4 'Spikes'

1st Marguerite: a Insert the hook into the 2nd chain from the hook, wrap the yarn round the hook and draw a loop through; repeat this step 3 more times into the 4th, 5th and 6th chains from the hook, (5 loops on the hook); **b** wrap the yarn and draw through all the loops; **c** make one chain firmly to close the Marguerite.

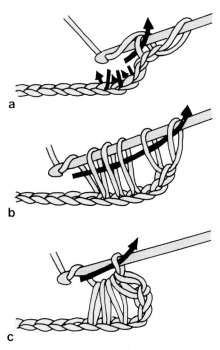

a

b

c

2nd and subsequent Marguerites: d Insert the hook, wrap the yarn and draw loops through as follows: into the loop which closed the previous Marguerite; into the same place as the previous Marguerite finished; and into each of the next 2 stitches (5 loops on the hook); **e** wrap the yarn, draw through all the loops on the hook and make a chain firmly to close the Marguerite.

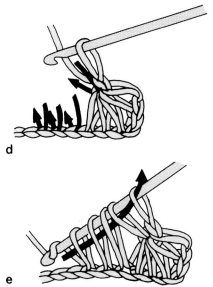

d

e

Raised (Relief) Stitches

Inserting the hook round the whole stem of a stitch creates raised or relief effects.

To work a 'raised' double crochet at the front of the fabric (1dc/rf)

a Wrap the yarn round the hook, insert the hook from in front and from right to left round the stem of the appropriate stitch; **b, c** and complete the stitch normally.

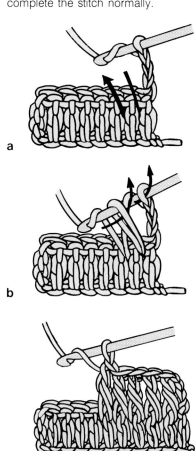

a

b

c

To work a 'raised' double crochet at the back of the fabric (1dc/rb)

d Wrap the yarn round the hook, insert the hook from behind and from right to left round the stem of the appropriate stitch; **e, f** and complete the stitch normally.

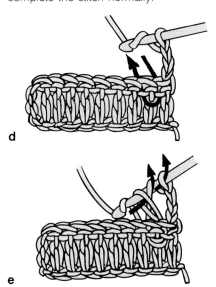

d

e

11

f

Any stitch can be worked in this way, singly, or in a group, or cluster. A 'raised' stitch may also be worked as a 'twin' cluster **g** together with a stitch worked normally under the top 2 loops of a stitch above.

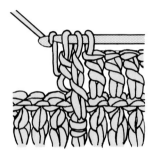

g

Working into Chain Spaces

When working a single stitch, or group, into a chain space, or chain loop, it is normal to **a** insert the hook into the space beneath the chain arch; this is quick and easy. It is important to notice, however, if the pattern instructions stipulate working into a particular chain, as you would, for instance, when working into the base chain **b**, since the technique may well change the result significantly (see 'Boxed Shell' and 'Boxed Block Stitch' on page 59).

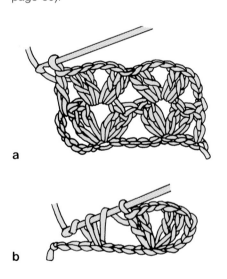

a

b

Crossed Stitch I

The simplest form of crossed stitch is made by inserting the hook into a previous stitch, wrapping the yarn and bringing a loop through and forward again in order to be able to complete the stitch normally. The threads of the new stitch thus made not only

cross over, but also sandwich previous stitches.

To work 2 crossed double crochet stitches (2Cdc)
a Skip 1 stitch, then work 1 double crochet; **b, c** work 1 double crochet into the stitch you skipped before the first double crochet; **d** repeat these steps to continue with the pattern of crossed pairs of double crochets.

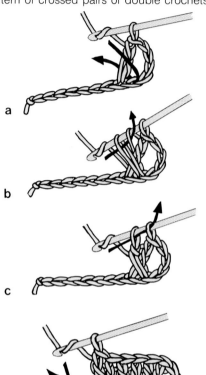

a

b

c

d

Crossed Stitch II

To make stitches which, although crossed, are not entangled with each other and so maintain a clear 'X' shape, **a** work the second stitch by taking the hook behind the first stitch **b** before inserting it.

a

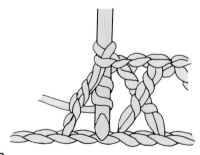

b

'X', 'Y' and 'λ' Shapes

In lacy stitch patterns long stitches are sometimes made into 'X' and 'Y' shapes without crossing them.

To make a Treble 'λ' and 'X' shape

a Wrap the yarn round the hook twice, insert the hook as required to make the lower part of the first 'leg'; **b** wrap the yarn, draw a loop through, wrap the yarn and draw through 2 loops (3 loops on the hook); wrap the yarn once more and insert the hook again as required to make the lower part of the second 'leg'; **c** wrap the yarn, draw a loop through, wrap the yarn and draw through 2 loops to complete both lower 'legs'; **d** wrap the yarn and draw through 2 loops; repeat this last step twice more to complete the first 'arm' — note that at this stage you have completed a 'λ' shape. **e** Make chains as required to take the hook to the top of the second 'arm', wrap the yarn once, insert the hook into the center of the cluster just completed, picking up 2 threads at the left-hand side, and draw a loop through; **f** wrap the yarn and draw through 2 loops; **g** repeat this last step to complete the second 'arm' and the whole 'X' shape.

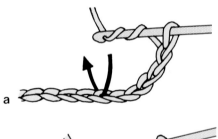

a

b

c

d

e

f

g

To make a Double treble 'Y' shape

a Work one complete double treble stitch for the lower 'leg' and first 'arm'; **b** make some chains as required to take the hook to the top of the second 'arm' and work 1 double crochet stitch into the center of the double treble to complete the second 'arm' and whole 'Y' shape in the same way as for the 'X' shape above.

a

b

Picots

A picot is normally a chain loop formed into a closed ring by a slip stitch, or single crochet. The number of chains in a picot varies. A common type of small picot shown here made with 3 chains is closed by inserting the hook down through the top of the previous stitch, wrapping the yarn and drawing a loop through all the loops on the hook.

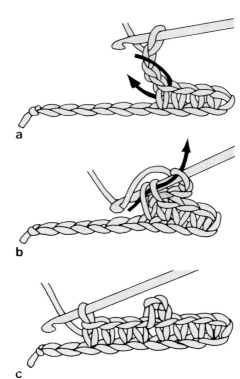

a

b

c

Lace Loops

Lace loops are most often used either as a decorative edging or for the kind of fabric-making sometimes called 'broomstick' crochet.

a Insert the hook, wrap the yarn over the hook and draw a loop through; wrap the yarn again, draw another loop through the first and lengthen this as required; repeat this procedure, keeping each loop on the hook, or **b** to help keep larger loops even in size, work from left to right and transfer each loop to a large size knitting needle (or 'broomstick').

c 2 or more lace loops can be made into clusters in various ways as an alternative to basic stitches.

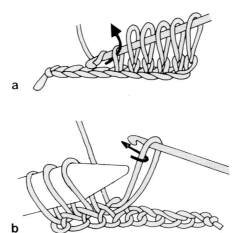

a

b

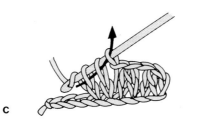

c

Solomon's Knot

A Solomon's Knot is a lengthened chain stitch locked with a single crochet stitch worked into its back loop.

a Make 1 chain and lengthen the loop as required; **b** wrap the yarn over the hook; **c** draw through the loop on the hook, keeping the single back thread of this long chain separate from the 2 front threads; **d** insert the hook under this single back thread and wrap the yarn again; **e** draw a loop through and wrap again; **f** draw through both loops on the hook to complete.

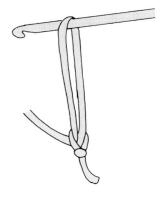

a

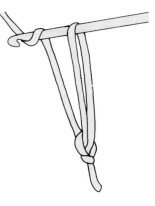

b

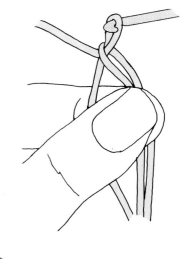

c

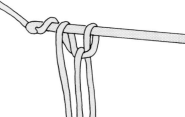

d

Stitch Variations

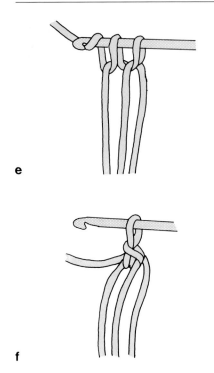

e

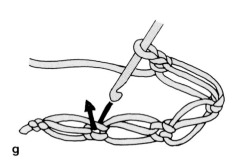

f

g It is necessary to work back into the 'knots' between the lengthened chains in order to make the classic Solomon's Knot fabric, see page 69.

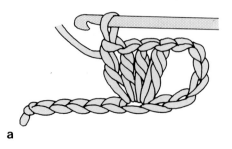

g

Popcorn

A popcorn is a group of complete stitches, usually worked into the same place, folded and closed at the top. The number and type of stitches included varies.

To make a popcorn with 4 double crochet stitches

a Work 4 double crochet stitches into one stitch normally; **b** take the hook out of the working loop, insert it under the top 2 loops of the first double crochet in the group just made, **c** pick up the working loop again and draw this through to close the group together and project it towards you. **Note:** On a 'wrong side' row insert the hook from behind and close the group so that it projects towards the back of the fabric.

a

b

Puff Stitch

A puff stitch is a cluster of half double crochet stitches (usually 3 to 5), worked into the same place, to make a soft lump.

b

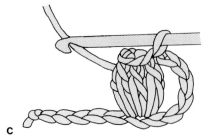

c

Bobble

A bobble is a cluster of stitches (usually 3 to 5) joined together at the top and also worked into the same place. Bobbles are thrown into relief most effectively when the stitches before and after them are shorter and they are worked on 'wrong side' rows.

To make a bobble of 3 double crochet stitches

a Work 3 double crochets, always inserting the hook into the same stitch and leaving the last loop of each on the hook as for a dc3tog cluster (see page 10); wrap the yarn over the hook and draw through all the loops on the hook to complete. **b** It often helps, particularly with the bulkier bobble clusters, to work an extra chain stitch to close them firmly.

To make a puff stitch of 3 half double crochet stitches

a Wrap the yarn over the hook, insert the hook, wrap the yarn again and draw a loop through, (3 loops on the hook); **b** repeat this step twice more, inserting the hook into the same stitch, (7 loops on the hook); wrap the yarn and draw through all the loops on the hook; **c** work an extra chain stitch to close the puff stitch firmly.

a

b

c

Bullion Stitch

Wrap the yarn over the hook as many times as specified (usually 7 to 10 times); insert the hook as required; wrap the yarn once again

and draw a loop through; wrap the yarn again and draw through all the loops on the hook, picking them off one at a time, if necessary; work a chain to complete the bullion stitch.

Loop (Fur) Stitch

Loop stitch is a variation of single crochet and is usually worked on 'wrong side' rows because the loops form at the back of the fabric.

a Using the left-hand finger to control the loop size insert the hook; pick up both threads of the loop and draw these through; **b** wrap the supply yarn over the hook; **c** and draw through all the loops on the hook to complete.

Note: When each loop is cut afterwards the texture of the fabric resembles fur.

Linked Stitches

The stems of all basic stitches, except single crochet, may be linked to each other in the middle. This gives the resulting fabric greater firmness and stability.

To make linked trebles: **a** Insert the hook down through the upper of 2 horizontal loops round the stem of the previous stitch, wrap the yarn over the hook and draw a loop through; insert the hook down through the lower horizontal loop of the same stitch, wrap the yarn and draw another loop through. **b** Treat these 2 loops as the wrappings which are required for an ordinary treble and complete the stitch in the normal way.

To make the first linked treble following the turning chain, insert the hook into the 2nd then the 4th chs from the hook in order to pick up the 2 preliminary loops.

Both double crochets and longer stitches are made in the same way with the appropriate number of preliminary linked and wrapped loops.

stitches in the 'wrong' direction, ie from left to right for righthanders.

After a right side row do not turn. **a** Always starting with the hook facing downwards insert the hook back into the next stitch to the right. Pull the yarn through twisting the hook to face upwards at the same time. **b** Wrap the yarn and draw through to finish off the sc as normally. **c** Insert hook ready for next stitch. **d** The direction of working causes the stitches to twist and create the decorative effect.

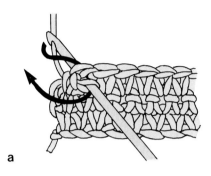

a

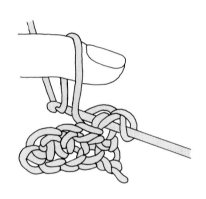

a

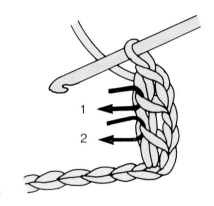

a

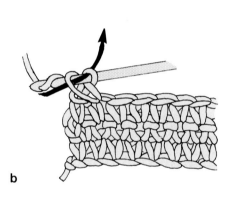

b

b

b

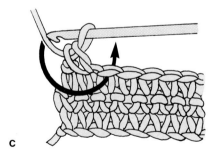

c

c

Corded or Reversed Single Crochet

Corded single crochet is used as a decorative texture (Corded Rib), or edging (Corded Edge). It consists of working single crochet

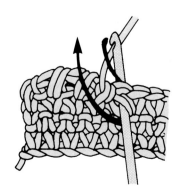

d

Following Crochet Patterns

Most crochet pattern instructions are written out in words. In order to follow these, you must be able to understand the simple jargon, abbreviations and standard conventions. You are expected to know how to make the basic stitches and to be familiar with basic fabric-making procedures; anything more advanced or specialised is always spelled out in individual pattern instructions.

Common abbreviations with which you should be familiar include:

alt = alternate
approx = approximate(ly)
beg = begin(ning)
cm = centimedce(s)
cont = continue
folls = follows
rem = remaining
rep = repeat
tog = together

Important terms and abbreviations for crochet stitches and stitch-making are as follows:

st(s) = stitch(es)
ch(s) = chain(s)
ch sp = chain space
tch = turning chain
stch = starting chain
sl st = slip stitch
sc = single crochet
hdc = half double crochet
dc = double crochet
tr = treble
dtr = double treble
ttr = triple treble
quad tr = quadruple treble
quin tr = quintuple treble
gr = group
CL = cluster
dec = decrease
inc = increase
yo = yarn over

Base (Foundation) chain = the length of chain made at the beginning of a piece of crochet as a basis for constructing the fabric.

Turning/starting chain = one, or more chains, depending upon the length of stitch required, worked at the beginning of a row (or end of the previous row) as preparation for the new row; sometimes counts as the first stitch in the new row. Called 'starting chain' when working 'in the round'.

Group = several stitches worked into the same place; sometimes called 'shell', 'fan', etc.

Cluster = two, or more, stitches, often started in different places, made leaving the last loop of each temporarily on the hook until finally one loop is drawn through them all, joining them together into one stitch at their top.

Picot = a run of chain stitches normally brought back on itself and fixed into a decorative loop with a slip stitch, or single crochet.

Note: Terms such as 'group', 'cluster', 'picot', and even 'shell', 'fan', 'flower', 'petal', 'leaf', 'bobble', etc, do not denote a fixed arrangement of stitches. Exactly what they mean may be different for each pattern. The procedure is therefore always spelled out at the beginning of each set of instructions and

is valid only for that set, unless stated otherwise.

Yarn over = the stitch-making instruction to wrap the yarn from the ball over the hook (or manipulate the hook round the yarn) in order to make a new loop; always done in an anti-clockwise direction, unless otherwise stated.

Work straight = work over an existing row of stitches without 'increasing' (i.e. adding stitches and so making the fabric wider), or 'decreasing' (i.e reducing the number of stitches and so making the fabric narrower). Precise methods of increasing and decreasing vary according to each stitch pattern and circumstances and are detailed in pattern instructions.

right/wrong side = the 'right side' is the surface of the fabric intended to be the outside of the finished article and therefore shown in the photographs; the 'wrong side' is the inside. If there is a difference, the instructions state which side is facing you as you work the first row and that surface of the fabric is identified and fixed from then on.

Hint: Crochet stitches are not the same back and front and so the two sides of a fabric may well be quite different. Even when a stitch pattern has no particular 'right side', however, it is wise to make a positive decision in respect of all separate pieces of the same article, so that the 'grain' of the rows can be matched exactly, when you join the pieces together.

front/back = 'front' and 'back' mean the front and back surfaces of a fabric for the time being as you hold and look at it; these change over every time you turn the work.

Note: In garment pattern instructions the terms 'Front' and 'Back' denote the different pieces of the garment.

Multiple: All but the simplest crochet stitch patterns are built around repeated sequences of stitches. In order to make sense of the instructions you must have exactly the right number of stitches in your base row. This number is a multiple of the number of stitches required for one complete sequence — sometimes plus an extra edge stitch, or two — and is given at the beginning of each set of instructions.

The number of chains you need for the base chain, in order to be able to create the appropriate number of stitches in the base row is also given. For example, 'Multiple of 2 sts + 1, (add 1 for base chain)' = make 4, 6, 8, etc chains for a base row of 3, 5, 7, etc, stitches; or 'Multiple of 8 sts + 3, (add 2 for base chain)' = make 13, 21, 29, etc, chains for a base row of 11, 19, 27, etc, stitches.

Color Note: Capital letters A, B, C, D, etc, are used to indicate different yarn colors; when only two colors are involved and one of these is intended to dominate, the terms 'main (M)' and 'contrast (C)' may be used instead.

Asterisks (*) and Brackets [ ]: These are used to simplify repetition. Instructions are put inside brackets and these are to be worked the number of times stated, for example: '[1ch, skip 1ch, 1dc into next st] 5 times'.

A sequence of stitches after an asterisk means that the whole sequence between that asterisk and the next semi-colon is to be repeated as many times as necessary to reach the end of the row, for example: '*1ch, skip 1ch, 1dc into next st, 1ch, skip

1ch, 1dc into each of next 3 sts; rep from * to end, turn'.

If no further details are given, as in this case, the end of the sequence will coincide exactly with the end of the row. If there are stitches remaining unworked after the last complete repeat sequence, details of how to complete the row are given, for example: 'Rep from * to last 4 sts, ending 1ch, skip 1ch, 1dc into each of last 3 sts, turn'. 'Rep from * 4 more times,' means work that sequence 5 times in all.

Charts: Filet crochet patterns, which are based on a regular grid of double crochet and chain stitches, are much easier to follow from a squared chart, when you understand the basic procedures (see page 18). This type of chart is also used to indicate different colors in Jacquard and Fair Isle patterns, which are usually based on a plain single crochet fabric (see page 20).

Stitch Diagrams: Accurate stitch diagrams show the overall picture at a glance and at the same time indicate precisely every detail of construction. To follow them you need to be familiar with the symbols which represent each individual stitch (see page 17).

Hint: Always read through the whole pattern before starting to crochet. This will give you a valuable overall picture of how the stitch pattern works and how the whole article is put together.

Gauge

Whenever you are following crochet pattern instructions, whatever form they take, probably the most important single factor in your success is obtaining the 'gauge' or 'tension' that the designer worked to. If you do not obtain the same gauge as indicated your work will not come to the measurement given.

The gauge is usually specified as a number of stitches and a number of rows to a given measurement (usually 10 cm).

The quick way to check is to make a square of fabric about 15 cm wide in the correct pattern and with the correct yarn and suggested hook size, lay this down on a flat surface and measure it — first horizontally (for stitch gauge) and then vertically (for row gauge). If your square has too few stitches or rows to the measurement, your gauge is too loose and you should try again with a size smaller hook. If it has too many stitches try a size larger hook. (**Hint:** Stitch gauge is generally much more important than row gauge in crochet.)

Note that the hook size quoted in instructions is a suggestion only. You must use whichever hook gives you the correct gauge.

Stitch Diagrams

Stitch diagrams are detailed 'maps' of fabric showing the right side uppermost. They enable you to see at a glance what you are going to do before you start and also where you are at any moment. To follow them you must first become familiar with all the basic stitches and fabric-making procedures needed for following written instructions.

The Stitches

As soon as you know the stitches themselves, it is easy to identify the symbols which represent them. From double crochet onwards the number of short angled strokes crossing the stems represents the number of times the yarn is wrapped before the hook is inserted.

Chain	o
Slip stitch	●
Single crochet	+
Half double crochet	T
Double crochet	∓
Treble	∓
Double treble	∓
Triple treble	∓
Quadruple treble	∓
Quintuple treble	∓
Bullion stitch	◊
Lace loop	◊
Solomon's Knot	◊

Groups, Clusters and Picots, etc, are usually obvious (though you may often have to remind yourself exactly how to work a complex cluster combination).

Single crochet

Half double crochet

Double crochet

Treble

Double treble

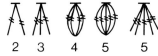

Back/front loop: Stitches which are to be made by inserting the hook under only one of the top two loops are indicated by heavy and lightweight stitch symbols with under-lining. A lightweight symbol in conjunction with an underline means pick up the loop nearest the right side of the fabric, i.e. front loop on right side rows, but back loop on wrong side rows. A heavyweight symbol with an underline means pick up the loop nearest the wrong side, i.e. back loop on right side rows, but front loop on wrong side rows.

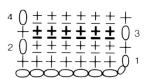

Spikes: The stitch symbol is extended downwards to show where the hook is to go through the fabric.

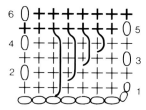

Marguerites: The individual parts of the marguerite clusters have barbs.

Popcorns: The tops of the group of stitches forming the popcorn are linked into an oval.

Half double treble

Double crochet

Treble

Raised (relief) stitches: When a stitch is to be worked by inserting the hook behind a stem (instead of under the top two loops), the stitch symbol ends in a 'crook' round the appropriate stem. The direction of the crook indicates which side of the fabric the hook is to be inserted. On a right side row work a raised stitch with a right side crook at the front, and one with a wrong side crook at the back (vice versa on a wrong side row).

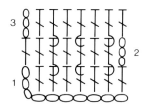

Crossed stitches: When stitch symbols cross each other, work as for Crossed Stitch I (see page 12), except when a stitch is broken — in which case take the hook behind the previous stitch as for Crossed Stitch II — or when the crossbars are drawn both above and below the crossing point of the stitches — work then as for an 'X' shape (see page 12).

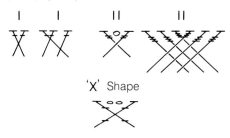

'X' Shape

Picots: When a single picot loop occurs after a solid stitch, note the usual method of working the closing slip stitch shown on page 13.

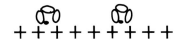

Distortion: Stitch symbols are drawn and laid out realistically as far as possible with consistent relative length and width, but there are times when they have to be distorted for the sake of clarity. Sometimes, for example, single crochet stitches may look extra long. This is only to show clearly where they go and you should not try to make artificially long stitches.

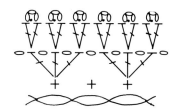

When the diagram represents a fabric, which is not intended to lie flat — for instance, a 'gathered' or frilled edging — since the drawing itself has to remain flat, the stitch symbols have to be stretched.

Figures: Figures indicate row (or round) numbers.

Motifs: When the base ring of a motif is drawn as a plain circle make it by looping the yarn around a finger (see page 8).

Color: Letters A, B, etc, and also light and heavy stitch symbols confirm changes of color.

Arrows: Once you are familiar with the basic fabric-making procedures, it is usually clear where a stitch pattern diagram begins and ends, which direction a row goes (Hint: Look for the turning chain), etc. If there is any doubt, additional directions are given with the help of various arrows.

Stitch Diagrams

Filet Crochet with Charts

Filet crochet is based on a simple network, or 'ground' with a regular, square grid, made of double crochet and chain stitches. Pattern instructions are therefore usually presented in the form of squared charts, in which the vertical lines represent double crochet stitches and the horizontal lines (the tops of the rows) chain stitches. Designs of all kinds — flowers, geometric patterns, lettering and even whole scenes — are created by 'filling in' some of the squares, or spaces with double crochet stitches instead of chains.

In earlier times people used to work with very fine hooks and yarns, but on a large scale, and so they often produced highly elaborate scenes with exquisite detailing, perhaps incorporating lengthy texts, such as The Lord's Prayer. Simple filet crochet designs are also effective, however, when only a few features, or just a single element, such as those depicted in the examples in this book, are repeated over the whole fabric, or as a border.

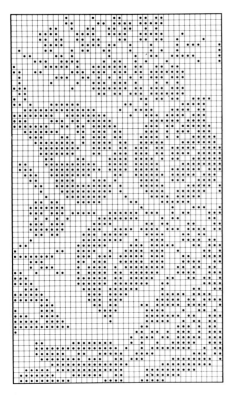

The chart represents a view of the finished fabric with the right side facing — you are to imagine having made it from the bottom upwards working to and fro. Even-numbered rows have therefore to be 'read' from left to right.

Each open square represents 2 double crochet stitches with a space between of 2 chains (or as specified — see below). When a square is filled by a dot (or otherwise marked) the 2 chain space is replaced by 2 double crochet stitches, making a single 'block' of 4 double crochets. 2 'blocks' together make 7 double crochets and 3 make 10 double crochets and so on.

The base row consists of a multiple of 3 stitches + 1, (— you multiply the number of squares, □, by 3 and add 1).

If the first square to be worked is a 'space', add 4 for the base chain and work the first double crochet into the 8th chain from the hook.

If the first square is a solid 'block', add only 2 for the base chain, work the first double crochet into the 4th chain from the hook and also 1 double crochet into each of the next 2 chains.

From the 2nd row onwards work spaces and blocks as follows: (see Diagram a):

A space over a space in the previous row.

At the beginning of the row = '5ch (count as 1dc and 2ch sp), skip 1 st and 2ch, 1dc into next dc, etc.'

At the end of the row = ' . . . 1dc into last dc, 2ch, skip 2ch, 1dc into 3rd of 5ch, turn.'

A space over a block in the previous row.

At the beginning of the row = '5ch (count as 1dc and 2ch sp), skip first 3 sts, 1dc into next dc, etc.'

At the end of the row = ' . . . over last 4 sts work 1dc into dc, 2ch, skip 2dc, 1dc into top of tch, turn.'

A block over a space in the previous row.

At the beginning of the row = '3ch (count as 1dc), skip 1 st, 1dc into each of next 2ch, 1dc into next dc, etc.'

At the end of the row = ' . . . 1dc into last dc, 1dc into each of next 3ch of 5ch, turn.'

A block over a block in the previous row.

At the beginning of the row = '3ch (count as 1dc), skip 1 st, 1dc into each of next 3dc, etc.'

At the end of the row = ' . . . 1dc into each of last 3dc and then into top of tch, turn.'

Lacets and Bars: (see Diagram b)

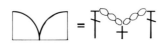

These are variations in the basic network — called 'lacets' and 'bars'. They are both worked over 2 squares of the grid and are used in conjunction with each other.

Lacet = 3ch, skip 2 sts, 1sc into next st, 3ch, skip 2 sts, 1dc into next dc.

Bar = 5ch, skip next lacet (or next 2sps), 1dc into next dc.

To re-establish the basic network after a bar work: 2ch, 1dc into 3rd of next 5ch, 2ch, 1dc into next dc.

Hint: Any squared chart can be adapted for filet crochet. Furthermore you can choose to work it upwards, downwards, or sideways according to your needs. Using plain graph paper it is a simple matter to draw in and plot your own designs and compositions, but

note that your basic network is not likely to work out exactly square, whatever combination of chain spaces and stitch lengths you use.

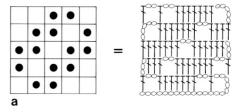

a

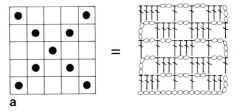

a

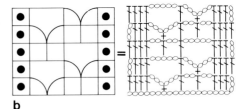

b

Provided you are completely consistent within any given piece of work, it is possible to interpret the space in each square of the chart as 1, or 3 chains, rather than 2 chains as we have done here. A single square then represents 3, or 5 (instead of 4) stitches. Equally the vertical stitches could be trebles. In these cases adjustments have to be made to the base and turning chains.

Color Work with Charts

When squared charts are used for color work they are to be 'read' in the same general way as for Filet charts, that is, working from the bottom upwards to and fro. It is however the square spaces which represent the stitches. Usually single crochet stitches are used because they are small and compact. In this case it may be preferable not to treat the turning chain as a stitch.

In practice no crochet stitch works out 'square' — single crochet is too shallow; half double crochet too deep — and this should be born in mind before you begin. Double crochet stitches, which are even taller, are sometimes represented on squared charts by two squares per row.

The squares may be blocked or hatched in, numbered or colored in different ways. A key is always given showing you what each square represents. For mechanical details of how to handle different color yarns, see page 7.

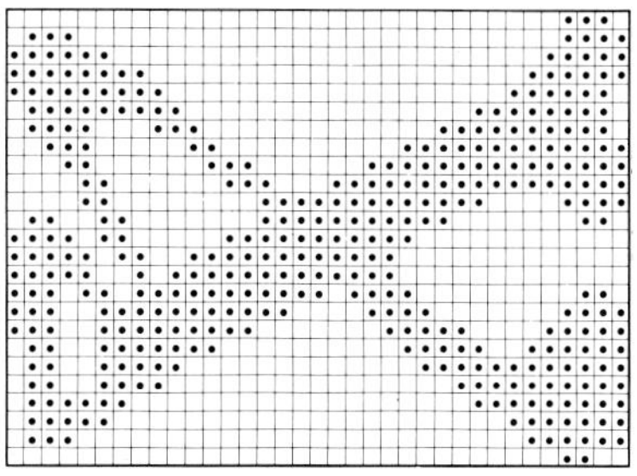
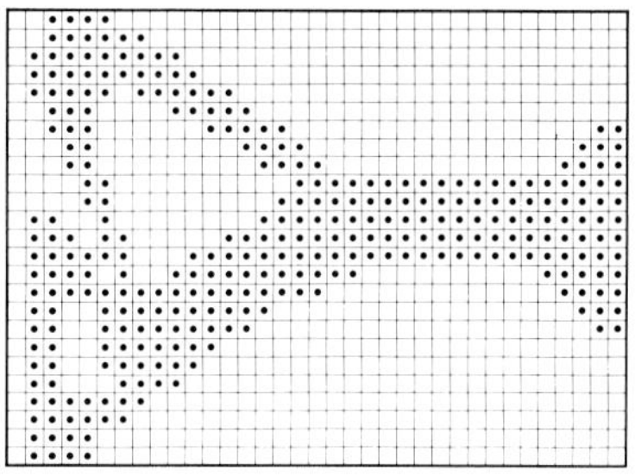
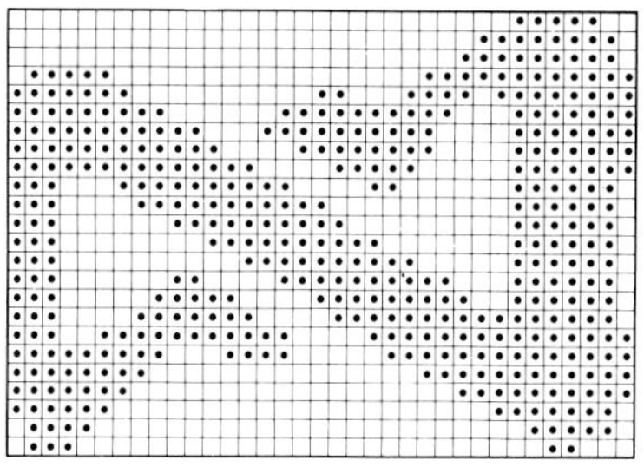
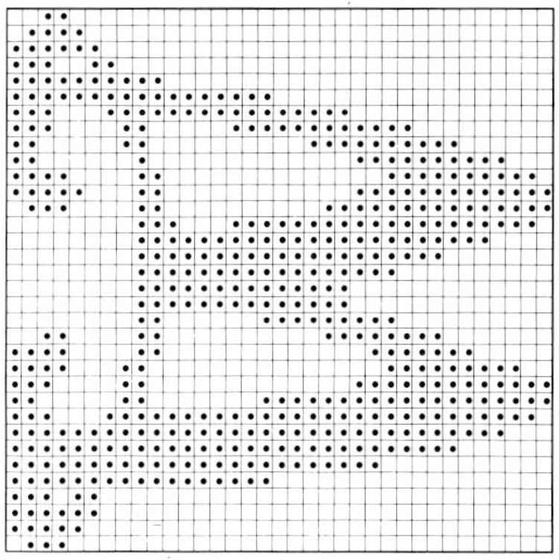
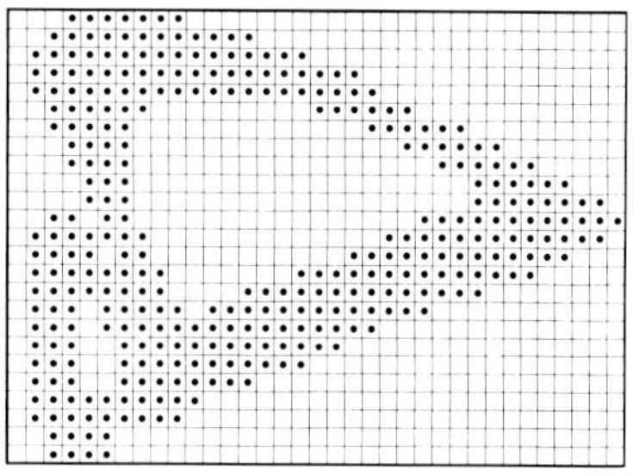
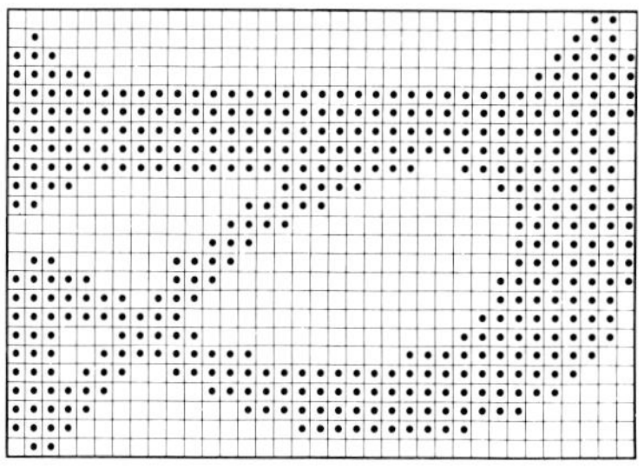
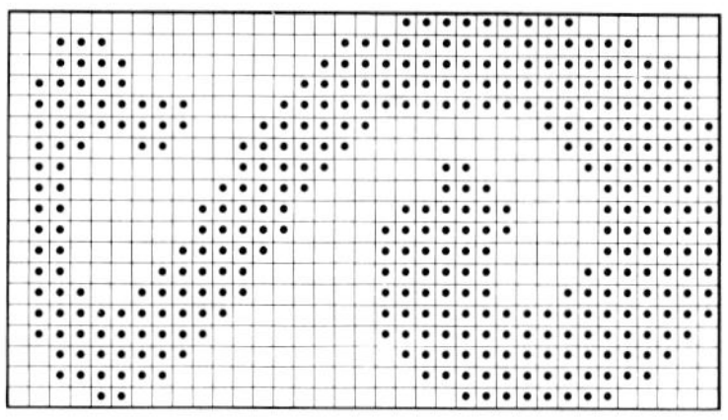
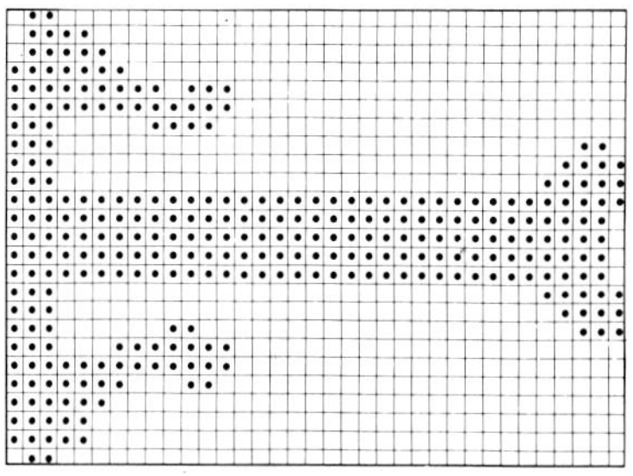
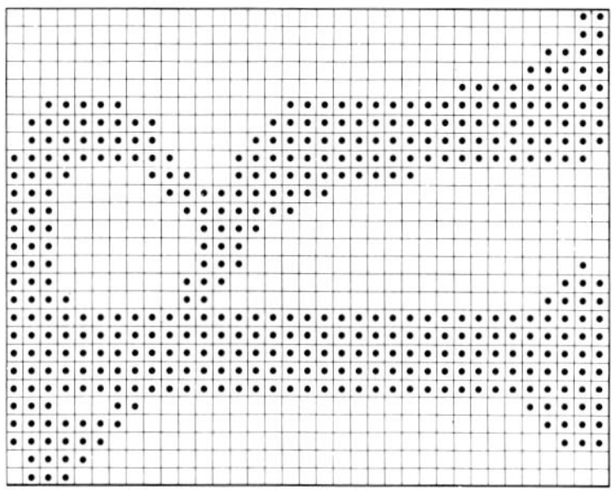
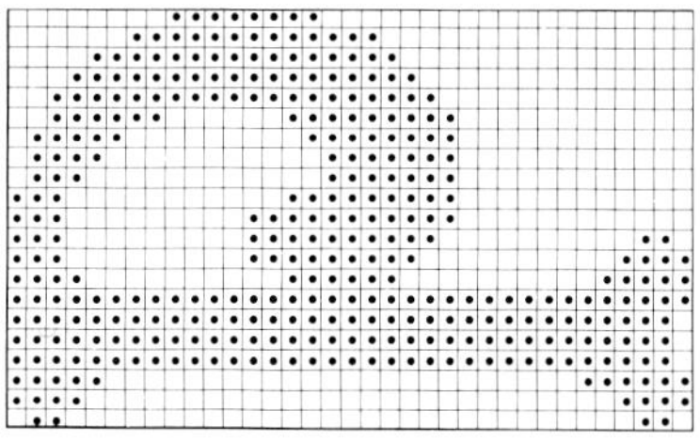
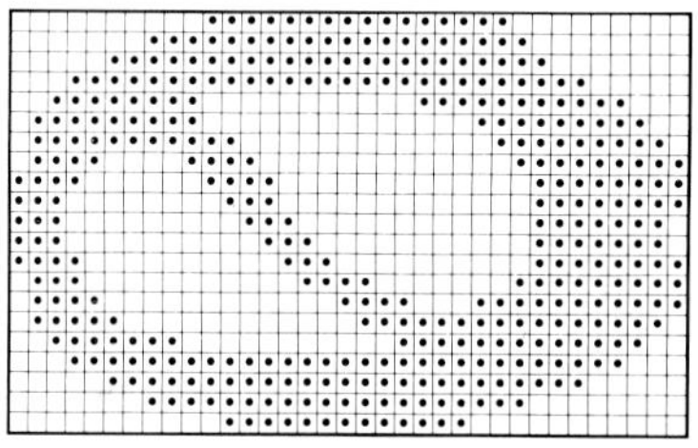
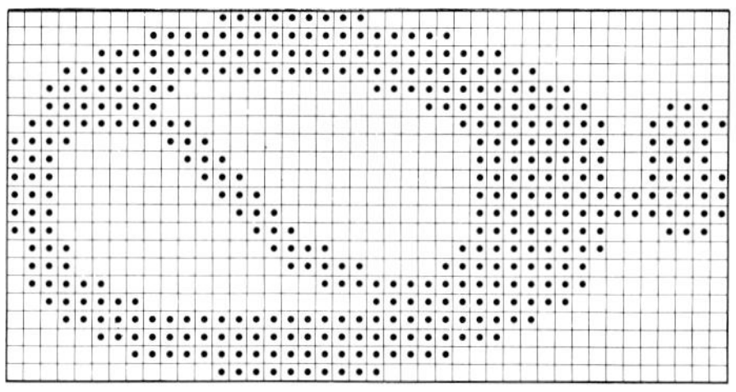
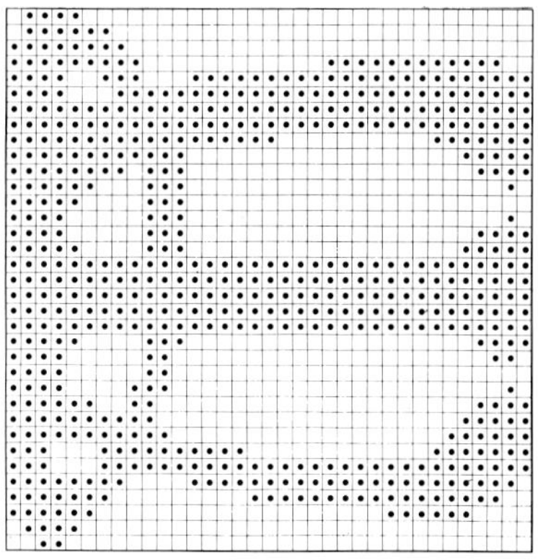
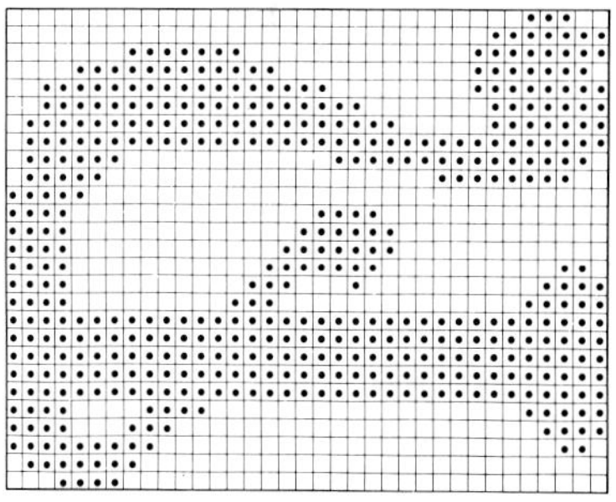
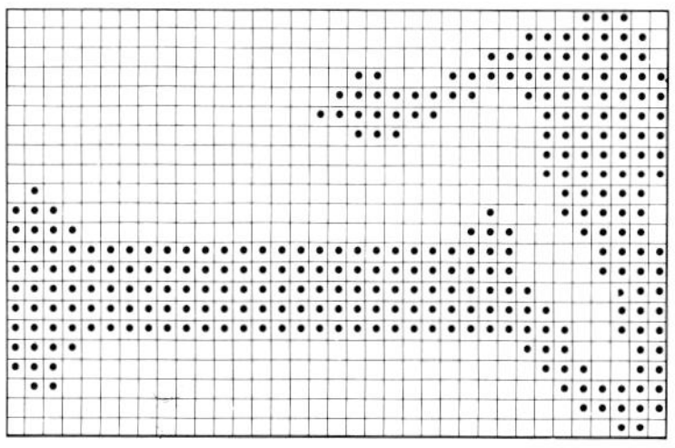
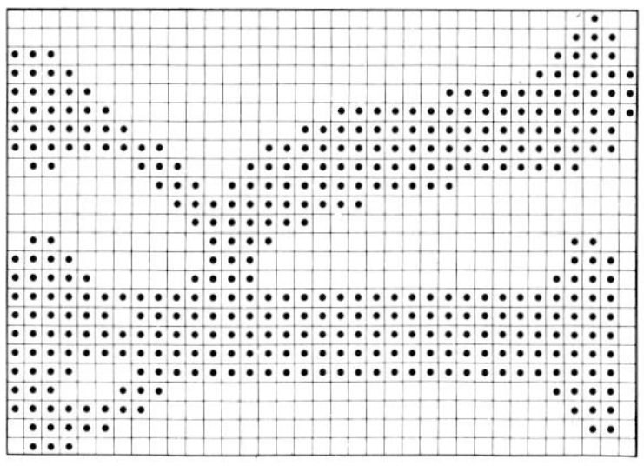
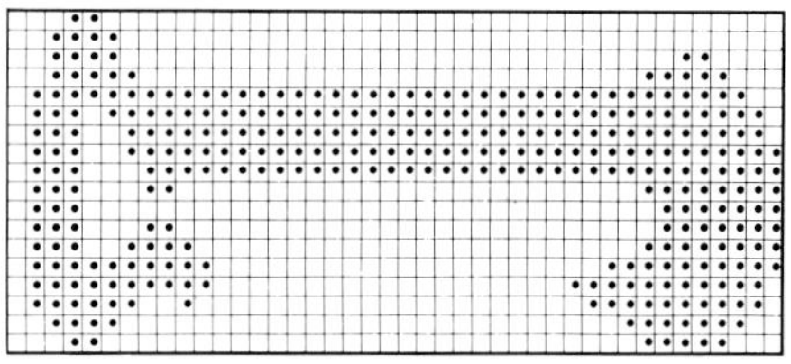
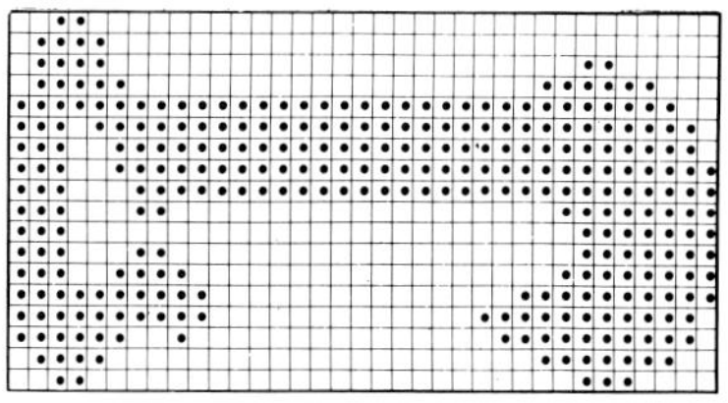
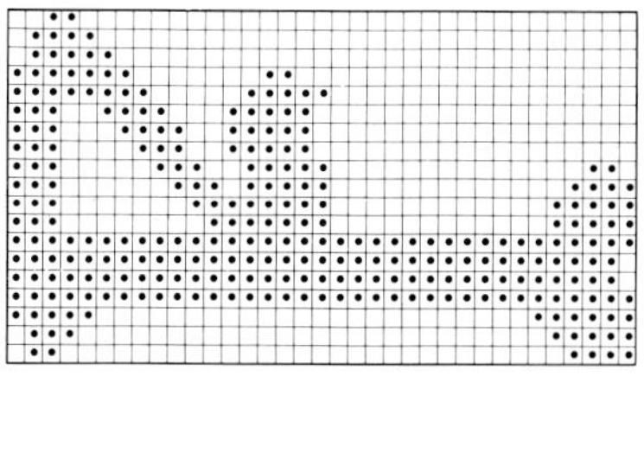
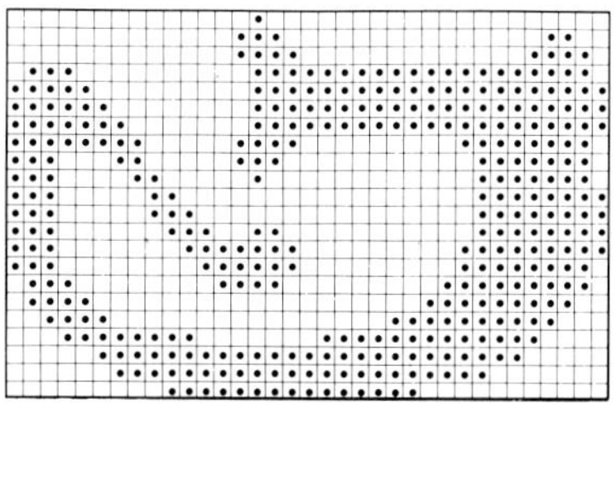
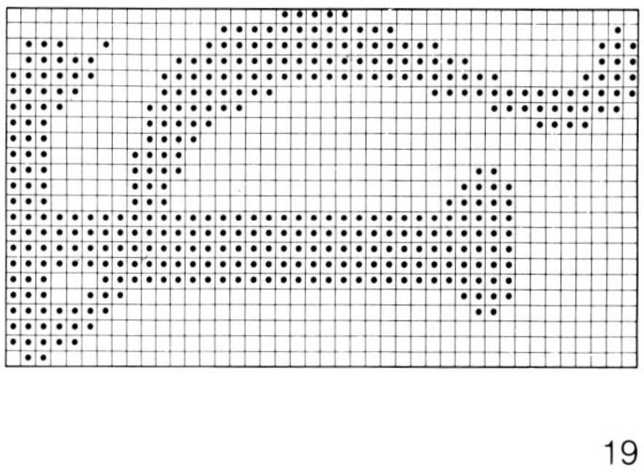

Basic Stitches

Basic Single Crochet

Any number of sts.
(add 1 for base chain)
1st row: Skip 2ch (count as 1sc), 1sc into next and each ch to end, turn.
2nd row: 1ch (counts as 1sc), skip 1 st, 1sc into next and each st to end working last st into tch, turn.
Rep 2nd row.

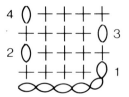

Hint: In some patterns the turning chain does **not** count as a stitch when working single crochet. In these cases the first sc is worked into the second ch from hook on the first row, and thereafter into the first sc of the previous row.

Basic Half Double Crochet

Any number of sts.
(add 1 for base chain)
1st row: Skip 2ch (count as 1hdc), 1hdc into next and each ch to end, turn.
2nd row: 2ch (count as 1hdc), skip 1 st, 1hdc into next and each st to end working last st into top of tch, turn.
Rep 2nd row.

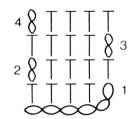

Basic Double Crochet

Any number of sts.
(add 2 for base chain)
1st row: Skip 3ch (count as 1dc), 1dc into next and each ch to end, turn.
2nd row: 3ch (count as 1dc), skip 1 st, 1dc into next and each st to end working last st into top of tch, turn.
Rep 2nd row.

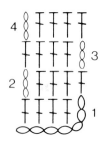

Basic Trebles

Any number of sts.
(add 3 for base chain)
1st row: Skip 4ch (count as 1tr), 1tr into next and each ch to end, turn.
2nd row: 4ch (count as 1tr), skip 1 st, 1tr into next and each st to end, working last st into top of tch, turn.
Rep 2nd row.

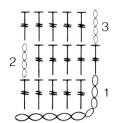

Back Loop Single Crochet

Worked as Basic Single Crochet except from 2nd row insert hook into back loop only of each st.

Front Loop Single Crochet

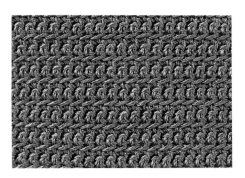

Worked as Basic Single Crochet except from 2nd row insert hook into front loop only of each st.

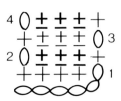

○ Chain ● Slip stitch + Single crochet T Half double crochet ╪ Double crochet ╪ Treble ╪ Double treble

Back and Front Loop Single Crochet

Multiple of 2 sts.
(add 1 for base chain)

1st row: Skip 2ch (count as 1sc), 1sc into next and each ch to end, turn.

2nd row: 1ch (counts as 1sc), skip 1 st, *1sc into back loop only of next st, 1sc into front loop only of next st; rep from * ending 1sc into top of tch, turn.

Rep 2nd row.

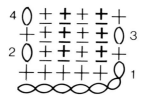

Shallow Single Crochet

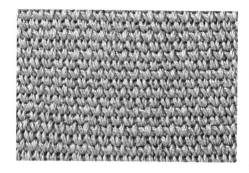

Worked as Basic Single Crochet except from 2nd row insert hook low into body of each st below 3 horizontal loops and between 2 vertical threads.

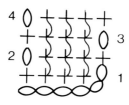

Back Loop Half Double Crochet

Worked as Basic Half Double Crochet except from 2nd row insert hook into back loop only of each st.

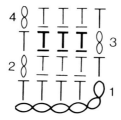

Back and Front Loop Half Double Crochet

Multiple of 2 sts.
(add 1 for base chain)

1st row: Skip 2ch (count as 1hdc), 1hdc into next and each ch to end, turn.

2nd row: 2ch (count as 1hdc), skip 1 st, *1hdc into back loop only of next st, 1hdc into front loop only of next st; rep from * ending 1hdc into top of tch, turn.

Rep 2nd row.

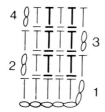

Linked Half DCs

Any number of sts.
(add 1 for base chain)

Special Abbreviation

꜀ **Lhdc (Linked Half Double Crochet)** = insert hook into single vertical thread at left-hand side of previous st, yo, draw loop through, insert hook normally into next st, yo, draw loop through st, yo, draw through all 3 loops on hook.

Note: To make first Lhdc at beg of row treat 2nd ch from hook as a single vertical thread.

1st row: 1Lhdc into 3rd ch from hook (picking up loop through 2nd ch from hook), 1Lhdc into next and each ch to end, turn.

2nd row: 2ch (count as 1hdc), skip 1 st, 1Lhdc into next and each st to end, working last st into top of tch, turn.

Rep 2nd row.

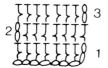

Herringbone Half Double Crochet

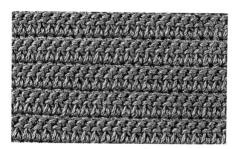

Any number of sts.
(add 1 for base chain)

Special Abbreviation

꜀ **HBhdc (Herringbone Half Double Crochet)** = yo, insert hook, yo, draw through st and first loop on hook, yo, draw through both loops on hook.

1st row: Skip 2ch (count as 1hdc), 1HBhdc into next and each ch to end, turn.

2nd row: 2ch (count as 1hdc), skip 1 st, 1HBhdc into next and each st to end working last st into top of tch, turn.

Rep 2nd row.

Variations

Wide Doubles

Worked as Basic Double Crochets but after 1st row insert hook between stems and below all horizontal threads connecting sts.

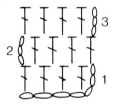

Note: Base chain should be worked loosely to accommodate extra width.

Herringbone Double Crochets

Any number of sts.
(add 2 for base chain)

Special Abbreviation
⚡ **HBdc (Herringbone Double Crochet)** = yo, insert hook, yo, draw through st and first loop on hook, yo, draw through 1 loop, yo, draw through both loops on hook.

1st row: Skip 3ch (count as 1dc), 1HBdc into next and each ch to end, turn.

2nd row: 3ch (count as 1dc), skip 1 st, 1HBdc into next and each st to end, working last st into top of tch, turn.
Rep 2nd row.

Alternative Doubles

Any number of sts.
(add 2 for base chain)

Special Abbreviation
⚡ **Alt dc (Alternative Double Crochet)** = yo, insert hook, yo, draw loop through, yo, draw through 1 loop only, yo, draw through all 3 loops on hook.

1st row: Skip 3ch (count as 1dc), 1dc into next and each ch to end, turn.

2nd row: 3ch (count as 1dc), skip 1 st, work 1 Alt dc into next and each st to end, working last st into top of tch, turn.
Rep 2nd row.

Linked Trebles

Any number of sts.
(add 3 for base chain)

Special Abbreviation
⚡ **Ltr (Linked Treble)** = insert hook down through upper of 2 horizontal loops round stem of last st made, yo, draw loop through, insert hook down through lower horizontal loop of same st, yo, draw loop through, insert hook normally into next st, yo, draw loop through st, (4 loops on hook), [yo, draw through 2 loops] 3 times (see also page 15).
Note: To make first Ltr (at beg of row) treat

2nd and 4th chs from hook as upper and lower horizontal loops.

1st row: 1Ltr into 5th ch from hook (picking up loops through 2nd and 4th chs from hook), 1Ltr into next and each ch to end, turn.

2nd row: 4ch (count as 1tr), skip 1 st, 1Ltr into next and each st to end, working last st into top of tch, turn.
Rep 2nd row.

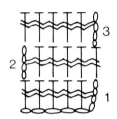

Singles and Doubles

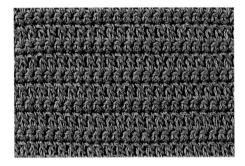

Any number of sts.
(add 1 for base chain)

1st row (wrong side): Skip 2ch (count as 1sc), 1sc into next and each ch to end, turn.

2nd row: 3ch (counts as 1dc), skip 1 st, 1dc into next and each st to end, working last st into top of tch, turn.

3rd row: 1ch (counts as 1sc), skip 1 st, 1sc into next and each st to end, working last st into top of tch, turn.

Rep 2nd and 3rd rows.

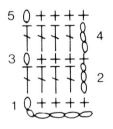

Hint: This is one of the simplest and most effective combination stitch patterns. It is also one of the easiest to get wrong! Concentration is required as you work the ends of the rows to avoid increasing or decreasing, or working two rows of the same stitch running by mistake.

○ Chain ● Slip stitch + Single crochet T Half double crochet ⊺ Double crochet ⧧ Treble ⧣ Double treble

Track Stitch

Any number of sts.
(add 1 for base chain)

1st row (wrong side): Skip 2ch (count as 1sc), 1sc into next and each ch to end, turn.

2nd row: 5ch (count as 1dtr), skip 1 st, 1dtr into next and each st to end, working last st into top of tch, turn.

3rd, 4th and 5th rows: 1ch (counts as 1sc), skip 1 st, 1sc into next and each st to end, working last st into top of tch, turn.

Rep 2nd to 5th rows.

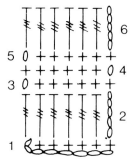

Single Crotchet Cluster Stitch I

Multiple of 2 sts + 1.
(add 1 for base chain)

Note: For description of sc2tog see page 10 (Clusters).

1st row (wrong side): 1sc into 2nd ch from hook, *1ch, skip 1ch, 1sc into next ch; rep from * to end, turn.

2nd row: 1ch, 1sc into first st, 1ch, sc2tog inserting hook into each of next 2 ch sps, 1ch, *sc2tog inserting hook first into same ch sp as previous st then into next ch sp, 1ch; rep from * ending 1sc into last st, skip tch, turn.

3rd row: 1ch, 1sc into first st, *1ch, skip 1ch, 1sc into next st; rep from * to end, skip tch, turn.

Rep 2nd and 3rd rows.

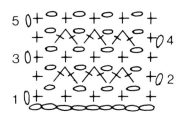

Single Crochet Cluster Stitch II

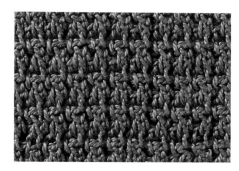

Multiple of 2 sts + 1.
(add 1 for base chain)

Note: For description of sc2tog see page 10 (Clusters).

1st row: Skip 1ch, *sc2tog inserting hook into each of next 2ch, 1ch; rep from * ending 1sc into last ch, turn.

2nd row: 1ch, sc2tog inserting hook into first st then into next ch sp, 1ch, *sc2tog inserting hook first before and then after the vertical thread between the next 2 clusters, 1ch; rep from * ending 1sc into last sc, skip tch, turn.

Rep 2nd row.

Single Crochet Cluster Stitch III

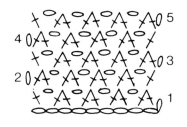

Multiple of 2 sts.
(add 1 for base chain)

Note: For description of sc2tog see page 10 (Clusters).

1st row: Skip 2ch (count as 1hdc), *sc2tog inserting hook into each of next 2ch, 1ch; rep from * ending with 1hdc into last ch, turn.

2nd row: 2ch (count as 1hdc), skip 1 st, *sc2tog inserting hook into back loop only of next ch then into back loop only of next st, 1ch; rep from * ending with 1hdc into top of tch, turn.

Rep 2nd row.

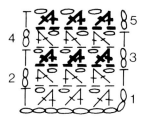

Single Crochet Cluster Stitch IV

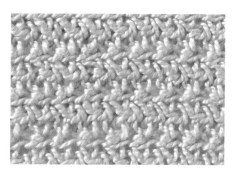

Multiple of 2 sts + 1.
(add 1 for base chain)

Special Abbreviation

⅄ **SC (Slip Cluster)** = insert hook into ch or st as indicated, yo, draw loop through, insert hook again as indicated, yo, draw loop through st and through next loop on hook, yo, draw through last 2 loops on hook.

1st row: 1SC inserting hook into 2nd and then 3rd ch from hook, 1ch; *1SC inserting hook into each of next 2ch, 1ch; rep from * ending 1sc into last ch, turn.

2nd row: 1ch (counts as 1sc), skip 1 st, *1SC inserting hook into front loop only of next ch then front loop only of next st, 1ch; rep from * ending 1sc into top of tch, turn.

Rep 2nd row.

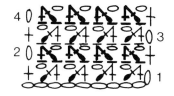

Clusters

Trinity Stitch I

Multiple of 2 sts + 1.
(add 1 for base chain)
Note: For description of sc3tog see page 10 (Clusters).

1st row: 1sc into 2nd ch from hook, sc3tog inserting hook first into same ch as previous sc, then into each of next 2ch, *1ch, sc3tog inserting hook first into same ch as 3rd leg of previous cluster, then into each of next 2ch; rep from * to last ch, 1sc into same ch as 3rd leg of previous cluster, turn.

2nd row: 1ch, 1sc into first st, sc3tog inserting hook first into same place as previous sc, then into top of next cluster, then into next ch sp, *1ch, sc3tog inserting hook first into same ch sp as 3rd leg of previous cluster, then into top of next cluster, then into next ch sp; rep from * to end working 3rd leg of last cluster into last sc, 1sc into same place, skip tch, turn.

Rep 2nd row.

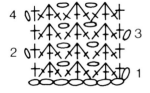

Trinity Stitch II

Worked as Trinity Stitch I.
Work 1 row each in colors A, B and C throughout.

> **Hint:** Normally the maximum number of stitches which may be worked together into a single crochet cluster is 3. (Longer stitches may have more).
> Remember that working stitches together into clusters is often the best way to decrease.

Half Double Crochet Cluster Stitch I

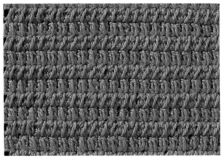

Any number of sts.
(add 1 for base chain)
Note: For description of hdc2tog see page 14 (Puff Stitch).

1st row: Skip 2ch (count as 1hdc), *hdc2tog all into next ch; rep from * to end, turn.

2nd row: 2ch (count as 1hdc), skip 1 st, hdc2tog all into next and each st, ending with hdc2tog into top of tch, turn.

Rep 2nd row.

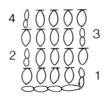

Half Double Crochet Cluster Stitch II

Any number of sts.
(add 2 for base chain)
Note: For description of hdc2tog see page 10 (Clusters).

1st row: Skip 2ch (count as 1hdc), hdc2tog inserting hook into each of next 2ch, *hdc2tog inserting hook first into same ch as previous cluster then into next ch; rep from * until 1ch remains, 1hdc into last ch, turn.

2nd row: 2ch (count as 1hdc), hdc2tog inserting hook first into first st then into next st, *hdc2tog inserting hook first into same st as previous cluster then into next st; rep from * ending 1hdc into top of tch, turn.

Rep 2nd row.

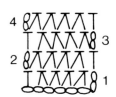

Half Double Crochet Cluster Stitch III

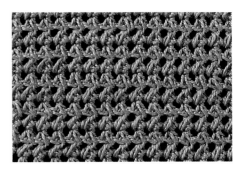

Multiple of 2 sts.
(add 1 for base chain)
Note: For description of hdc2tog see page 10 (Clusters).

1st row: Skip 2ch (count as 1hdc), *hdc2tog inserting hook into each of next 2ch, 1ch; rep from * ending 1hdc into last ch, turn.

2nd row: 2ch (count as 1hdc), skip 1 st, *hdc2tog inserting hook into next ch sp then into next st, 1ch; rep from * ending 1hdc into top of tch, turn.

Rep 2nd row.

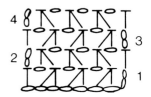

Forked Cluster Stitch

Any number of sts.
(add 2 for base chain)

o Chain   ● Slip stitch   + Single crochet   T Half double crochet   ╀ Double crochet   ╪ Treble   ╪╪ Double treble

Special Abbreviation

⅄ **FC (Forked Cluster)** = [yo, insert hook into ch or st as indicated, yo, draw loop through] twice (5 loops on hook), [yo, draw through 3 loops] twice.

1st row: Skip 2ch (count as 1dc), work 1FC inserting hook into each of next 2ch, *work 1FC inserting hook into same ch as previous FC then into next ch; rep from * until 1ch remains, 1dc into last ch, turn.

2nd row: 3ch (count as 1dc), 1FC inserting hook into each of first 2 sts, *1FC inserting hook into same st as previous FC then into next st; rep from * ending 1dc into top of tch, turn.

Rep 2nd row.

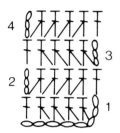

Odd Forked Cluster Stitch

Any number of sts.
(add 2 for base chain)

Special Abbreviation

⅄ **OFC (Odd Forked Cluster)** = yo, insert hook into ch or st as indicated, yo, draw loop through, yo, draw through 2 loops, insert hook into next ch or st, yo, draw loop through, yo, draw through all 3 loops on hook.

1st row: Skip 2ch (count as 1hdc), 1OFC inserting hook first into 3rd then 4th ch from hook, *1OFC inserting hook first into same ch as previous OFC then into next ch; rep from * until 1ch remains, 1hdc into last ch, turn.

2nd row: 2ch (count as 1hdc), 1OFC inserting hook into first st then into next st, *1OFC inserting hook into same st as previous OFC then into next st; rep from * ending 1hdc into top of tch, turn.

Rep 2nd row.

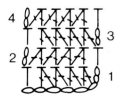

Mixed Cluster Stitch

Multiple of 2 sts + 1.
(add 1 for base chain)

Special Abbreviation

⌐ **MC (Mixed Cluster)** = yo, insert hook into first st as indicated, yo, draw loop through, yo, draw through 2 loops, skip 1 st, [yo, insert hook into next st, yo, draw loop through] twice all into same st, (6 loops on hook), yo, draw through all loops on hook.

1st row (wrong side): Skip 2ch (count as 1sc), 1sc into next and each ch to end, turn.

2nd row: 2ch (count as 1hdc), 1MC inserting hook into first then 3rd st, *1ch, 1MC inserting hook first into same st as previous MC; rep from * ending last rep in top of tch, 1hdc into same place, turn.

3rd row: 1ch (counts as 1sc), skip 1 st, 1sc into next and each st to end, working last st into top of tch, turn.

Rep 2nd and 3rd rows.

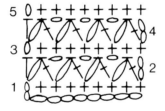

Double Crochet Cluster Stitch I

Multiple of 2 sts.
(add 2 for base chain)

Special Abbreviation

DcC (Double Crochet Cluster) = *yo, insert hook into ch or st as indicated, yo, draw loop through, yo, draw through 2 loops*, skip 1 ch or st, rep from * to * into

next st, yo, draw through all 3 loops on hook.

1st row: Skip 2ch (count as 1dc), work 1DcC inserting hook first into 3rd ch, 1ch, *work 1DcC inserting hook first into same ch as previous DcC, 1ch; rep from * ending 1dc into last ch, turn.

2nd row: 3ch (counts as 1dc), 1DcC inserting hook first into first st, 1ch, *1DcC inserting hook first into same st as previous DcC, 1ch; rep from * ending 1dc into top of tch, turn.

Rep 2nd row.

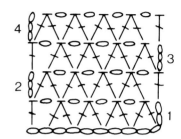

Double Crochet Cluster Stitch II

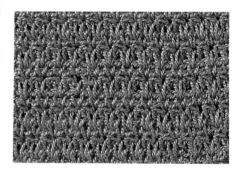

Multiple of 2 sts.
(add 2 for base chain)

Special Abbreviation

DcC (Double Crochet Cluster) worked as under Double Crochet Cluster Stitch I.

1st row (right side): Skip 2ch (count as 1dc), work 1DcC inserting hook into 3rd ch then 5th ch, 1ch, *work 1DcC inserting hook first into same ch as previous DcC, 1ch; rep from * ending 1dc into last ch, turn.

2nd row: 1ch (counts as 1sc), skip 1 st, *1sc into next ch sp, 1ch, skip 1 st; rep from * ending 1sc into top of tch, turn.

3rd row: 3ch (count as 1dc), 1DcC inserting hook first into first st, 1ch, *1DcC inserting hook first into same st as previous DcC, 1ch; rep from * ending 1dc into top of tch, turn.

Rep 2nd and 3rd rows.

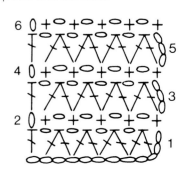

Textured Stitches

Double Crochet Cluster Stitch III

Any number of sts.
(add 2 for base chain)
Note: For description of dc2tog see page 10 (Clusters).
1st row: Skip 3ch (count as 1dc), work dc2tog into next and each ch until 1ch remains, 1dc into last ch, turn.
2nd row: 3ch (count as 1dc), dc2tog between first dc and next cluster, *dc2tog between next 2 clusters; rep from * ending 1dc into top of tch, turn.
Rep 2nd row.

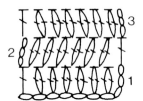

Crunch Stitch

Multiple of 2 sts.
(add 1 for base chain)
1st row: Skip 2ch (count as 1hdc), *sl st into next ch, 1hdc into next ch; rep from * ending sl st into last ch, turn.
2nd row: 2ch (count as 1hdc), skip 1 st, *sl st into next hdc, 1hdc into next sl st; rep from * ending sl st into top of tch, turn.
Rep 2nd row.

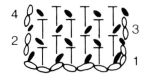

Floret Stitch I

Multiple of 2 sts + 1.
(add 2 for base chain)
1st row (right side): Skip 3ch (count as 1dc), 1dc into next and each ch to end, turn.
2nd row: 1ch, skip 1 st, *1dc into next st, sl st into next st; rep from * ending last rep into top of tch, turn.
3rd row: 3ch (count as 1dc), skip 1 st, *1dc into next dc, 1dc into next sl st; rep from * ending last rep into tch, turn.
Rep 2nd and 3rd rows.

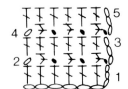

Floret Stitch II

Worked as Floret Stitch I.
Work 1 row each in colors A and B alternately throughout.

Floret Stitch III

Worked as Floret Stitch I.
Work 1 row each in colors A, B and C throughout.

Griddle Stitch

Multiple of 2 sts.
(add 2 for base chain)
1st row: Skip 3ch (count as 1dc), *1sc into next ch, 1dc into next ch; rep from * ending 1sc into last ch, turn.
2nd row: 3ch (count as 1dc), skip 1 st, *1sc into next dc, 1dc into next sc; rep from * ending 1sc into top of tch, turn.
Rep 2nd row.

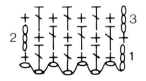

Crumpled Griddle Stitch

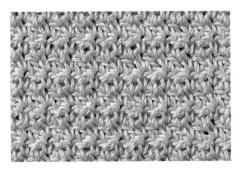

Multiple of 2 sts + 1.
(add 2 for base chain)
1st row: Skip 3ch (count as 1dc), *1sc into next ch, 1dc into next ch; rep from * to end, turn.
2nd row: 3ch (count as 1dc), skip 1 st, *1sc into next sc, 1dc into next dc; rep from * ending last rep into top of tch, turn.
Rep 2nd row.

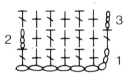

⚬ Chain ● Slip stitch + Single crochet T Half double crochet ⊤ Double crochet ⧧ Treble ⧦ Double treble

Solid Shell Stitch

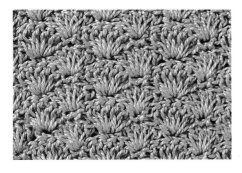

Multiple of 6 sts + 1.
(add 1 for base chain)

1st row: 1sc into 2nd ch from hook, *skip 2ch, 5dc into next ch, skip 2ch, 1sc into next ch; rep from * to end, turn.

2nd row: 3ch (count as 1dc), 2dc into first st, *skip 2dc, 1sc into next dc, skip 2dc, 5dc into next sc; rep from * ending last rep with 3dc into last sc, skip tch, turn.

3rd row: 1ch, 1sc into first st, *skip 2dc, 5dc into next sc, skip 2dc, 1sc into next dc; rep from * ending last rep with 1sc into top of tch, turn.

Rep 2nd and 3rd rows.

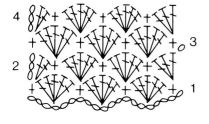

Wavy Shell Stitch I

Multiple of 14 sts + 1.
(add 2 for base chain)

Note: See Wavy Shell Stitch II for stitch diagram.

1st row (right side): Skip 2ch (count as 1dc), 3dc into next ch, *skip 3ch, 1sc into each of next 7ch, skip 3ch, 7dc into next ch; rep from * ending last rep with 4dc into last ch, turn.

2nd row: 1ch, 1sc into first st, 1sc into each st to end, finishing with 1sc into top of tch, turn.

3rd row: 1ch, 1sc into each of first 4 sts, *skip 3 sts, 7dc into next st, skip 3 sts, 1sc into each of next 7 sts; rep from * to last 11 sts, skip 3 sts, 7dc into next st, skip 3 sts,

1sc into each of last 4 sc, skip tch, turn.

4th row: 1ch, 1sc into first st, 1sc into next and each st to end, skip tch, turn.

5th row: 3ch (count as 1dc), 3dc into first st, *skip 3 sts, 1sc into each of next 7 sts, skip 3 sts, 7dc into next st; rep from * ending last rep with 4dc into last sc, skip tch, turn.

Rep 2nd, 3rd, 4th and 5th rows.

Wavy Shell Stitch II

Worked as Wavy Shell Stitch I.
Work 1 row each in colors A, B and C throughout.

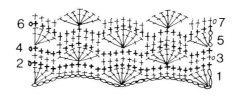

Catherine Wheel I

Multiple of 10 sts + 6.
(add 1 for base chain)

Special Abbreviation

CL (Cluster) = work [yo, insert hook, yo, draw loop through, yo, draw through 2 loops] over the number of sts indicated, yo, draw through all loops on hook (see also page 10 (Clusters).

1st row (wrong side): 1sc into 2nd ch from hook, 1sc into next ch, *skip 3ch, 7dc into next ch, skip 3ch, 1sc into each of next 3ch; rep from * to last 4 ch, skip 3 ch, 4dc into last ch, turn.

2nd row: 1ch, 1sc into first st, 1sc into next st, *3ch, 1CL over next 7 sts, 3ch, 1sc into

each of next 3 sts; rep from * to last 4 sts, 3ch, 1CL over last 4 sts, skip tch, turn.

3rd row: 3ch (count as 1dc), 3dc into first st, *skip 3ch, 1sc into each of next 3sc, skip 3ch, 7dc into loop which closed next CL; rep from * to end finishing with skip 3ch, 1sc into each of last 2sc, skip tch, turn.

4th row: 3ch (count as 1dc), skip first st, 1CL over next 3 sts, *3ch, 1sc into each of next 3 sts, 3ch, 1CL over next 7 sts; rep from * finishing with 3ch, 1sc into next st, 1sc into top of tch, turn.

5th row: 1ch, 1sc into each of first 2sc, *skip 3ch, 7dc into loop which closed next CL, skip 3ch, 1sc into each of next 3sc; rep from * ending skip 3ch, 4dc into top of tch, turn.

Rep 2nd, 3rd, 4th and 5th rows.

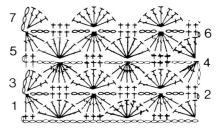

Catherine Wheel II

Worked as Catherine Wheel I.
Make base chain and work first row in color A. Thereafter work 2 rows each in color B and color A.

Catherine Wheel III

Worked as Catherine Wheel I.
Work 1 row each in colors A, B and C throughout.

Textured Stitches

Catherine Wheel IV

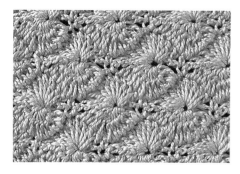

Multiple of 8 sts + 1.
(add 1 for base chain)

Special Abbreviation

CL (Cluster) worked as under Catherine Wheel I.

1st row (right side): 1sc into 2nd ch from hook, *skip 3ch, 9dc into next ch, skip 3ch, 1sc into next ch; rep from * to end, turn.
2nd row: 3ch (count as 1dc), skip first st, 1CL over next 4 sts, *3ch, 1sc into next st, 3ch, 1CL over next 9 sts; rep from * ending last rep with 1CL over last 5 sts, skip tch, turn.
3rd row: 3ch (count as 1dc), 4dc into first st, *skip 3ch, 1sc into next sc, skip 3ch, 9dc into loop which closed next CL; rep from * ending last rep with 5dc into top of tch, turn.
4th row: 1ch, 1sc into first st, *3ch, 1CL over next 9 sts, 3ch, 1sc into next st; rep from * ending last rep with 1sc into top of tch, turn.
5th row: 1ch, 1sc into first st, *skip 3ch, 9dc into loop which closed next CL, skip 3ch, 1sc into next sc; rep from * to end, skip tch, turn.
Rep 2nd, 3rd, 4th and 5th rows.

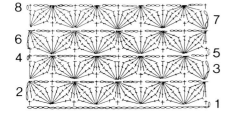

Silt Stitch

Multiple of 3 sts + 1.
(add 2 for base chain)

1st row (right side): Skip 3ch (count as 1dc), 1dc into next and each ch to end, turn.
2nd row: 1ch (counts as 1sc), 2dc into first st, *skip 2 sts, work [1sc, 2dc] into next st; rep from * to last 3 sts, skip 2 sts, 1sc into top of tch, turn.
3rd row: 3ch (count as 1dc), skip 1 st, 1dc into next and each st to end, working last st into top of tch, turn.
Rep 2nd and 3rd rows.

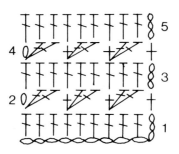

Hexagon Stitch

Multiple of 8 sts + 4.
(add 1 for base chain)

Special Abbreviations

CL (Cluster) = work [yo, insert hook, yo, draw loop through loosely] over number and position of sts indicated, ending yo, draw through all loops, 1ch tightly to close Cluster. See also page 10 (Clusters).

Picot = 5ch, 1sc into 2nd ch from hook, 1sc into each of next 3ch.

1st row (wrong side): 1sc into 2nd ch from hook, 1sc into each of next 3ch (counts as Picot), skip 3ch, 3dc into next ch, skip 3ch, 1sc into next ch, *skip 3ch, into next ch work [3dc, 1 Picot, 3dc], skip 3ch, 1sc into next ch; rep from * to end, turn.
2nd row: 4ch (count as 1tr), 1CL over each of first 8 sts, 3ch, 1sc into top of Picot, *3ch, 1CL over next 15 sts inserting hook into underside of each of 4ch of Picot, into next 3dc, 1sc, 3dc and 4sc of next Picot, then 3ch, 1sc into top of Picot; rep from * to end, turn.
3rd row: 1ch, 1sc into first st, *skip 3ch, into loop which closed next CL work [3dc, 1 Picot, 3dc], skip 3ch, 1sc into next st; rep from * ending skip 3ch, 4dc into loop which closed last CL, skip tch, turn.
4th row: 7ch (count as 1tr and 3ch), starting into 5th ch from hook work 1CL over next 15 sts as before, *3ch, 1sc into top of Picot, 3ch, 1CL over next 15 sts; rep from * ending last rep with 1CL over last 8 sts, skip tch, turn.
5th row: 8ch, 1sc into 2nd ch from hook, 1sc into each of next 3ch (counts as 1dc and 1 Picot), 3dc into first st, skip 3ch, 1sc into next sc, *skip 3ch, into loop which closed next CL work [3dc, 1 Picot, 3dc], skip 3ch, 1sc into next sc; rep from * ending last rep with 1sc into 4th ch of tch, turn.
Rep 2nd, 3rd, 4th and 5th rows.

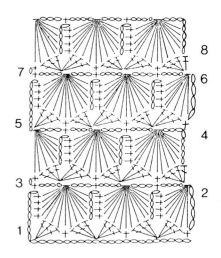

Grit Stitch I

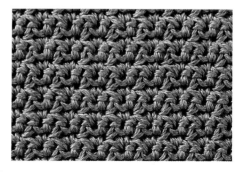

Multiple of 2 sts + 1.
(add 2 for base chain)

1st row: Skip 2ch (count as 1sc), 1sc into next ch, *skip 1ch, 2sc into next ch; rep from * to last 2ch, skip 1ch, 1sc into last ch, turn.

2nd row: 1ch (counts as 1sc), 1sc into first st, *skip 1sc, 2sc into next sc; rep from * to last 2 sts, skip 1sc, 1sc into top of tch, turn.
Rep 2nd row.

⬯ Chain ⬤ Slip stitch + Single crochet T Half double crochet ⊤ Double crochet ⸾ Treble ⹀ Double treble

Grit Stitch II

Multiple of 2 sts + 1.
(add 2 for base chain)

1st row: Skip 2ch (count as 1sc), 1dc into next ch, *skip 1ch, work [1sc and 1dc] into next ch; rep from * to last 2ch, skip 1ch, 1sc into last ch, turn.

2nd row: 1ch (counts as 1sc), 1dc into first st, *skip 1dc, work [1sc and 1dc] into next sc; rep from * to last 2 sts, skip 1dc, 1sc into top of tch, turn.

Rep 2nd row.

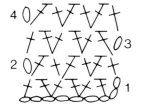

Sedge Stitch I

Multiple of 3 sts + 1.
(add 2 for base chain)

1st row: Skip 2ch (count as 1sc), work [1hdc, 1dc] into next ch, *skip 2ch, work [1sc, 1hdc, 1dc] into next ch; rep from * to last 3ch, skip 2ch, 1sc into last ch, turn.

2nd row: 1ch (counts as 1sc), work [1hdc, 1dc] into first st, *skip [1dc and 1hdc], work [1sc, 1hdc, 1dc] into next sc; rep from * to last 3 sts, skip [1dc and 1hdc], 1sc into top of tch, turn.

Rep 2nd row.

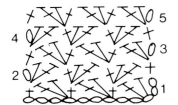

Sedge Stitch II

Multiple of 3 sts + 1.
(add 2 for base chain)

1st row: Skip 2ch (count as 1sc), 2dc into next ch, *skip 2ch, [1sc, 2dc] into next ch; rep from * to last 3ch, skip 2ch, 1sc into last ch, turn.

2nd row: 1ch (counts as 1 sc), 2dc into first st, *skip 2dc, [1sc, 2dc] into next sc; rep from * to last 3 sts, skip 2dc, 1sc into top of tch, turn.

Rep 2nd row.

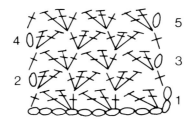

Wattle Stitch

Multiple of 3 sts + 2.
(add 1 for base chain)

1st row: Skip 2ch (count as 1sc), *work [1sc, 1ch, 1dc] into next ch, skip 2ch; rep from * ending 1sc into last ch, turn.

2nd row: 1ch (counts as 1sc), skip first sc and next dc, *work [1sc, 1ch, 1dc] into next ch sp, skip 1sc and 1dc; rep from * ending with [1sc, 1ch, 1dc] into last ch sp, skip next sc, 1sc into top of tch, turn.

Rep 2nd row.

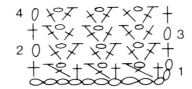

Wedge Stitch I

Multiple of 6 sts + 1.
(add 1 for base chain)

Special Abbreviation

WP (Wedge Picot) = work 6ch, 1sc into 2nd ch from hook, 1hdc into next ch, 1dc into next ch, 1tr into next ch, 1dtr into next ch.

1st row (wrong side): 1sc into 2nd ch from hook, *1WP, skip 5ch, 1sc into next ch; rep from * to end, turn.

2nd row: 5ch (count as 1dtr), *1sc into top of WP, over next 5ch at underside of WP work 1sc into next ch, 1hdc into next ch, 1dc into next ch, 1tr into next ch, 1dtr into next ch, skip next sc; rep from * omitting 1dtr at end of last rep when 2 sts remain, **[yo] 3 times, insert hook into last ch at underside of WP, yo, draw loop through, [yo, draw through 2 loops] 3 times, rep from ** into next sc, yo, draw through all 3 loops on hook, skip tch, turn.

3rd row: 1ch, 1sc into first st, *1WP, skip next 5 sts, 1sc into next st; rep from * ending last rep with 1sc into top of tch, turn.

Rep 2nd and 3rd rows.

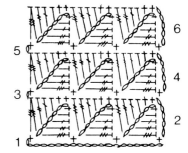

Wedge Stitch II

Worked as Wedge Stitch I.

Make base chain and work first row in color A. Thereafter work 2 rows each in color B and color A.

Textured Stitches

Crosshatch Stitch I

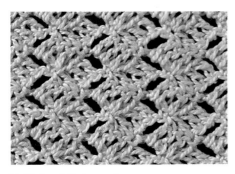

Multiple of 7 sts + 4.
(add 3 for base chain)

1st row: Skip 2ch (count as 1dc), 2dc into next ch, *skip 3ch, 1sc into next ch, 3ch, 1dc into each of next 3ch; rep from * to last 4ch, skip 3ch, 1sc into last ch, turn.

2nd row: 3ch (count as 1dc), 2dc into first sc, *skip 3dc, 1sc into first of 3ch, 3ch, 1dc into each of next 2ch, 1dc into next sc; rep from * ending skip 2dc, 1sc into top of tch, turn.

Rep 2nd row.

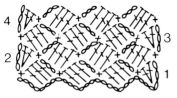

Crosshatch Stitch II

Worked as Crosshatch Stitch I.
Work 1 row each in colors A, B and C throughout.

Ridged Chevron Stitch

Multiple of 12 sts.
(add 3 for base chain)

Note: For description of dc2tog see page 10 (Clusters).

1st row: Skip 3ch (count as 1dc), 1dc into next ch, *1dc into each of next 3ch, [over next 2ch work dc2tog] twice, 1dc into each of next 3ch, [2dc into next ch] twice; rep from * ending last rep with 2dc once only into last ch, turn.

2nd row: 3ch (count as 1dc), 1dc into first st, always inserting hook into back loop only of each st *1dc into each of next 3 sts, [over next 2 sts work dc2tog] twice, 1dc into each of next 3 sts, [2dc into next st] twice; rep from * ending last rep with 2dc once only into top of tch, turn.

Rep 2nd row.

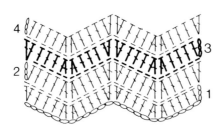

Sharp Chevron Stitch

Multiple of 14 sts.
(add 2 for base chain)

Note: For description of dc3tog see page 10 (Clusters).

1st row: Skip 2ch (count as 1dc), 2dc into next ch, *1dc into each of next 3ch, [over next 3ch work dc3tog] twice, 1dc into each of next 3ch, [3dc into next st] twice; rep from * ending last rep with 3dc once only into last ch, turn.

2nd row: 3ch (count as 1dc), 2dc into first st, *1dc into each of next 3 sts, [over next 3 sts work dc3tog] twice, 1dc into each of next 3 sts, [3dc into next st] twice; rep from * ending last rep with 3dc once only into top of tch, turn.

Rep 2nd row.

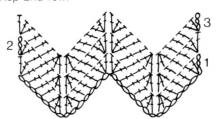

Close Chevron Stitch

Multiple of 11 sts + 1.
(add 1 for base chain)
Work 4 rows each in colors A and B alternately throughout.

1st row (right side): 2sc into 2nd ch from hook, *1sc into each of next 4ch, skip 2ch, 1sc into each of next 4ch, 3sc into next ch; rep from * ending last rep with 2sc only into last ch, turn.

2nd row: 1ch, 2sc into first st, *1sc into each of next 4 sts, skip 2 sts, 1sc into each of next 4 sts, 3sc into next st; rep from * ending last rep with 2sc only into last st, skip tch, turn.

Rep 2nd row.

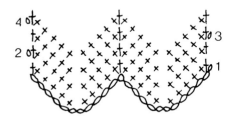

Peephole Chevron Stitch

Multiple of 10 sts.
(add 2 for base chain)

1st row: Skip 2ch (count as 1dc), 1dc into each of next 4ch, *skip 2ch, 1dc into each of next 4ch, 2ch, 1dc into each of next 4ch; rep from * to last 6ch, skip 2ch, 1dc into each of next 3ch, 2dc into last ch, turn.

2nd row: 3ch (count as 1dc), 1dc into first st, 1dc into each of next 3 sts, *skip 2 sts, 1dc into each of next 3 sts, [1dc, 2ch, 1dc] into 2ch sp, 1dc into each of next 3 sts; rep

o Chain ● Slip stitch + Single crochet T Half double crochet ⊤ Double crochet ⧧ Treble ⧧ Double treble

from * to last 6 sts, skip 2 sts, 1dc into each of next 3 sts, 2dc into top of tch, turn.
Rep 2nd row.

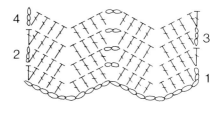

Crunchy Chevron Stitch

Multiple of 8 sts.
(add 1 for base chain)
Note: For description of hdc2tog see page 14 (Puff Stitch).
Work 1 row each in colors A, B, C, D and E throughout.

1st row: 1sc into 2nd ch from hook, 1sc into each of next 3ch, *hdc2tog all into each of next 4ch, 1sc into each of next 4ch; rep from * to last 4ch, hdc2tog all into each of last 4ch, turn.

2nd row: 1ch, then starting in first st, *1sc into each of next 4 sts, hdc2tog all into each of next 4sc; rep from * to end, skip tch, turn.
Rep 2nd row.

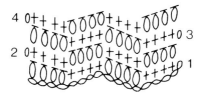

Simple Chevron Stitch

Multiple of 10 sts + 1.
(add 2 for base chain)
Note: For description of dc3tog see page 10 (Clusters).

1st row: Skip 2ch (count as 1dc), 1dc into next ch, *1dc into each of next 3ch, over next 3ch work dc3tog, 1dc into each of next 3ch, 3dc into next ch; rep from * ending last rep with 2dc into last ch, turn.

2nd row: 3ch (count as 1dc), 1dc into first st, *1dc into each of next 3dc, over next 3 sts work dc3tog, 1dc into each of next 3dc, 3dc into next dc; rep from * ending last rep with 2dc into top of tch, turn.
Rep 2nd row.

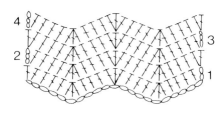

Textured Wave Stitch

Multiple of 20 sts.
(add 1 for base chain)
Special Abbreviation
2Cdc (2 crossed double crochets) = skip next st, 1dc into next st, 1dc into skipped st working over previous dc. See also page 12 (Crossed Stitch I).
Work 2 rows each in colors A and B alternately throughout.

1st base row (right side): Skip 2ch (count as 1sc), 1sc into next and each ch to end, turn.

2nd base row: 1ch (counts as 1sc), skip 1 st, 1sc into next and each st to end working last st into tch, turn.

Commence Pattern
1st row: 3ch (count as 1dc), skip 1 st, over next 4 sts work [2Cdc] twice, *1sc into each of next 10 sts, over next 10 sts work [2Cdc] 5 times; rep from * to last 15 sts, 1sc into each of next 10 sts, over next 4 sts work [2Cdc] twice, 1dc into tch, turn.

2nd row: As 1st row.

3rd and 4th rows: As 2nd base row.

5th row: 1ch (counts as 1sc), skip 1 st, 1sc into each of next 4 sts, *over next 10 sts work [2Cdc] 5 times, 1sc into each of next 10 sts; rep from * to last 15 sts, over next 10 sts work [2Cdc] 5 times, 1sc into each

of last 5 sts working last st into tch, turn.
6th row: As 5th row.
7th and 8th rows: As 2nd base row.
Rep these 8 rows.

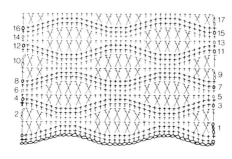

2 rows each in colors A and B

Long Wave Stitch

Multiple of 14 sts + 1.
(add 1 for base chain)
Special Abbreviations
Gr (Group) (worked over 14 sts) = 1sc into next st, [1hdc into next st] twice, [1dc into next st] twice, [1tr into next st] 3 times, [1dc into next st] twice, [1hdc into next st] twice, [1sc into next st] twice.

Rev Gr (Reverse Group) (worked over 14 sts) = 1tr into next st, [1dc into next st] twice, [1hdc into next st] twice, [1sc into next st] 3 times, [1hdc into next st] twice, [1dc into next st] twice, [1tr into next st] twice.

Work 2 rows each in colors A and B alternately throughout.

1st row (right side): Skip 2ch (count as 1sc), *1Gr over next 14ch; rep from * to end, turn.

2nd row: 1ch (counts as 1sc), skip first st, 1sc into next and each st to end working last st into top of tch, turn.

3rd row: 4ch (count as 1tr), skip first st, *1 Rev Gr over next 14 sts; rep from * ending last rep in tch, turn.

4th row: As 2nd row.

5th row: 1ch (counts as 1sc), skip first st, *1Gr over next 14 sts; rep from * ending last rep in tch, turn.

6th row: As 2nd row.
Rep 3rd, 4th, 5th and 6th rows.

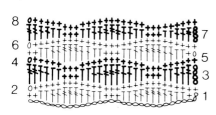

Textured Stitches

Smooth Wave Stitch

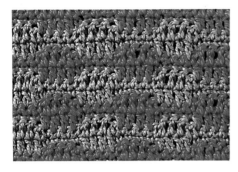

Multiple of 8 sts + 4.
(add 1 for base chain)

Work 2 rows each in colors A and B alternately throughout.

1st row (right side): Skip 2ch (count as 1sc), 1sc into each of next 3ch, *1dc into each of next 4ch, 1sc into each of next 4ch; rep from * to end, turn.

2nd row: 1ch (counts as 1sc), skip first st, 1sc into each of next 3 sts, *1dc into each of next 4 sts, 1sc into each of next 4 sts; rep from * to end working last st into top of tch, turn.

3rd row: 3ch (count as 1dc), skip first st, 1dc into each of next 3 sts, *1sc into each of next 4 sts, 1dc into each of next 4 sts; rep from * to end working last st into top of tch, turn.

4th row: As 3rd row.

5th and 6th rows: As 2nd row.

Rep 3rd, 4th, 5th and 6th rows.

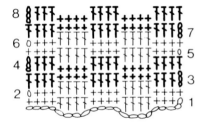

Wave and Chevron Stitch

Multiple of 6 sts + 1.
(add 1 for base chain)

Note: For description of sc2tog, sc3tog, tr2tog and tr3tog see page 10 (Clusters).

Work 2 rows each in colors A, B, C and D throughout.

Base row: (right side): Skip 2ch (count as 1sc), 1sc into next and each ch to end, turn.

Commence Pattern

1st row: 1ch (counts as 1sc), skip 1 st, *1hdc into next st, 1dc into next st, 3tr into next st, 1dc into next st, 1hdc into next st, 1sc into next st; rep from * to end, turn.

2nd row: 1ch, skip 1 st, 1sc into next st (counts as sc2tog), 1sc into each of next 2 sts, *3sc into next st, 1sc into each of next 2 sts, over next 3 sts work sc3tog, 1sc into each of next 2 sts; rep from * to last 5 sts, 3sc into next st, 1sc into each of next 2 sts, over last 2 sts work sc2tog, skip tch, turn.

3rd row: As 2nd row.

4th row: 4ch, skip 1 st, 1tr into next st (counts as tr2tog), *1dc into next st, 1hdc into next st, 1sc into next st, 1hdc into next st, 1dc into next st**, over next 3 sts work tr3tog; rep from * ending last rep at **, over last 2 sts work tr2tog, skip tch, turn.

5th row: 1ch (counts as 1sc), skip 1 st, 1sc into next and each st to end, turn.

6th row: As 5th row.

Rep these 6 rows.

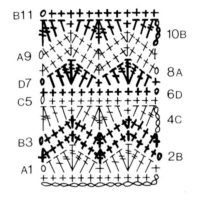

Crossed Double Crochet Stitch

Multiple of 2 sts.
(add 2 for base chain)

Special Abbreviation

2Cdc (2 crossed double crochets) worked as under Textured Wave Stitch (see page 31).

1st row (right side): Skip 3ch (count as 1dc), *2Cdc over next 2ch; rep from * ending 1dc into last ch, turn.

2nd row: 1ch (counts as 1sc), skip 1 st, 1sc into next and each st to end, working last st into top of tch, turn.

3rd row: 3ch (count as 1dc), skip 1 st, *work 2Cdc over next 2 sts; rep from * ending 1dc into tch, turn.

Rep 2nd and 3rd rows.

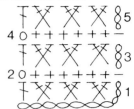

Woven Shell Stitch

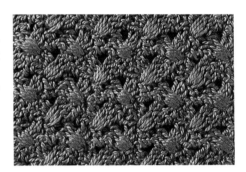

Multiple of 6 sts + 1.
(add 2 for base chain)

Special Abbreviation

CGr (Crossed Group) = skip 3dc and next st, 3dc into 2nd of next 3dc, 3ch, 3dc into 2nd of 3dc just skipped working back over last 3dc made.

1st row: Skip 3ch (count as 1dc), *skip next 3ch, 3dc into next ch, 3ch, 3dc into 2nd of 3ch just skipped working back over last 3dc made, skip 1ch, 1dc into next ch; rep from * to end, turn.

2nd row: 3ch (count as 1dc), 3dc into first st, 1sc into next 3ch arch, *1CGr, 1sc into next 3ch arch; rep from * ending 4dc into top of tch, turn.

3rd row: 3ch (count as 1dc), skip 1 st, 1CGr, *1sc into next 3ch loop, 1CGr; rep from * ending 1dc into top of tch, turn.

Rep 2nd and 3rd rows.

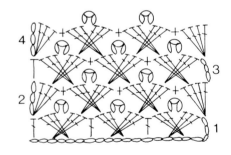

Crossbill Stitch

○ Chain   ● Slip stitch   + Single crochet   T Half double crochet   ⊤ Double crochet   ⨏ Treble   ⨎ Double treble

Multiple of 4 sts + 1.
(add 2 for base chain)

Special Abbreviation

2Cdc (2 crossed double crochets) = skip 2 sts, 1dc into next st, 1ch, 1dc into first of 2 sts just skipped working back over last dc made (see also page 12 — Crossed Stitch I).

1st row: Skip 3ch (count as 1dc), *work 2Cdc over next 3ch, 1dc into next ch; rep from * to end, turn.

2nd row: 3ch (count as 1dc), 1dc into first st, skip 1dc, *1dc into next ch, work 2Cdc over next 3dc, rep from * ending 1dc into last ch, skip 1dc, 2dc into top of tch, turn.

3rd row: 3ch (count as 1dc), skip 1 st, *work 2Cdc over next 3dc, 1dc into next ch; rep from * ending last rep into top of tch, turn.

Rep 2nd and 3rd rows.

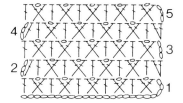

Sidesaddle Cluster Stitch

Multiple of 5 sts + 1.
(add 1 for base chain)

Note: For description of dc4tog see page 10 (Clusters).

1st row: 1sc into 2nd ch from hook, *3ch, dc4tog over next 4ch, 1ch, 1sc into next ch; rep from * to end, turn.

2nd row: 5ch, 1sc into next cluster, *3ch, dc4tog all into next 3ch arch, 1ch, 1sc into next cluster; rep from * ending 3ch, dc4tog all into next 3ch arch, 1dc into last sc, skip tch, turn.

3rd row: 1ch, skip 1 st, 1sc into next CL, *3ch, 1CL into next 3ch arch, 1ch, 1sc into next CL; rep from * ending last rep with 1sc into tch arch, turn.

Rep 2nd and 3rd rows.

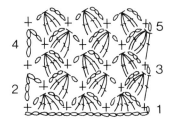

Crossed Cluster Stitch

Multiple of 8 sts + 4.
(add 1 for base chain)

Special Abbreviation

2CC (2 crossed clusters) = skip 1 st, into next st work *[yo, insert hook, yo, draw loop through] twice, yo, draw through all 5 loops on hook; rep from * into st just skipped working over previous cluster.

1st row (wrong side): Skip 2ch (count as 1sc), 1sc into next and each ch to end, turn.

2nd row: 3ch (count as 1dc), skip 1 st, *2CC over next 2 sts, 1dc into each of next 6 sts, rep from * to last 3 sts, 2CC over next 2 sts, 1dc into tch, turn.

3rd row: 1ch (counts as 1sc), skip 1 st, 1sc into next and each st to end, working last st into top of tch, turn.

4th row: 3ch (counts as 1dc), skip 1 st, 1dc into each of next 4 sts, *2CC over next 2 sts, 1dc into each of next 6 sts; rep from * to last 7 sts, 2CC over next 2 sts, 1dc into each of last 5 sts, working last st into tch, turn.

5th row: As 3rd row.

Rep 2nd, 3rd, 4th and 5th rows.

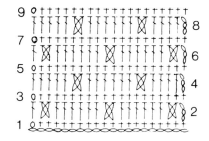

Diagonal Shell Stitch

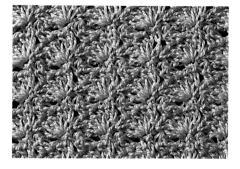

Multiple of 4 sts + 1.
(add 1 for base chain)

Special Abbreviation

Shell = [1sc, 3ch, 4dc] all into same st.
Note: For description of dc2tog see page 10 (Clusters).

1st row (right side): Work 1 shell into 2nd ch from hook, *skip 3ch, 1 shell into next ch; rep from * to last 4ch, skip 3ch, 1sc into last ch, turn.

2nd row: 3ch (count as 1dc), skip 1 st, *skip 1dc, over next 2 sts work dc2tog, 3ch, skip 1dc, 1sc into top of 3ch; rep from * to end, turn.

3rd row: 1ch, 1 shell into first st, *skip 3ch and next st, 1 shell into next sc; rep from * ending skip 3ch and next st, 1sc into top of tch, turn.

Rep 2nd and 3rd rows.

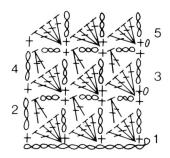

Sidesaddle Shell Stitch

Multiple of 6 sts + 1.
(add 3 for base chain)

Special Abbreviation

Shell = 3dc, 1ch, [1sc, 1hdc, 1dc] all into side of last of 3dc just made.

1st row (wrong side): Skip 3ch (count as 1dc), 3dc into next ch, skip 2ch, 1sc into next ch, *skip 2ch, Shell into next ch, skip 2ch, 1sc into next ch; rep from * to last 3ch, skip 2ch, 4dc into last ch, turn.

2nd row: 1ch (counts as 1sc), skip 1 st, *skip next 3 sts, Shell into next sc, skip 3 sts, 1sc into next ch sp; rep from * ending last rep with 1sc into top of tch, turn.

3rd row: 3ch (count as 1dc), 3dc into first st, skip 3 sts, 1sc into next ch sp, *skip 3 sts, Shell into next sc, skip 3 sts, 1sc into next ch sp; rep from * ending skip 3 sts, 4dc into tch, turn.

Rep 2nd and 3rd rows.

Spikes

Interlocking Block Stitch I

Multiple of 6 sts + 3.
(add 2 for base chain)

Special Abbreviation

Sdc (Spike double crochet) = work dc over ch sp by inserting hook into top of next row below (or base chain).

Work 1 row each in colors A, B and C throughout.

1st row: Skip 3ch (count as 1dc), 1dc into each of next 2ch, *3ch, skip 3ch, 1dc into each of next 3ch; rep from * to end, turn.
2nd row: *3ch, skip 3 sts, 1Sdc over each of next 3 sts; rep from * to last 3 sts, 2ch, skip 2 sts, sl st into top of tch, turn.
3rd row: 3ch (count as 1Sdc), skip 1 st, 1Sdc over each of next 2 sts, *3ch, skip 3 sts, 1Sdc over each of next 3 sts; rep from * to end, turn.
Rep 2nd and 3rd rows.

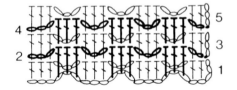

Interlocking Block Stitch II

Worked as Interlocking Block Stitch I.
Work 1 row each in colors A and B alternately throughout. Do not break yarn when changing color, but begin row at same end as color.

Diagonal Spike Stitch

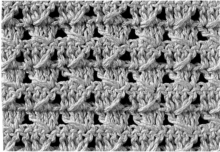

Multiple of 4 sts + 2.
(add 2 for base chain)

Special Abbreviation

Sdc (Spike double crochet) = yo, insert hook into same place that first dc of previous 3dc block was worked, yo, draw loop through and up so as not to crush 3dc block, [yo, draw through 2 loops] twice.

1st row: Skip 3ch (count as 1dc), *1dc into each of next 3ch, skip next ch and work 1Sdc over it instead; rep from * ending 1dc into last ch, turn.
2nd row: 3ch (count as 1dc), skip 1 st, *1dc into each of next 3 sts, skip next st and work 1Sdc over it instead; rep from * ending 1dc into top of tch, turn.
Rep 2nd row.

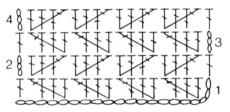

Alternating Spike Stitch I

Multiple of 2 sts.
(add 1 for base chain)

Special Abbreviation

Ssc (Spike single crochet) = insert hook below next st 1 row down (i.e. into same place as that st was worked), yo, draw loop

through and up to height of present row, yo, draw through both loops on hook (see also page 10 — Spikes).

1st row: Skip 2ch (count as 1sc), 1sc into next and each ch to end, turn.
2nd row: 1ch (counts as 1sc), skip 1 st, *1sc into next st, 1Ssc over next st; rep from * ending 1sc into tch, turn.
Rep 2nd row.

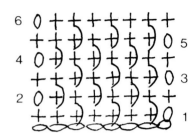

Alternating Spike Stitch II

Worked as Alternating Spike Stitch I.
Work 1 row each in colors A, B and C throughout.

Arrowhead Spike Stitch

Multiple of 6 sts + 2.
(add 1 for base chain)

Special Abbreviation

Ssc (Spike single crochet) = insert hook below next st 1 or more rows down (indicated thus: Ssc1, Ssc2, Ssc3, etc), yo, draw loop through and up to height of current row,

○ Chain ● Slip stitch + Single crochet T Half double crochet ╤ Double crochet ⧧ Treble ⧦ Double treble yo, draw through both loops on hook (see also page 10 — Spikes).

Work 6 rows each in colors A and B alternately throughout.

Base row (right side): Using A 1sc into 2nd ch from hook, 1sc into each ch to end, turn.

Commence Pattern

1st row: 1ch, 1sc into first and each st to end, skip tch, turn.

Work 4 rows as 1st row.

6th row: Using B 1ch, 1sc into first st, *1sc into next st, 1Ssc1 over next st, 1Ssc2 over next st, 1Ssc3 over next st, 1Ssc4 over next st, 1Ssc5 over next st; rep from * ending 1sc into last st, skip tch, turn.

Work 5 rows as 1st row.

12th row: Using A 1ch, 1sc into first st, *1Ssc5 over next st, 1Ssc4 over next st, 1Ssc3 over next st, 1Ssc2 over next st, 1Ssc1 over next st, 1sc into next st; rep from * ending 1sc into last st, skip tch, turn.

Rep these 12 rows.

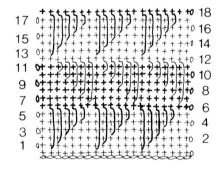

Spiked Squares

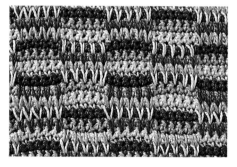

Multiple of 10 sts + 1.
(add 1 for base chain)

Special Abbreviation

Ssc (Spike single crochet) worked as under Arrowhead Spike Stitch. Note: when working Sscs over previous Sscs be careful to insert hook in centers of previous Sscs.

Work 2 rows each in colors A, B and C throughout.

Base row (right side): 1sc into 2nd ch from hook, 1sc into next and each ch to end, turn.

Commence Pattern

1st row: 1ch, 1sc into first and each st to end, skip tch, turn.

2nd row: 1ch, 1sc into first st, *1Ssc2 over each of next 5 sts, 1sc into each of next 5

---

sts; rep from * ending 1sc into last sc, skip tch, turn.

Rep the last 2 rows 3 times more.

9th row: As 1st row.

10th row: 1ch, 1sc into first st, *1sc into each of next 5 sts, 1Ssc2 over each of next 5 sts; rep from * ending 1sc into last sc, skip tch, turn.

Rep the last 2 rows 3 times more.

Rep these 16 rows.

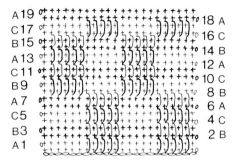

Spike Cluster Stitch

Multiple of 8 sts + 5.
(add 1 for base chain)

Special Abbreviation

SPC (Spike Cluster) = over next st pick up 5 spike loops by inserting hook as follows: 2 sts to right of next st and 1 row down; 1 st to right and 2 rows down; directly below and 3 rows down; 1 st to left and 2 rows down; 2 sts to left and 1 row down, (6 loops on hook); now insert hook into top of next st itself, yo, draw loop through, yo, draw through all 7 loops on hook (see also page 10).

Work 4 rows each in colors A and B alternately throughout.

Base row (right side): 1sc into 2nd ch from hook, 1sc into each ch to end, turn.

Commence Pattern

1st row: 1ch, 1sc into first and each st to end, skip tch, turn.

2nd and 3rd rows: As 1st row.

4th row: 1ch, 1sc into each of first 4 sts, *1SPC over next st, 1sc into each of next 7 sts (Hint: be careful not to pick up any of the spikes of the previous SPC); rep from * ending 1sc into last st, skip tch, turn.

5th, 6th and 7th rows: As 1st row.

8th row: 1ch, 1sc into each of first 8 sts, *1SPC over next st, 1sc into each of next 7 sts; rep from * to last 5 sts, 1SPC over next st, 1sc into each of last 4 sts, skip tch, turn.

Rep these 8 rows.

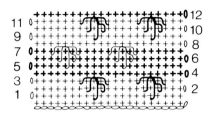

5-Star Marguerite Stitch

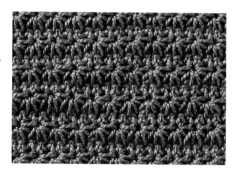

Multiple of 2 sts + 1.
(add 1 for base chain)

Special Abbreviation

M5C (Marguerite Cluster with 5 spike loops) = pick up spike loops (ie: yo and draw through) inserting hook as follows: into loop which closed previous M5C, under 2 threads of last spike loop of same M5C, into same place that last spike loop of same M5C was worked, into each of next 2 sts (6 loops on hook), yo, draw through all loops on hook (see also page 11 — Marguerites).

1st row (wrong side): 1sc into 2nd ch from hook, 1sc into next and each ch to end, turn.

2nd row: 3ch, 1M5C inserting hook into 2nd and 3rd chs from hook and then first 3 sts to pick up 5 spike loops, *1ch, 1M5C; rep from * to end, skip tch, turn.

3rd row: 1ch, 1sc into loop which closed last M5C, *1sc into next ch, 1sc into loop which closed next M5C; rep from * ending 1sc into each of next 2ch of tch, turn.

Rep 2nd and 3rd rows.

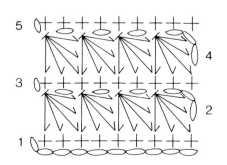

Relief Patterns

Simple Marguerite Stitch

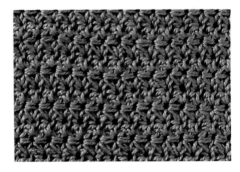

Multiple of 2 sts + 1.
(add 2 for base chain)
Special Abbreviation
↖ **M3C (Marguerite Cluster with 3 spike loops)** See text below and also page 11.
1st row: Make a spike loop (i.e. yo and draw through) into 2nd, 3rd and 5th chs from hook, yo and through all 4 loops (1M3C made), *1ch, make 1M3C picking up 1 loop in ch which closed previous M3C, 2nd loop in same place as last spike of previous M3C, skip 1ch, then last loop in next ch, yo and through all 4 loops; rep from * to end, turn.
2nd row: 3ch, make 1M3C picking up loops in 2nd and 3rd ch from hook and in ch which closed 2nd M3C on previous row, *1ch, work 1M3C picking up first loop in ch which closed previous M3C, 2nd loop in same place as last spike of previous M3C and last loop in ch which closed next M3C on previous row; rep from * to end, picking up final loop in top of ch at beg of previous row.
Rep 2nd row.

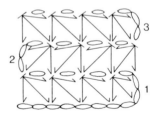

Granule Stitch

Multiple of 4 sts + 1.
(add 1 for base chain)
Special Abbreviation
Psc (Picot single crochet) = insert hook, yo, draw loop through, [yo, draw through 1 loop] 3 times to make 3ch, yo, draw through both loops on hook. Note: draw picot chain

loops to the back (right side) of fabric.
1st row (right side): 1sc into 2nd ch from hook, 1sc into each ch to end, turn.
2nd row: 1ch, 1sc into first st, *1Psc into next st, 1sc into next st; rep from * to end, skip tch, turn.
3rd row: 1ch, 1sc into first and each st to end, skip tch, turn. Hint: Hold down the picot chains at the front and you will see the top 2 loops of the Psc where you are to insert the hook.
4th row: 1ch, 1sc into each of first 2 sts, *1Psc into next st, 1sc into next st; rep from * to last st, 1sc into last st, skip tch, turn.
5th row: As 3rd row.
Rep 2nd, 3rd, 4th and 5th rows.

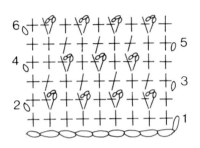

Relief Arch Stitch

Multiple of 8 sts + 1.
(add 1 for base chain)
1st row (wrong side): 1sc into 2nd ch from hook, 1sc into each of next 2ch, *7ch, skip 3ch, 1sc into each of next 5ch; rep from * to last 6ch, 7ch, skip 3ch, 1sc into each of last 3ch, turn.
2nd row: 3ch (count as 1dc), skip 1 st, 1dc into each of next 2 sts, *going behind 7ch loop work 1tr into each of next 3 base ch**, 1dc into each of next 5sc; rep from * ending last rep at ** when 3 sts remain, 1dc into each of last 3 sts, skip tch, turn.
3rd row: 1ch, 1sc into first st, *7ch, skip 3 sts, 1sc into next st at same time catching in center of 7ch loop of last-but-one row, 7ch, skip 3 sts, 1sc into next st; rep from * to end, turn.
4th row: 3ch (count as 1dc), skip 1 st, *going behind 7ch loop of last row work 1tr into each of next 3 sts of last-but-one row, 1dc into next sc; rep from * to end, skip tch, turn.
5th row: 1ch, 1sc into each of first 2 sts, *1sc into next st at same time catching in center of 7ch loop of last-but-one row, 7ch, skip 3 sts, 1sc into next st at same time catching in center of 7ch loop of last-but-one

row**, 1sc into each of next 3 sts; rep from * ending last rep at ** when 2 sts remain, 1sc into each of last 2 sts, turn.
6th row: As 2nd row working trs into last-but-one row.
Rep 3rd, 4th, 5th and 6th rows.

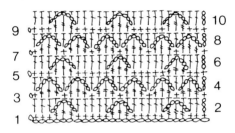

Thistle Pattern

Multiple of 10 sts + 1.
(add 1 for base chain)
Note: For description of sc2tog see page 10 (Clusters).
Special Abbreviation
Catch Loop = Catch 10ch loop of Thistle by inserting hook under ch at tip of loop **at the same time** as under the next st.
Base row (wrong side): Skip 2ch (count as 1sc), 1sc into each of next 4ch, *into next st work a Thistle of 1sc, [10ch, 1sc] 3 times**, 1sc into each of next 9ch; rep from * ending last rep at **, 1sc into each of last 5sc, turn.
Commence Pattern
Note: Hold loops of Thistle down at front of work on right side rows.
1st row: 1ch (count as 1sc), skip 1sc, 1sc into each of next 4sc, *skip 1sc of Thistle, work sc2tog over next 2sc, skip last sc of Thistle**, work 1sc into each of next 9 sts; rep from * ending last rep at **, 1sc into each of next 4sc, 1sc into tch, turn.
2nd, 4th, 8th and 10th rows: 1ch, skip 1 st, 1sc into each st to end, turn.
3rd row: 1ch, skip 1 st, 1sc into next sc, *catch first loop of Thistle in next sc, 1sc into each of next 5sc, skip center loop of Thistle, catch 3rd loop in next st**, 1sc into each of next 3sc; rep from * ending last rep at **, 1sc into each of last 2 sts, turn.
5th row: 1ch, skip 1 st, 1sc into each of next 4sc, *work 6dc into next sc and at the same time catch center loop**, 1sc into each of next 9sc; rep from * ending last rep at **, 1sc into each of last 5 sts, turn.
6th row: 1ch, skip 1 st, 1sc into each of first 4sc, *1ch, skip 6dc, 1sc into each of next 4sc**, work a Thistle into next sc, 1sc into each of next 4sc; rep from * ending last rep

○ Chain ● Slip stitch + Single crochet T Half double crochet ⊤ Double crochet ‡ Treble ‡ Double treble

at **, 1sc into last st, turn.

7th row: 1ch, skip 1 st, 1sc into each of next 9 sts, *work sc2tog over center 2 of next 4sc, skip 1sc, 1sc into each of next 9 sts; rep from * to last st, 1sc into last st, turn.

9th row: 1ch, skip 1 st, 1sc into each of next 6sc, *catch first loop into next sc, 1sc into each of next 5sc, catch 3rd loop into next sc**, 1sc into each of next 3sc; rep from * ending last rep at **, 1sc into each st to end, turn.

11th row: 1ch, skip 1 st, 1sc into each of next 9 sts, *work 6dc into next sc and catch center loop at the same time, 1sc into each of next 9sc; rep from * to last st, 1sc in last st, turn.

12th row: 1ch, skip 1 st, 1sc into each of next 4sc, *work a Thistle into next sc, 1sc into each of next 4sc**, 1ch, skip 6dc, 1sc into each of next 4sc; rep from * ending last rep at **, 1sc into last st, turn.

Rep these 12 rows.

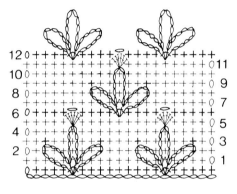

Corded Ridge Stitch

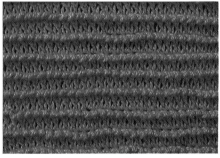

Any number of sts.
(add 2 for base chain)
Note: work all rows with right side facing, i.e. work even numbered rows from left to right (see also page 15 — Corded or Reversed Single Crochet).

1st row (right side): Skip 3ch (count as 1dc), 1dc into next and each ch to end. Do not turn.

2nd row: 1ch, 1sc into front loop only of last dc made, *1sc into front loop only of next dc to right; rep from * ending sl st into top of tch at beginning of row. Do not turn.

3rd row: 3ch (count as 1dc), skip 1 st, 1dc into back loop only of next and each st of last-but-one row to end. Do not turn.

Rep 2nd and 3rd rows.

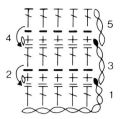

Astrakhan Stitch

Any number of sts.
(add 2 for base chain)
Note: work all rows with right side facing, i.e. work even numbered rows from left to right.

1st row (right side): Skip 3ch (count as 1dc), 1dc into each ch to end. Do not turn.

2nd row: *7ch, sl st into front loop only of next dc to right; rep from * ending 7ch, sl st into top of tch at beginning of row. Do not turn.

3rd row: 3ch (count as 1dc), skip 1 st, 1dc into back loop only of next and each st of last-but-one row to end. Do not turn.

Rep 2nd and 3rd rows.

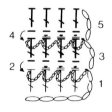

Embossed Roundels

Multiple of 8 sts + 5.
(add 2 for base chain)
Special Abbreviation
ERd (Embossed Roundel) = work [1dc, 2ch] 9 times all into same st, remove hook

from working loop, insert hook from back through top of first dc of Roundel and, keeping sts of Roundel at back of fabric, pick up working loop again and draw through to close Roundel.

1st row (right side): Skip 3ch (count as 1dc), 1dc into next and each ch to end, turn.

2nd row: 3ch (count as 1dc), skip 1 st, 1dc into each of next 3 sts, *1ERd into next st, 1dc into each of next 7 sts; rep from * ending 1dc into top of tch, turn.

3rd row: 3ch (count as 1dc), skip 1 st, 1dc into next and each st to end, working last st into top of tch, turn.

4th row: 3ch (count as 1dc), skip 1 st, *1dc into each of next 7 sts, 1ERd into next st; rep from * to last 4 sts, 1dc into each of last 4 sts, turn.

5th row: As 3rd row.
Rep 2nd, 3rd, 4th and 5th rows.

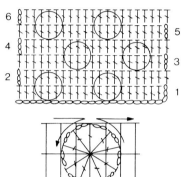

Embossed Pockets

Multiple of 3 sts + 1.
(add 2 for base chain)
Special Abbreviation
PGr (Pocket Group) = work [1sc, 1hdc, 3dc] round stem of indicated st.

1st row (wrong side): Skip 3ch (count as 1dc), 1dc into each ch to end, turn.

2nd row: 1PGr round first st, skip 2 sts, sl st into top of next st, *1PGr round same st as sl st, skip 2 sts, sl st into top of next st; rep from * to end, turn.

3rd row: 3ch (count as 1dc), skip 1 st, 1dc into each st to end, turn.

Rep 2nd and 3rd rows.

Relief Patterns

Single Rib

Multiple of 2 sts.
(add 2 for base chain)
Note: For description of dc/rf and dc/rb see page 11.
1st row (wrong side): Skip 3ch (count as 1dc), 1dc into next and each ch to end, turn.
2nd row: 2ch (count as 1dc), skip first st, *1dc/rf round next st, 1dc/rb round next st; rep from * ending 1dc into top of tch, turn.
Rep 2nd row.

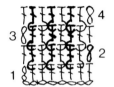

Zigzag Rib

Multiple of 4 sts + 2.
(add 2 for base chain)
Note: For description of dc/rf and dc/rb see page 11 (Raised Stitches).
Base row (wrong side): Skip 3ch (count as 1dc), 1dc into next and each ch to end, turn.
Commence Pattern
1st row: 2ch (count as 1dc), skip first st, *1dc/rf round each of next 2 sts, 1dc/rb round each of next 2 sts; rep from * ending 1dc into top of tch, turn.
2nd row: 2ch (count as 1dc), skip first st, 1dc/rb round next st, *1dc/rf round each of next 2 sts**, 1dc/rb round each of next 2 sts; rep from * ending last rep at ** when 2 sts remain, 1dc/rb round next st, 1dc into top of tch, turn.
3rd row: 2ch (count as 1dc), skip first st, *1dc/rb round each of next 2 sts, 1dc/rf round each of next 2 sts; rep from * ending 1dc into top of tch, turn.

4th row: 2ch (count as 1dc), miss first st, 1dc/rf round next st, *1dc/rb round each of next 2 sts**, 1dc/rf round each of next 2 sts; rep from * ending last rep at ** when 2 sts remain, 1dc/rf round next st, 1dc into top of tch, turn.
5th row: As 3rd row.
6th row: As 2nd row.
7th row: As 1st row.
8th row: As 4th row.
Rep these 8 rows.

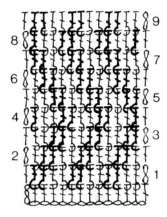

Ripple Stitch I

Multiple of 2 sts + 1.
(add 2 for base chain)
Note: For description of tr/rf see page 11.
1st row (right side): Skip 3ch (count as 1dc), 1dc into each ch to end, turn.
2nd row: 1ch (counts as 1sc), skip first st, 1sc into each st to end, working last st into top of tch, turn.
3rd row: 3ch (count as 1dc), skip first st, *1tr/rf round dc below next st, 1dc into next st; rep from * to end, turn.
4th row: As 2nd row.
5th row: 3ch (count as 1dc), skip first st, *1dc into next st, 1tr/rf round dc below next st; rep from * to last 2 sts, 1dc into each of last 2 sts, turn.
Rep 2nd, 3rd, 4th and 5th rows.

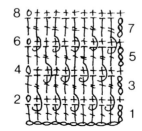

Ripple Stitch II

Worked as Ripple Stitch I.
Work 2 rows each in colors A and B alternately throughout.

Basketweave Stitch

Multiple of 8 sts + 2.
(add 2 for base chain)
Note: For description of dc/rf and dc/rb see page 11 (Raised Stitches).
Base row (wrong side): Skip 3ch (count as 1dc), 1dc into next and each ch to end, turn.
Commence Pattern
1st row: 2ch (count as 1dc), skip first st, *1dc/rf round each of next 4 sts, 1dc/rb round each of next 4 sts; rep from * ending 1dc into top of tch, turn.
Rep the last row 3 times.
5th row: 2ch (count as 1dc), skip first st, *1dc/rb round each of next 4 sts, 1dc/rf round each of next 4 sts; rep from * ending 1dc into top of tch, turn.
Rep the last row 3 times.
Rep these 8 rows.

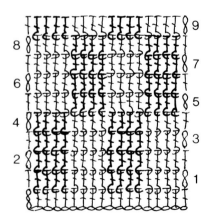

◦ Chain   • Slip stitch   + Single crochet   T Half double crochet   Ŧ Double crochet   ‡ Treble   ⹋ Double treble

Raised Chevron Stitch

Multiple of 16 sts + 1.
(add 2 for base chain)
Note: For description of dc/rb and dc/rf see page 11 (Raised Stitches). For dc2tog and dc3tog see page 10 (Clusters).

1st row (right side): Skip 3ch, dc2tog over next 2ch (counts as dc3tog), *1dc into each of next 5ch, [2dc, 1ch, 2dc] into next ch, 1dc into each of next 5ch**, dc5tog over next 5ch; rep from * ending last rep at ** when 3ch remain, dc3tog, turn.

2nd row: 3ch, skip first st, dc/rb2tog over next 2 sts (all counts as dc/rb3tog), *1dc/rf round each of next 5 sts, [2dc, 1ch, 2dc] into next ch sp, 1dc/rf round each of next 5 sts**, dc/rb5tog over next 5 sts; rep from * ending last rep at ** when 3 sts remain, dc/rb3tog, turn.

3rd row: 3ch, skip first st, dc/rf2tog over next 2 sts (all counts as dc/rf3tog), *1dc/rb round each of next 5 sts, [2dc, 1ch, 2dc] into next ch sp, 1dc/rb round each of next 5 sts**, dc/rf5tog over next 5 sts; rep from * ending last rep at ** when 3 sts remain, dc/rf3tog, turn.

Rep 2nd and 3rd rows.

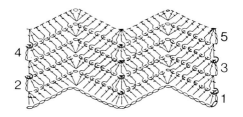

Crinkle Stitch I

Multiple of 2 sts.
(add 1 for base chain)
Note: For description of sc/rf and sc/rb see page 11 (Raised Stitches).

1st row (wrong side): Skip 2ch (count as 1hdc), 1hdc into each ch to end, turn.
2nd row: 1ch, 1sc into first st, *1sc/rf round next st, 1sc/rb round next st; rep from * ending 1sc into top of tch, turn.
3rd row: 2ch (count as 1hdc), skip first st, 1hdc into next and each st to end, skip tch, turn.
4th row: 1ch, 1sc into first st, *1sc/rb round next st, 1sc/rf round next st; rep from * ending 1sc into top of tch, turn.
5th row: As 3rd row.
Rep 2nd, 3rd, 4th and 5th rows.

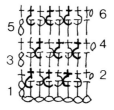

Crinkle Stitch II

Worked as Crinkle Stitch I, but using wrong side of fabric as right side.

Crossed Ripple Stitch

Multiple of 3 sts + 2.
(add 1 for base chain)
Note: For description of dc/rf see page 11 (Raised Stitches).

1st base row (wrong side): 1sc into 2nd ch from hook, 1sc into each ch to end, turn.
2nd base row: 3ch (count as 1dc), skip first st, *skip next 2 sts, 1dc into next st, 1ch, 1dc back into first of 2 sts just skipped — called Crossed Pair; rep from * ending 1dc into last st, skip tch, turn.
Commence Pattern
1st row: 1 ch, 1sc into first st, 1sc into next and each st and each ch sp to end working last st into top of tch, turn.
2nd row: As 2nd base row, except as 2nd st of each Crossed Pair work 1dc/rf loosely round first st of corresponding Crossed Pair 2 rows below.
Rep these 2 rows.

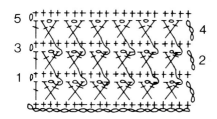

Leafhopper Stitch

Multiple of 4 sts + 1.
(add 2 for base chain)
Special Abbreviation
LCL (Leafhopper Cluster) = *[yo, insert hook at front and from right to left behind stem of st before next st, yo, draw loop through and up to height of hdc] twice, yo, draw through 4 loops**, skip next st, rep from * to ** round stem of next st, ending yo, draw through all 3 loops on hook.

1st row (wrong side): Skip 3ch (count as 1dc), 1dc into next and each ch to end, turn.
2nd row: 3ch (count as 1dc), skip first st, 1dc into next st, *1LCL over next st, 1dc into each of next 3 sts; rep from * omitting 1dc from end of last rep, turn.
3rd row: 3ch (count as 1dc), skip first st, 1dc into next and each st to end, working last st into top of tch, turn.
4th row: 3ch (count as 1dc), skip first st, *1dc into each of next 3 sts, 1LCL over next st; rep from * ending 1dc into each of last 4 sts, working last st into top of tch, turn.
5th row: As 3rd row.
Rep 2nd, 3rd, 4th and 5th rows.

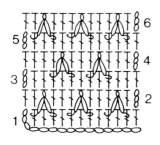

Relief Patterns

Gwenyth's Cable

Worked over 19 sts on a background of basic double crochets with any number of sts.

Note: For description of tr/rf and tr/rb see page 11 (Raised Stitches). For going behind previous stitches see page 12 (Crossed Stitch II).

1st row (right side): 1tr/rf round first st, 1dc into next st, skip next 3 sts, 1dtr into each of next 3 sts, going behind last 3dtrs work 1dtr into each of 3 sts just skipped, 1dc into next st, 1tr/rf round next st, 1dc into next st, skip next 3 sts, 1dtr into each of next 3 sts, going in front of last 3dtrs but not catching them work 1dtr into each of 3 sts just skipped, 1dc into next st, 1tr/rf round next st.

2nd row: As 1st row, except work 1tr/rb instead of rf over first, 10th and 19th sts to keep raised ridges on right side of fabric.

Rep 1st and 2nd rows.

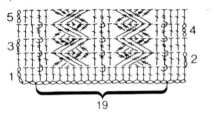

Dots and Diamonds

Multiple of 4 sts + 3.
(add 1 for base chain)

Special Abbreviation

Psc (Picot single crochet) = insert hook, yo, draw loop through, [yo, draw through 1 loop] 3 times, yo, draw through both loops on hook. Note: draw picot ch loops to front (right side) of fabric.

Note: For description of tr/rf see page 11 (Raised Stitches). For tr2tog see page 10 (Clusters).

Base row (right side): 1sc into 2nd ch from hook, 1sc into each of next 2ch, *psc into

next ch, 1sc into each of next 3ch; rep from * to end, turn.

Commence Pattern

1st row: 3ch (count as 1dc), skip first st, 1dc into each st to end, skip tch, turn.

2nd row: 1ch, 1sc into first st, *psc into next st, 1sc into next st**, tr/rf2tog over next st inserting hook round 2nd sc in last-but-one row for first leg and round following 4th sc for 2nd leg (skipping 3 sts between), 1sc into next st; rep from * ending last rep at ** in top of tch, turn.

3rd row: As 1st row.

4th row: 1ch, 1sc into first st, 1tr/rf over next st inserting hook round top of first raised cluster 2 rows below, *1sc into next st, psc into next st, 1sc into next st**, tr/rf2tog over next st inserting hook round same cluster as last raised st for first leg and round top of next raised cluster for 2nd leg; rep from * ending last rep at ** when 2 sts remain, 1tr/rf over next st inserting hook round top of same cluster as last raised st, 1sc into top of tch, turn.

5th row: As 1st row.

6th row: As 2nd row, except to make new raised clusters insert hook round previous raised clusters instead of scs.

Rep 3rd, 4th, 5th and 6th rows.

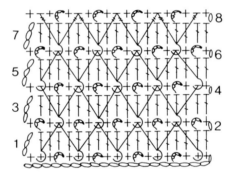

Crossed Puff Cables

Worked over 11 sts on a background of basic double crochets with any number of sts.

Note: For description of tr/rb and tr/rf see page 11 (Raised Stitches); for hdc5tog see page 14 (Puff Stitch).

1st row (right side): 1dc into each st.

2nd row: *1tr/rb round next st, work a Puff st of hdc5tog all into next st, 1tr/rb round next st**, 1dc into next st; rep from * once and from * to ** again.

3rd row: *Leaving last loop of each st on hook work [1dc into next st, skip Puff st, work 1tr/rf round next st] ending yo, draw through all 3 loops on hook, 1dc into top of Puff st, leaving last loop of each st on hook work

[1tr/rf round st before same Puff st and 1dc into top of st after Puff st] ending yo, draw through all 3 loops on hook**, 1dc into next st; rep from * once and from * to ** again.

4th row: As 2nd row, but make new tr/rbs by inserting hook under raised stems only of previous sts.

Rep 3rd and 4th rows.

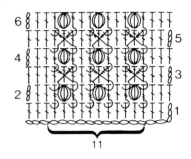

Tulip Cable

Worked over 15 sts on a background of basic double crochets with any number of sts.

Special Abbreviations

Note: For description of tr/rf and tr/rb see page 11 (Raised Stitches). For Puff Stitch see page 14.

FCL (Forward Cluster) = leaving last loop of each st on hook work 1dc into next st and 1tr/rf or rb (see Note below) round next st after that, ending yo, draw through all 3 loops on hook.

BCL (Backward Cluster) = leaving last loop of each st on hook work 1tr/rf or rb round st below dc just made and 1dc into next st.

Note: Raised legs of these clusters are to be worked at front (rf) on right side rows and at back (rb) on wrong side rows as indicated in the text thus: FCL/rf, FCL/rb, BCL/rf, BCL/rb.

TCL (Triple Cluster) = leaving last loop of each st on hook work 1tr/rf round st below dc just made, 1dc/rf round next Puff st, and 1tr/rf round next st, ending yo, draw through all 4 loops on hook.

1st row: (right side): 1tr/rf round next st, 1dc into next st, 1tr/rf round next st, 1dc into each of next 2 sts, [1FCL/rf] twice, 1dc into next st, [1BCL/rf] twice, 1dc into each of next 2 sts, 1tr/rf round next st, 1dc into next st, 1tr/rf round next st.

2nd row: [1tr/rb round next st, 1dc into next st] twice, [1FCL/rb] twice, 1dc into each of next 3 sts, [1BCL/rb] twice, [1dc into next st, 1tr/rb round next st] twice.

3rd row: [1tr/rf round next st, 1dc into next st] twice, 1tr/rf round each of next 2 sts, 1dc into each of next 3 sts, 1tr/rf round each of

○ Chain ● Slip stitch + Single crochet T Half double crochet ⊺ Double crochet ⧸ Treble ⧸ Double treble

next 2 sts, [1dc into next st, 1tr/rf round next st] twice.

4th row: 1tr/rb round next st, 1dc into next st, 1tr/rb round next st, 1dc into each of next 2 sts, [1BCL/rb] twice, work a Puff st of hdc5tog all into next st, [1FCL/rb] twice, 1dc into each of next 2 sts, 1tr/rb round next st, 1dc into next st, 1tr/rb round next st.

5th row: 1tr/rf round next st, 1dc into next st, 1tr/rf round next st, 1dc into each of next 3 sts, 1BCL/rf, 1TCL, 1FCL/rf, 1dc into each of next 3 sts, 1tr/rf round next st, 1dc into next st, 1tr/rf round next st.

6th row: *1tr/rb round next st, 1dc into next st, 1tr/rb round next st**, 1dc into each of next 9 sts, rep from * to **
Rep these 6 rows.

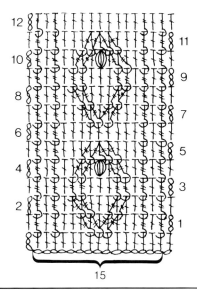

Puff Stitch Plaits

Multiple of 8 sts + 1.
(add 1 for base chain)
Note: For description of hdc3tog see page 14 (Puff Stitch).

1st row (right side): Skip 2ch (count as 1hdc), 1hdc into each of next 2ch, *1ch, skip 1ch, hdc3tog all into next ch, 1ch, skip 1ch**, 1hdc into each of next 5ch; rep from * ending last rep at ** when 3ch remain, 1hdc into each of last 3ch, turn.

2nd row: 2ch (count as 1hdc), skip first st, 1hdc into each of next 2 sts, *hdc3tog into next ch sp, 1ch, skip 1 st, hdc3tog into next ch sp**, 1hdc into each of next 5 sts; rep from * ending last rep at ** when 3 sts remain including tch, 1hdc into each of last 3 sts, turn.

3rd row: 2ch (count as 1hdc), skip first st, 1hdc into each of next 2 sts, *1ch, skip 1 st, hdc3tog into next ch sp, 1ch, skip 1 st**, 1hdc into each of next 5 sts; rep from * end-

ing last rep at ** when 3 sts remain including tch, 1hdc into each of last 3 sts, turn.
Rep 2nd and 3rd rows.

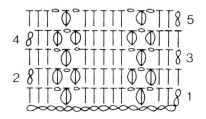

Aligned Puff Stitch

Multiple of 2 sts + 1.
(add 1 for base chain)
Note: For description of hdc4tog see page 14 (Puff Stitch).

1st row (right side): 1sc into 2nd ch from hook, *1ch, skip 1ch, 1sc into next ch; rep from * to end, turn.

2nd row: 2ch (count as 1hdc), skip first st, *hdc4tog all into next ch sp, 1ch, skip 1sc; rep from * ending hdc4tog into last ch sp, 1hdc into last sc, skip tch, turn.

3rd row: 1ch, 1sc into first st, *1ch, skip 1 st, 1sc into next ch sp; rep from * ending in top of tch, turn.
Rep 2nd and 3rd rows.

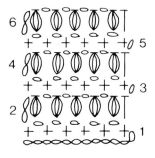

Boxed Puff Stitch

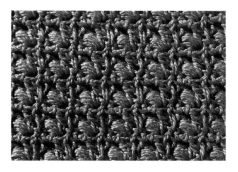

Multiple of 3 sts + 1.
(add 4 for base chain)
Special Abbreviation
Puff Stitch = hdc4tog all into same st and closed with 1ch drawn tightly.
Note: For description of Puff Stitch see page 14.

1st row (right side): Puff st into 5th ch from hook, *skip 2ch, [1dc, 2ch, puff st] all into next ch; rep from * ending skip 2ch, 1dc into last ch, turn.

2nd row: 1ch, skip first st, *work 1dc loosely over next row into first of 2 skipped sts in row below, 1sc into puff st, 1sc into next 2ch sp; rep from * ending 1sc into 3rd ch of tch, turn.

3rd row: 5ch (count as 1dc and 2ch), puff st into first st, *skip 2sc, [1dc, 2ch, puff st] all into next dc; rep from * ending skip 2sc, 1dc into last dc, skip tch, turn.

Rep 2nd and 3rd rows.

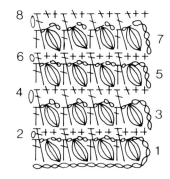

Aligned Cobble Stitch

Multiple of 2 sts + 1.
(add 1 for base chain)
1st row (right side): 1sc into 2nd ch from hook, 1sc into each ch to end, turn.

2nd row: 1ch, 1sc into first st, *1tr into next st, 1sc into next st; rep from * to end, skip tch, turn.

3rd row: 1ch, 1sc into first st, 1sc into next and each st to end, skip tch, turn.
Rep 2nd and 3rd rows.

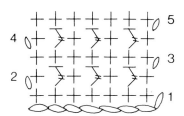

Knobbles and Bobbles

Wavy Puff Stitch Sprays

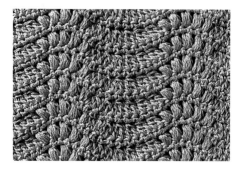

Multiple of 17 sts.
(add 2 for base chain)

Note: For description of dc2tog and hdc4tog see page 10 (Clusters), and page 14 (Puff Stitch).

1st row (right side): 1dc into 4th ch from hook (counts as dc2tog), [dc2tog over next 2ch] twice, *[1ch, work hdc4tog into next ch] 5 times, 1ch**, [dc2tog over next 2ch] 6 times; rep from * ending last rep at ** when 6ch remain, [dc2tog over next 2ch] 3 times, turn.

2nd row: 1ch, 1sc into first st and then into each st and each ch sp to end excluding tch, turn.

3rd row: 3ch, skip first st, 1dc into next st (counts as dc2tog), [dc2tog over next 2 sts] twice, *[1ch, work hdc4tog into next st] 5 times, 1ch**, [dc2tog over next 2 sts] 6 times; rep from * ending last rep at ** when 6 sts remain, [dc2tog over next 2 sts] 3 times, skip tch, turn.

Rep 2nd and 3rd rows.

V-Twin Popcorn Stitch

Multiple of 11 sts + 3.
(add 2 for base chain)

Note: For description of 5dc popcorn see page 14; for tr/rb and tr/rf see page 11 (Raised Stitches).

1st row (right side): Skip 3ch (count as 1dc), 1dc into each of next 2ch, *2ch, skip 3ch, 5dc popcorn into next ch, 1ch, 5dc popcorn into next ch, 1ch, skip 2ch, 1dc into each of next 3ch; rep from * to end, turn.

2nd row: 3ch (count as 1dc), skip first st, 1tr/rb round next st, 1dc into next st, *3ch, skip 1ch and 1 popcorn, 2sc into next ch sp, 3ch, skip 1 popcorn and 2ch, 1dc into next st, 1tr/rb round next st; rep from * ending last rep in top of tch, turn.

3rd row: 3ch (count as 1dc), skip first st, 1tr/rf round next st, 1dc into next st, *2ch, skip 3ch, 5dc popcorn into next sc, 1ch, 5dc popcorn into next sc, 1ch, skip 3ch, 1dc into next st, 1tr/rf round next st, 1dc into next st; rep from * ending last rep in top of tch, turn.

Rep 2nd and 3rd rows.

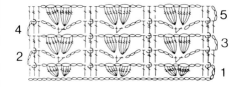

Blackberry Salad Stitch

Multiple of 4 sts + 1.
(add 2 for base chain)

Note: For description of dc5tog see page 14 (Bobble).

1st row (right side): Skip 3ch (count as 1dc), 1dc into each ch to end, turn.

2nd row: 1ch, 1sc into each of first 2 sts, *work dc5tog into next st, 1sc into each of next 3 sts; rep from * to last 3 sts, work dc5tog into next st, 1sc into each of last 2 sts (including top of tch), turn.

3rd row: 3ch (count as 1dc), skip first st, 1dc into each st to end, skip tch, turn.

4th row: 1ch, 1sc into each of first 4 sts, *work dc5tog into next st, 1sc into each of next 3 sts; rep from * ending 1sc into top of tch, turn.

5th row: As 3rd row.
Rep 2nd, 3rd, 4th and 5th rows.

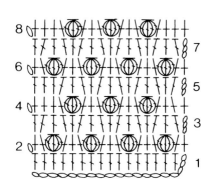

Bullion Diagonals

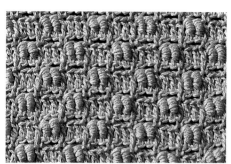

Multiple of 6 sts + 2.
(add 1 for base chain)

Note: For description of bullion st see page 14. Make Bullion sts with [yo] 7 times.

1st row (wrong side): 1sc into 2nd ch from hook, 1ch, skip 1ch, 1sc into next ch, *2ch, skip 2ch, 1sc into next ch; rep from * to last 2ch, 1ch, skip 1ch, 1sc into last ch, turn.

2nd row: 3ch (count as 1dc), skip first st, 1dc into next ch sp, *1dc into next sc, 1 Bullion st into each of next 2ch, 1dc into next sc**, 1dc into each of next 2ch; rep from * ending last rep at ** when 1 ch sp remains, 1dc into next ch, 1dc into last sc, skip tch, turn.

3rd row: 1ch, 1sc into first st, 1ch, skip 1 st, 1sc into next st, *2ch, skip 2 sts, 1sc into next st; rep from * to last 2 sts, 1ch, skip 1 st, 1sc into top of tch, turn.

4th row: 3ch (count as 1dc), skip first st, 1 Bullion st into next ch sp, *1dc into next sc, 1dc into each of next 2ch, 1dc into next sc**, 1 Bullion st into each of next 2ch; rep from * ending last rep at ** when 1ch sp remains, 1 Bullion st into next sp, 1dc into last sc, skip tch, turn.

5th row: As 3rd row.
Rep 2nd, 3rd, 4th and 5th rows.

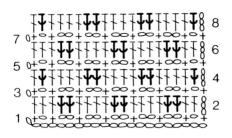

Diagram Note
Ŧ Bullion Stitch with [yo] 7 times.

○ Chain ● Slip stitch + Single crochet T Half double crochet Ŧ Double crochet ‡ Treble ‡ Double treble

Popcorn Waffle Stitch

Multiple of 4 sts + 1.
(add 1 for base chain)

Note: For description of 5dc popcorn see page 14.

1st row (right side): 1sc into 2nd ch from hook, *3ch, 5dc popcorn into same place as previous sc, skip 3ch, 1sc into next ch; rep from * to end, turn.

2nd row: 3ch (count as 1dc), skip first st, *1sc into each of next 2ch, 1hdc into next ch, 1dc into next sc; rep from * to end, skip tch, turn.

3rd row: 1ch, 1sc into first st, *3ch, 5dc popcorn into same place as previous sc, skip next 3 sts, 1sc into next dc; rep from * ending last rep in top of tch, turn.

Rep 2nd and 3rd rows.

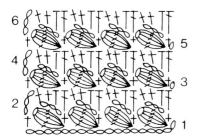

Diagonal Trip Stitch

Multiple of 6 sts + 2.
(add 1 for base chain)

1st row (right side): 1sc into 2nd ch from hook, 1sc into each ch to end, turn.

2nd row: 1ch, 1sc into first st, *1tr into next

st, 1sc into next st, 1tr into next st, 1sc into each of next 3 sts; rep from * ending 1sc into last sc, skip tch, turn.

3rd row: 1ch, 1sc into first st, 1sc into next and each st to end, skip tch, turn.

4th row: 1 ch, 1sc into each of first 2 sts, *1tr into next st, 1sc into next st, 1tr into next st, 1sc into each of next 3 sts; rep from * to end, skip tch, turn.

5th row: As 3rd row.

6th row: 1 ch, 1sc into each of first 3 sts, *1tr into next st, 1sc into next st, 1tr into next st, 1sc into each of next 3 sts; rep from * to end, omitting 1sc at end of last rep, skip tch, turn.

Continue in this way, working the pairs of tr 1 st further to the left on every wrong side row.

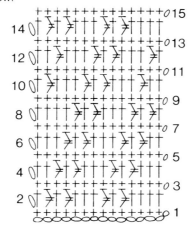

Bobble Braid Stitch

Worked over 13 sts on a background of any number of sts worked in basic double crochet on right side rows and single crochet on wrong side rows.

Note: For description of tr/rf see page 11 (Raised Stitches); for dc5tog see page 14 (Bobble).

1st row (right side): 1dc into each of first 4 sts, [1ch, skip 1 st, 1dc into next st] 3 times, 1dc into each of last 3 sts.

2nd row: 1sc into each of first 4 sts, work dc5tog into next ch sp, 1sc into next dc, 1sc into next sp, 1sc into next dc, dc5tog into next sp, 1sc into each of last 4 sts.

3rd row: 1tr/rf round first st 2 rows below (ie: 1st row), 1dc into next st on previous (ie: 2nd) row, 1tr/rf round next st 2 rows below,

[1ch, skip 1 st, 1dc into next st on previous row] 3 times, 1ch, skip 1 st, 1tr/rf round next st 2 rows below, 1dc into next st on previous row, 1tr/rf round next st 2 rows below.

4th row: 1sc into each of first 6 sts, work dc5tog into next st, 1sc into each of last 6 sts.

5th row: [1tr/rf round corresponding raised st 2 rows below, 1dc into next st] twice, [1ch, skip 1 st, 1dc into next st] 3 times, 1tr/rf round corresponding raised st 2 rows below, 1dc into next st, 1tr/rf round corresponding raised st 2 rows below.

Continue as set on 2nd, 3rd, 4th and 5th rows.

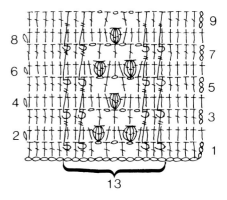

Loop or Fur Stitch

Multiple of 8 sts.
(add 2 for base chain)

Note: For description of Loop St see page 15. For plain loop stitch do not cut loops.

1st row (right side): Skip 3ch (count as 1dc), 1dc into next and each ch to end, turn.

2nd row: 1ch, 1sc into each of first 2 sts, *1 Loop st into each of next 4 sts**, 1sc into each of next 4 sts; rep from * ending last rep at **, 1sc into each of last 2 sts including top of tch, turn.

3rd row: 3ch (count as 1dc), skip 1 st, 1dc into next and each st to end, skip tch, turn.

Rep 2nd and 3rd rows.

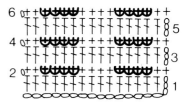

Diagram Note

 Sc Loop Stitch

Patterns for Texture and Color

Interweave Stitch

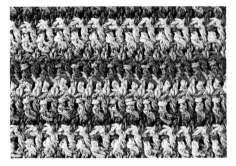

Multiple of 2 sts + 1.
(add 2 for base chain)

Note: For description of tr/rf see page 11. Work 1 row each in colors A, B and C throughout.

1st row (right side): Skip 3ch (count as 1dc), 1dc into next and each ch to end, turn.
2nd row: 3ch (count as 1dc), skip first st, *1tr/rf round next st, 1dc into next st; rep from * ending last rep in top of tch, turn.
Rep 2nd row.

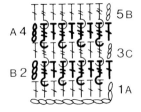

Little Wave Stitch

Multiple of 4 sts + 1.
(add 1 for base chain)

Work 2 rows each in colors A and B alternately.

1st row (right side): 1sc into 2nd ch from hook, *1hdc into next ch, 1dc into next ch, 1hdc into next ch, 1sc into next ch; rep from * to end, turn.
2nd row: 1ch, 1sc into first st, *1hdc into next hdc, 1dc into next dc, 1hdc into next hdc, 1sc into next sc; rep from * to end, skip tch, turn.
3rd row: 3ch (count as 1dc), skip first st, *1hdc into next hdc, 1sc into next dc, 1hdc into next hdc, 1dc into next sc; rep from * to end, skip tch, turn.
4th row: 3ch (count as 1dc), skip first st, *1hdc into next hdc, 1sc into next sc, 1hdc

into next hdc, 1dc into next dc; rep from * ending last rep in top of tch, turn.
5th row: 1ch, 1sc into first st, *1hdc into next hdc, 1dc into next sc, 1hdc into next hdc, 1sc into next dc; rep from * ending last rep in top of tch, turn.
Rep 2nd, 3rd, 4th and 5th rows.

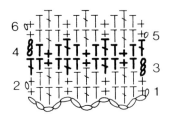

Interlocking Diamond Stitch

Multiple of 6 sts + 1.
(add 1 for base chain)

Work 1st row in color A, then 2 rows each in colors B and A alternately throughout.

1st row (wrong side): Sl st into 2nd ch from hook, *3ch, skip 2ch, 1dc into next ch, 3ch, skip 2ch, sl st into next ch; rep from * to end, turn.
2nd row: 4ch (count as 1dc and 1ch), 1dc into first sl st, *skip 3ch, sl st into next dc**, skip 3ch, work [1dc, 1ch, 1dc, 1ch, 1dc] into next sl st; rep from * ending last rep at ** in last dc, skip 3ch, work [1dc, 1ch, 1dc] into last sl st, turn.
3rd row: 6ch (count as 1dc and 3ch), skip [first st, 1ch and 1dc], *sl st into next sl st**, 3ch, skip 1dc and 1ch, 1dc into next dc, 3ch, skip 1ch and 1dc; rep from * ending last rep at ** in last sl st, 3ch, skip 1dc and 1ch, 1dc into next ch of tch, turn.
4th row: Sl st into first st, *skip 3ch, [1dc, 1ch, 1dc, 1ch, 1dc] all into next sl st, skip 3ch, sl st into next dc; rep from * ending in 3rd ch of tch loop, turn.
5th row: *3ch, skip 1dc and 1ch, 1dc into next dc, 3ch, skip 1ch and 1dc, sl st into next sl st; rep from * to end, turn.
Rep 2nd, 3rd, 4th and 5th rows.

Interlocking Shell Stitch

Multiple of 6 sts + 1.
(add 2 for base chain)

Note: For description of dc5tog see page 10 (Clusters).

Work 1 row each in colors A and B alternately; fasten off each color at end of each row.

1st row (right side): Skip 2ch (count as 1dc), 2dc into next ch, skip 2ch, 1sc into next ch, *skip 2ch, 5dc into next ch, skip 2ch, 1sc into next ch; rep from * to last 3ch, skip 2ch, 3dc into last ch, turn.
2nd row: 1ch, 1sc into first st, *2ch, dc5tog over next 5 sts, 2ch, 1sc into next st; rep from * ending last rep in top of tch, turn.
3rd row: 3ch (count as 1dc), 2dc into first st, 1sc into next cluster, *skip 2ch, 5dc into next sc, skip 2ch, 1sc into next cluster; rep from * to last cluster, skip 2ch, 3dc into last sc, skip tch, turn.
Rep 2nd and 3rd rows.

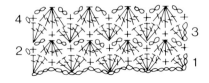

Zigzig Pip Stitch

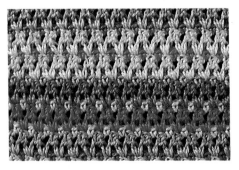

Multiple of 4 sts + 1.
(add 1 for base chain)

Note: For description of dc2tog see page 10 (Clusters).

Work 1 row each in colors A, B, C, D and E throughout.

1st row (right side): 1sc into 2nd ch from hook, *1ch, skip 1ch, 1sc into next ch; rep from * to end, turn.

○ Chain ● Slip stitch + Single crochet T Half double crochet ⊤ Double crochet ⧘ Treble ⧚ Double treble

2nd row: 3ch, 1dc into next ch sp (counts as dc2tog), *1ch, dc2tog inserting hook into same sp as previous st for first leg and into next sp for 2nd leg; rep from * to last sp, ending 1ch, dc2tog over same sp and last sc, skip tch, turn.

3rd row: 1ch, 1sc into first st, *1sc into next sp, 1ch, skip next cluster; rep from * ending 1sc into last sp, 1sc into last st, skip tch, turn.

4th row: 3ch (count as 1dc), dc2tog inserting hook into first st for first leg and into next sp for 2nd leg, *1ch, dc2tog inserting hook into same sp as previous st for first leg and into next sp for 2nd leg; rep from * ending with 2nd leg of last cluster in last sc, 1dc into same place, skip tch, turn.

5th row: 1ch, 1sc into first st, *1ch, skip next cluster, 1sc into next sp; rep from * working last sc into top of tch, turn.

Rep 2nd, 3rd, 4th and 5th rows.

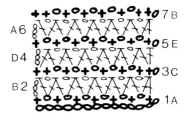

Aligned Railing Stitch

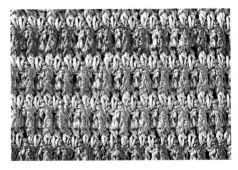

Multiple of 2 sts + 1.
(add 2 for base chain)

On a background of basic double crochets in color M work raised rows — one row each in colors A, B and C throughout.

Note: For description of Raised Stitches see page 11.

Work 2 rows basic double crochets in M.

Commence Pattern

1st row (right side): Put working loop temporarily on a stitch holder or safety pin, draw loop of contrast color through top of last background st completed, 1ch, work 1tr/rf round stem of 2nd st in last-but-one row, *1ch, skip 1 st, 1tr/rf round stem of next st in last-but-one row; rep from * ending sl st into top of tch at beg of last background row worked. Fasten off but do not turn work.

2nd row: Replace hook in working loop of M. 3ch, work 1dc inserting hook through top of raised st and background st at the same time, *work 1dc inserting hook under contrast color ch and top of next st in background color at the same time, work 1dc

inserting hook under top of next raised st and background st as before; rep from * to end. Work 1 row in basic double crochets. Rep these 3 rows.

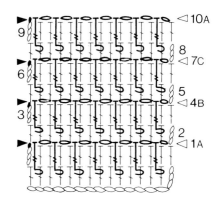

Shadow Tracery Stitch

Multiple of 6 sts + 1.
(add 1 for base chain)

Special Abbreviation

Puff stitch = work hdc5tog all into same place ending with 1ch drawn tightly to close.

Note: For description of hdc5tog see page 14.

Work 1 row each in colors A and B alternately throughout. Do not break yarn when changing color, but fasten off temporarily and begin row at same end as new color.

1st row (right side in A): 1sc into 2nd ch from hook, *3ch, skip 2ch, puff st into next ch, 3ch, skip 2ch, 1sc into next ch; rep from * to end. Do not turn.

2nd row (right side in B): Join yarn into first st, 1ch, 1sc into first st, *3ch, skip 3ch, 1sc into next puff st, 3ch, skip 3ch, 1sc into next sc; rep from * to end. Do not turn.

3rd row (wrong side in A): 6ch (count as 1dc and 3ch), skip first st and 3ch, 1sc into next sc, *3ch, skip 3ch, puff st into next sc, 3ch, skip 3ch, 1sc into next sc; rep from * ending 3ch, skip 3ch, 1dc into last sc. Do not turn.

4th row (wrong side in B): Pick up yarn in 3rd ch of tch, 1ch, 1sc into same place, *3ch, skip 3ch, 1sc into next sc, 3ch, skip 3ch, 1sc into next st; rep from * to end, turn.

5th row (right side in A): 1ch, 1sc into first st, *3ch, skip 3ch, puff st into next sc, 3ch, skip 3ch, 1sc into next sc; rep from * to end. Do not turn.

Rep 2nd, 3rd, 4th and 5th rows.

Fleur de Lys Stitch

Multiple of 6 sts + 1.
(add 2 for base chain)

Special Abbreviations

FC/rf (Fleur Cluster raised at front) = leaving last loop of each st on hook work 1dc/rf round next dc, skip 1ch, 1dc into top of next sc, skip 1ch, 1dc/rf round next dc (4 loops on hook), yo, draw through all loops.

FC/rb (Fleur Cluster raised at back) = as for FC/rf except insert hook at back for first and 3rd legs.

Note: For description of dc/rf and dc/rb see page 11 (Raised Stitches).

Work 1 row each in colors A and B alternately throughout. Do not break yarn when changing color, but fasten off temporarily and begin row at same end as new color.

1st row (right side in A): Skip 2ch (count as 1dc), 1dc into next ch, *1ch, skip 2ch, 1sc into next ch, 1ch, skip 2ch**, 3dc into next ch; rep from * ending last rep at **, 2dc into last ch. Do not turn.

2nd row (right side in B): Join new yarn into top of tch, 1ch, 1sc into same place, *2ch, FC/rb, 2ch, 1sc into next dc; rep from * to end, turn.

3rd row (wrong side in A): 3ch (count as 1dc), 1dc into first st, *1ch, skip 2ch, 1sc into next cluster, 1ch, skip 2ch**, 3dc into next sc; rep from * ending last rep at **, 2dc into last sc. Do not turn.

4th row (wrong side in B): Rejoin new yarn at top of 3ch, 1ch, 1sc into same place, *2ch, FC/rf, 2ch, 1sc into next dc; rep from * to end, turn.

5th row (right side in A): 3ch (count as 1dc), 1dc into first st, *1ch, skip 2ch, 1sc into next cluster, 1ch, skip 2ch**, 3dc into next sc; rep from * ending last rep at **, 2dc into last sc. Do not turn.

Rep 2nd, 3rd, 4th and 5th rows.

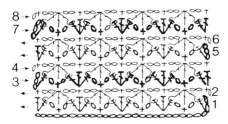

Patterns for Texture and Color

Picot Coronet Stitch

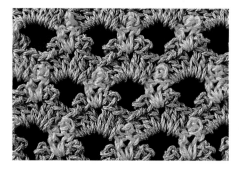

Multiple of 7 sts + 1.
(add 3 for base chain)
Work 1 row each with colors A and B alternately throughout; fasten off each color at end of each row.

1st row (right side): Skip 3ch (count as 1dc), 1dc into next ch, work a picot of [3ch, insert hook down through top of dc just made and work a sl st to close], 2dc into same ch, *skip 6ch, work a Coronet of [3dc, picot, 1ch, 1dc, picot, 2dc] into next ch; rep from * to last 7ch, skip 6ch, [3dc, picot, 1dc] into last ch, turn.

2nd row: 3ch (count as 1dc), 1dc into first st, *3ch, work a picot V st of [1dc, picot, 1dc] into 1ch sp at center of next Coronet; rep from * ending 3ch, 2dc into top of tch, turn.

3rd row: 2ch (count as 1hdc), skip first 2 sts, *Coronet into next 3ch sp, skip next picot V st; rep from * ending Coronet into last sp, 1hdc into top of tch, turn.

4th row: 4ch (count as 1dc and 1ch), *picot V st into sp at center of next Coronet, 3ch; rep from * ending picot V st into last Coronet, 1ch, 1dc into top of tch, turn.

5th row: 3ch (count as 1dc), skip first st, [1dc, picot, 2dc] into 1ch sp, *skip next picot V st, Coronet into next sp; rep from * ending skip last picot V st, 3dc into next ch, picot, 1dc into next ch of tch, turn.

Rep 2nd, 3rd, 4th and 5th rows.

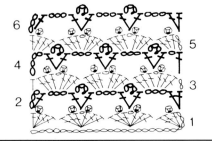

Relief Squares

Multiple of 10 sts + 4.
(add 1 for base chain)

Note: For description of dtr/rf and quin tr/rf see page 11 (Raised Stitches).

1st base row (right side): Using A, 1sc into 2nd ch from hook, 1sc into next and each ch to end, turn.

2nd base row: 1ch, 1sc into first and each st to end, skip tch, turn.

Commence Pattern

Change to B and rep the 2nd base row twice.

Change to C and rep the 2nd base row 4 times.

7th row: Using B, 1ch, 1sc into each of first 3 sts, *[1dtr/rf round st corresponding to next st 5 rows below, i.e. last row worked in B] twice, 1sc into each of next 4 sts, [1dtr/rf round st corresponding to next st 5 rows below] twice, 1sc into each of next 2 sts; rep from * ending 1sc into last st, skip tch, turn.

8th row: Using B rep 2nd base row.

9th row: Using A, 1ch, 1sc into first st, *[1quin tr/rf round st corresponding to next st 9 rows below, ie last row worked in A] twice, 1sc into each of next 8 sts; rep from * to last 3 sts, [1quin tr/rf round st corresponding to next st 9 rows below] twice, 1sc into last st, skip tch, turn.

10th row: Using A rep 2nd base row.
Rep these 10 rows.

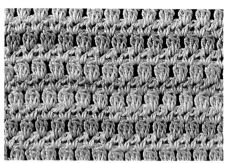

Multi-Colored Parquet Stitch

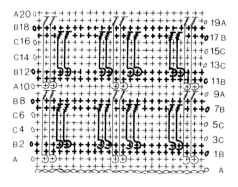

Multiple of 3 sts + 1.
(add 1 for base chain)

Work 1 row each in colors A, B and C alternately throughout.

1st row (right side): 1sc into 2nd ch from hook, *3ch, 1dc into same place as previous sc, skip 2ch, 1sc into next ch; rep from * to end, turn.

2nd row: 3ch (count as 1dc), 1dc into first st, 1sc into next 3ch arch, *3ch, 1dc into same 3ch arch, 1sc into next 3ch arch; rep

---

from * ending 2ch, 1dc into last sc, skip tch, turn.

3rd row: 1ch, 1sc into first st, 3ch, 1dc into next 2ch sp, *work [1sc, 3ch, 1dc] into next 3ch arch; rep from * ending 1sc into top of tch, turn.
Rep 2nd and 3rd rows.

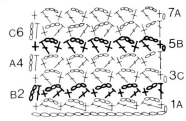

Zigzag Lozenge Stitch

Multiple of 2 sts + 1.
(add 2 for base chain)

Work 1 row each in colors A, B and C alternately throughout.

Note: For description of dc2tog and dc3tog see page 14 (Bobble).

1st row (wrong side): Skip 2ch (count as 1hdc), 1hdc into next ch, *skip 1ch, [1hdc, 1ch, 1hdc] into next ch; rep from * to last 2 ch, skip 1ch, 2hdc into last ch, turn.

2nd row: 3ch, 1dc into first st (counts as dc2tog), *1ch, work dc3tog into next ch sp; rep from * to last sp, ending 1ch, dc2tog into top of tch, turn.

3rd row: 2ch (count as 1hdc), skip first st, *work [1hdc, 1ch, 1hdc] into next ch sp; rep from * ending 1hdc into top of tch, turn.

4th row: 3ch (count as 1dc), skip first st, *work dc3tog into next sp, 1ch; rep from * ending 1dc into top of tch, turn.

5th row: 2ch (count as 1hdc), 1hdc into first st, *work [1hdc, 1ch, 1hdc] into next ch sp; rep from * ending 2hdc into top of tch, turn.
Rep 2nd, 3rd, 4th and 5th rows.

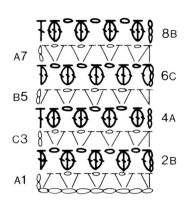

○ Chain ● Slip stitch + Single crochet T Half double crochet Ŧ Double crochet ‡ Treble ‡ Double treble

Filet Crochet Lace

For help with making Filet Crochet Lace fabrics from squared charts please refer to 'Filet Crochet with Charts', page 18.

☐ = space (2ch)
⌐¬ = bar
◠ = lacet
⊡ = block

Greek Key Frieze

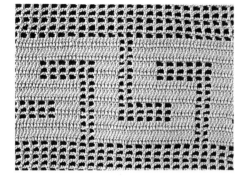

Base Row
Multiple of 3 sts per square + 1
Pattern Repeat = 12 squares

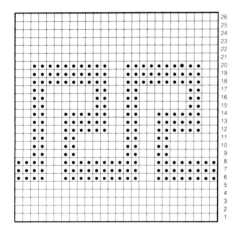

Alternating Tiles

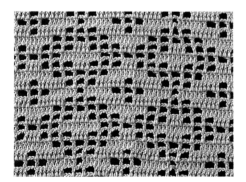

Base Row
Multiple of 3 sts per square + 1
Pattern Repeat = 8 squares

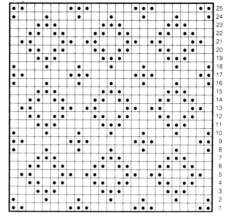

Southern Cross

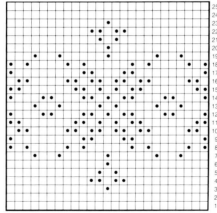

Base Row
Multiple of 3 sts per square + 1
Pattern Repeat = 15 squares

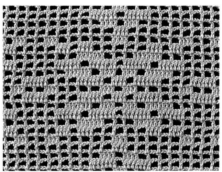

Orchid Blooms

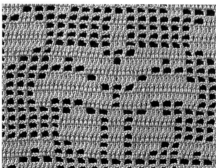

Base Row
Multiple of 3 sts per square + 1
Pattern Repeat = 22 squares

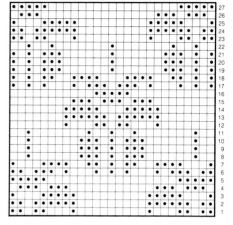

Blocks and Lacets

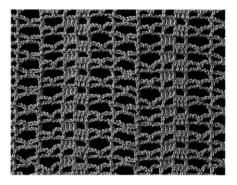

Base Row
Multiple of 3 sts per square + 1
Pattern Repeat = 8 squares wide by 2 squares deep

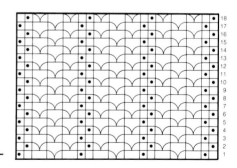

Hint: Larger items, such as curtains and bedspreads, can easily be made in Filet. Work a small piece of alternate blocks and spaces to ascertain the number of blocks and rows to the inch. From that you can calculate the number of squares you will need in Filet to cover the area you require and this can then be drawn onto graph paper. Any of the designs suggested here can then be added, either singly or in repeats, or you can design your own exclusive pattern!

Filet Crochet

Flowerpots

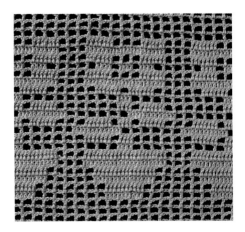

Base Row
Multiple of 3 sts per square + 1
Pattern Repeat = 10 squares

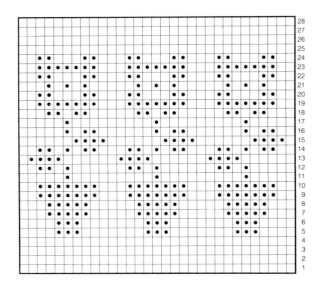

Butterfly

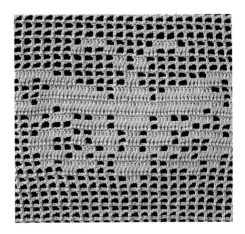

Base Row
Multiple of 3 sts per square + 1
Pattern Repeat = 31 squares

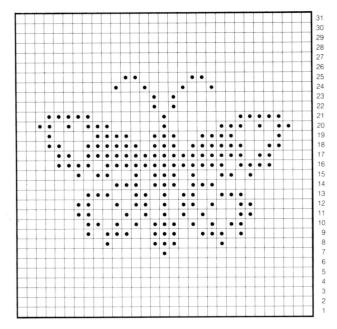

Peace Rose

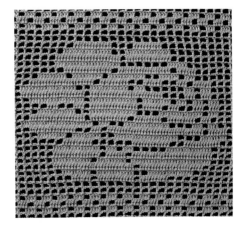

Base Row
Multiple of 3 sts per square + 1
Pattern Repeat = 30 squares

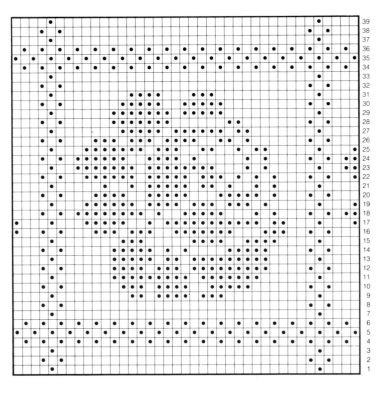

□ = space (2ch)   ▭ = bar   ▽ = lacet   ▪ = block   For more information refer to page 18.

Pokerwork

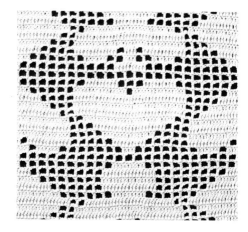

Base Row

Multiple of 3 sts per square + 1

Pattern Repeat = 24 squares wide by 23 squares deep

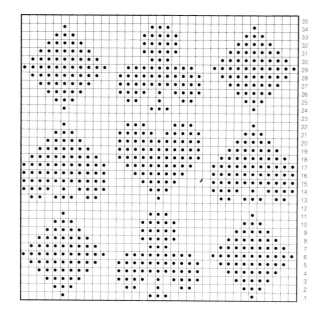

Letterform

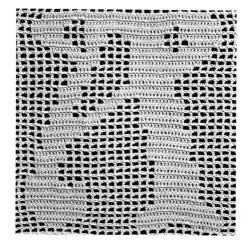

Base Row

Multiple of 3 sts per square + 1

Remaining letter charts are shown on page 19.

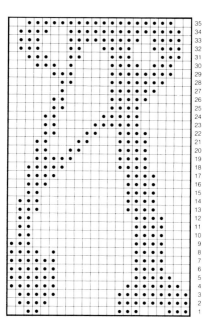

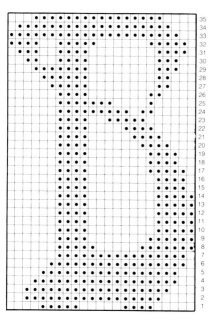

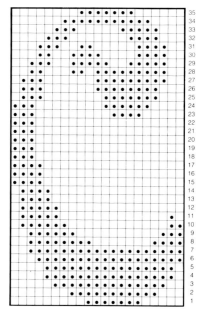

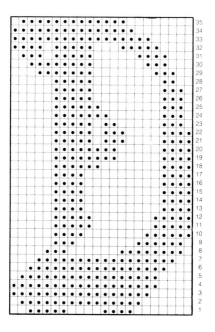

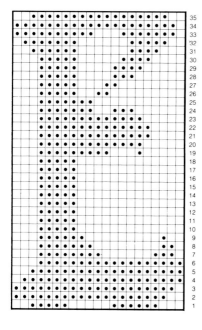

Openwork and Lace Patterns

Offset Filet Network

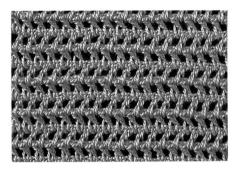

Multiple of 2 sts.
(add 3 for base chain)

1st row (right side): 1dc into 6th ch from hook, *1ch, skip 1ch, 1dc into next ch; rep from * ending 1dc into last ch, turn.

2nd row: 4ch (count as 1dc and 1ch), skip first 2 sts, 1dc into next ch sp, *1ch, skip 1dc, 1dc into next sp; rep from * to tch, 1dc into next ch, turn.

Rep 2nd row.

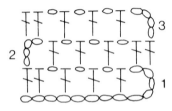

String Network

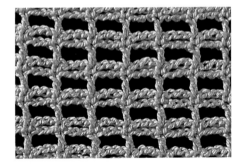

Multiple of 4 sts + 1.
(add 5 for base chain)

1st row (right side): 1dc into 10th ch from hook, *3ch, skip 3ch, 1dc into next ch; rep from * to end, turn.

2nd row: 1ch, 1sc into first st, *3ch, skip 3ch, 1sc into next dc; rep from * ending 3ch, 1sc into 4th ch of tch, turn.

3rd row: 6ch (count as 1dc and 3ch), skip first st and 3ch, 1dc into next sc, *3ch, skip 3ch, 1dc into next sc; rep from * to end, turn.

Rep 2nd and 3rd rows.

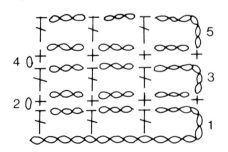

Double Crochet and Popcorn Squares

Multiple of 8 sts + 3.
(add 2 for base chain)

Notes

For description of Popcorn see page 14. Popcorns occur on both right and wrong side rows. Be sure to push them all out on the right side of the fabric as you complete them.

1st row (right side): 5dc Popcorn into 4th ch from hook, *1dc into each of next 7ch, 5dc Popcorn into next ch; rep from * ending 1dc into last ch, turn.

2nd row: 4ch (count as 1dc and 1ch), skip first st and next Popcorn, 1dc into next st, *2ch, skip 2 sts, 5dc Popcorn into next st, 2ch, skip 2 sts, 1dc into next st, 1ch, skip next Popcorn, 1dc into next st; rep from * ending last rep in tch, turn.

3rd row: 4ch (count as 1dc and 1ch), skip first st and next ch, 1dc into next st, *1ch, skip 1ch, 5dc Popcorn into next ch, 1ch, skip Popcorn, 5dc Popcorn into next ch, [1ch, skip next ch, 1dc into next st] twice; rep from * ending last rep in tch, turn.

4th row: 4ch (count as 1dc and 1ch), skip first st and next ch, 1dc into next st, *2ch, 5dc Popcorn into ch sp between next 2 Popcorns, 2ch, 1dc into next dc, 1ch, skip 1ch, 1dc into next st; rep from * ending last rep in tch, turn.

5th row: 3ch (count as 1dc), skip first st, 5dc Popcorn into next ch, *1dc into next dc, 1dc into each of next 2ch, 1dc into next Popcorn, 1dc into each of next 2ch, 1dc into next dc, 5dc Popcorn into next ch; rep from * ending 1dc into next ch of tch, turn.

Rep 2nd, 3rd, 4th and 5th rows.

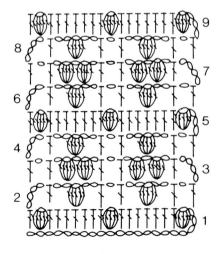

Picot Ridge Stitch

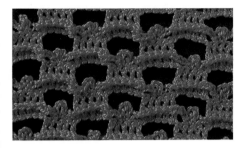

Multiple of 10 sts + 7.
(add 2 for base chain)

Note: For description of dc/rf see page 11.

1st row (right side): Skip 3ch (count as 1dc), *1dc into each of next 5ch, 3ch, skip 2ch, [1sc, 4ch, 1sc] into next ch, 3ch, skip 2ch; rep from * ending 1dc into last ch, turn.

2nd row: 8ch (count as 1dc and 5ch), skip first st and next 3ch arch, *1dc/rf round each of next 5 sts, 5ch, skip next 3 arches; rep from * ending 1dc/rf round each of last 5dcs, 1dc into top of tch, turn.

3rd row: 6ch, skip first 3 sts, *[1sc, 4ch, 1sc] into next st, 3ch, skip 2 sts, 1dc into each of next 5ch**, 3ch, skip 2 sts; rep from * ending last rep at **, 1dc into next ch of tch, turn.

4th row: 3ch (count as 1dc), skip first st, *1dc/rf round each of next 5 sts, 5ch**, skip next 3 arches; rep from * ending last rep at **, skip next 2 arches, 1dc into tch arch, turn.

5th row: 3ch (count as 1dc), skip first st, *1dc into each of next 5ch, 3ch, skip 2 sts, [1sc, 4ch, 1sc] into next st, 3ch, skip 2 sts; rep from * ending 1dc into top of tch, turn.

Rep 2nd, 3rd, 4th and 5th rows.

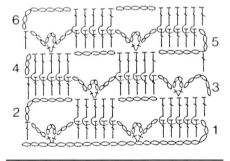

Fancy Picot Stitch

Multiple of 10 sts + 1.
(add 2 for base chain)

1st row (right side): Skip 3ch (count as 1dc), *1dc into each of next 2ch, work a picot of [3ch, insert hook down through top of last st made and sl st to close], [1ch, skip 1ch,

○ Chain ● Slip stitch + Single crochet T Half double crochet ⊤ Double crochet ⧚ Treble ⧚ Double treble

1dc into next ch, picot] twice, 1ch, skip 1ch, 1dc into each of next 2ch**, 1ch, skip 1ch; rep from * ending last rep at **, 1dc into last ch, turn.

2nd row: 3ch (count as 1dc), skip first st, *1dc into each of next 2 sts, [picot, 1ch, skip next ch and picot, 1dc into next dc] 3 times, 1dc into next dc**, 1ch, skip 1ch; rep from * ending last rep at **, 1dc into top of tch, turn.

Rep 2nd row.

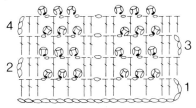

Squares and Ladders

Multiple of 16 sts + 5.
(add 3 for base chain)
Note: For description of dc3tog see page 10.

Base row (right side): 1dc into 6th ch from hook, *1ch, skip 1ch, 1dc into next ch; rep from * to end, turn.

Commence Pattern

1st row: 4ch (count as 1dc and 1ch), skip first st and next ch, 1dc into next dc, 1ch, skip 1ch, 1dc into next dc, *5ch, skip 5 sts, dc3tog into next dc, 5ch, skip 5 sts, 1dc into next dc, [1ch, skip 1ch, 1dc into next st] twice; rep from * ending last rep in tch, turn.

2nd row: 4ch (count as 1dc and 1ch), skip first st and next ch, 1dc into next dc, 1ch, skip 1ch, 1dc into next dc, *4ch, 1sc into 5ch arch, skip cluster, 1sc into next 5ch arch, 4ch, 1dc into next dc, [1ch, skip 1ch, 1dc into next st] twice; rep from * ending last rep in tch, turn.

3rd row: 4ch (count as 1dc and 1ch), skip first st and next ch, 1dc into next dc, 1ch, skip 1ch, 1dc into next dc, *4ch, 1sc into 4ch arch, 1sc between 2sc, 1sc into next 4ch arch, 4ch, 1dc into next dc, [1ch, skip 1ch, 1dc into next st] twice; rep from * ending last rep in tch, turn.

4th row: 4ch (counts as 1dc and 1ch), skip first st and next ch, 1dc into next dc, 1ch, skip 1ch, 1dc into next dc, *5ch, dc3tog into 2nd of 3sc, 5ch, 1dc into next dc, [1ch, skip 1ch, 1dc into next st] twice; rep from * ending last rep in tch, turn.

5th row: 4ch (count as 1dc and 1ch), skip first st and next ch, 1dc into next dc, *1ch, skip 1ch, 1dc into next st; rep from * ending last rep in tch, turn.

6th row: As 5th row.

Rep these 6 rows.

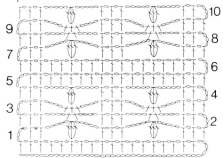

Shell Network

Multiple of 8 sts + 3.
(add 3 for base chain)

1st row (right side): 1dc into 6th ch from hook, *skip 2ch, 5dc into next ch, skip 2ch, 1dc into next ch, 1ch, skip 1ch, 1dc into next ch; rep from * to end, turn.

2nd row: 4ch (count as 1dc and 1ch), skip first st and next ch, 1dc into next dc, *skip 2dc, 5dc into next dc, skip 2dc, 1dc into next dc, 1ch, skip 1ch, 1dc into next dc; rep from * ending last rep in 2nd ch of tch, turn.

Rep 2nd row.

Sieve Stitch

Multiple of 2 sts + 1.
(add 1 for base chain)
Base row (wrong side): 1sc into 2nd ch from hook, *1ch, skip 1ch, 1sc into next ch; rep from * to end, turn.

Commence Pattern

1st row: 1ch, skip 1 st, *2sc into next ch sp, skip next sc; rep from * until 1 ch sp remains, 1sc into last ch sp, 1sc into next sc, skip tch, turn.

2nd row: 1ch, skip 1 st, 1sc into next st, *1ch, skip 1 st, 1sc into next sc; rep from * until only tch remains, 1sc into tch, turn.

3rd row: 1ch, skip first 2 sts, *2sc into next ch sp, skip next sc; rep from * until only tch remains, 2sc into tch, turn.

4th row: As 2nd row.

5th row: 1ch, 1sc into first st, *skip next sc, 2sc into next ch sp; rep from * ending last rep in tch, turn.

6th row: 1ch, skip 1 st, *1sc into next sc, 1ch, skip 1sc; rep from * ending 1sc into tch, turn.

7th row: 1ch, skip 1 st, 1sc into next ch sp, *skip 1sc, 2sc into next sp; rep from * ending skip last sc, 1sc into tch, turn.

8th row: 1ch, 1sc into first st, *1ch, skip 1sc, 1sc into next st; rep from * to end working last st into top of tch, turn.

Rep these 8 rows.

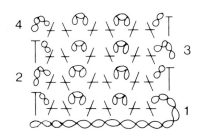

Winkle Picot Stitch

Multiple of 3 sts + 2.
(add 4 for base chain)

1st row (right side): 1sc into 6th ch from hook, *skip 1ch, 1sc into next ch, 3ch, 1sc into next ch; rep from * until 3ch remain, skip 1ch, 1sc into next ch, 2ch, 1hdc into last ch, turn.

2nd row: 4ch, 1sc into next 2ch sp, *[1sc, 3ch, 1sc] into next 3ch arch; rep from * ending [1sc, 2ch, 1hdc] into last ch arch, turn.
Rep 2nd row.

Openwork and Lace Patterns

Half Double Crochet V Stitch

Multiple of 2 sts.
(add 2 for base chain)

1st row (right side): [1hdc, 1ch, 1hdc] into 4th ch from hook, *skip 1ch, [1hdc, 1ch, 1hdc] into next ch; rep from * until 2ch remain, skip 1ch, 1hdc into last ch, turn.

2nd row: 2ch, *skip 2 sts, [1hdc, 1ch, 1hdc] into next ch sp; rep from * to last ch sp, skip 1 st, 1hdc into tch, turn.

Rep 2nd row.

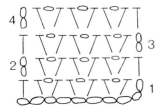

Double Crochet V

Multiple of 2 sts.
(add 2 for base chain)

1st row (right side): 2dc into 4th ch from hook, *skip 1ch, 2dc into next ch; rep from * to last 2ch, skip 1ch, 1dc into last ch, turn.

2nd row: 3ch, *skip 2 sts, 2dc between 2nd skipped st and next st; rep from * to last 2 sts, skip 1 st, 1dc into top of tch, turn.

Rep 2nd row.

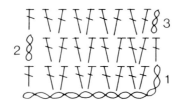

Offset V Stitch

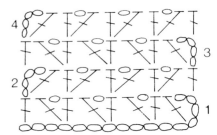

Multiple of 3 sts + 1.
(add 3 for base chain)

1st row (right side): 1dc into 4th ch from hook, *skip 2ch, work a V st of [1dc, 1ch, 1dc] into next ch; rep from * to last 3ch, skip 2ch, 1dc into last ch, turn.

2nd row: 4ch, 1dc into first st, *V st into 2nd dc of next V st; rep from * until 1dc and tch remain, skip 1dc and 1ch, 1dc into next ch, turn.

Rep 2nd row.

Twin V Stitch

Multiple of 4 sts + 2.
(add 2 for base chain)

1st row (right side): 2dc into 5th ch from hook, 2dc into next ch, *skip 2ch, 2dc into each of next 2ch; rep from * to last 2ch, skip 1ch, 1dc into last ch, turn.

2nd row: 3ch, *skip 2 sts, 2dc into each of next 2 sts; rep from * to last 2 sts, skip 1 st, 1dc into tch, turn.

Rep 2nd row.

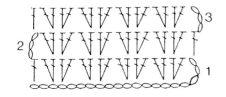

Three-and-Two Stitch

Multiple of 6 sts + 2.
(add 2 for base chain)

1st row (right side): Work a V st of [1dc, 1ch, 1dc] into 5th ch from hook, *skip 2ch, 3dc into next ch, skip 2ch, work a V st into next ch; rep from * to last 5ch, skip 2ch, 3dc into next ch, skip 1ch, 1dc into last ch, turn.

2nd row: 3ch, *skip 2 sts, work 3dc into center dc of next 3dc, work a V st into ch sp at center of next V st; rep from * ending 1dc into top of tch, turn.

3rd row: 3ch, *V st into sp of next V st, 3dc into center dc of next 3dc; rep from * ending 1dc into top of tch, turn.

Rep 2nd and 3rd rows.

Basket Stitch

Multiple of 3 sts + 2.
(add 2 for base chain)

Note: For description of working double crochet stitches together see page 10.

1st row (wrong side): Work a V st of [1dc, 1ch, 1dc] into 5th ch from hook, *skip 2ch, work V st into next ch; rep from * to last 2ch,

○ Chain ● Slip stitch + Single crochet T Half double crochet ⊤ Double crochet ⧧ Treble ⧉ Double treble

skip 1ch, 1dc into last ch, turn.

2nd row: 3ch, skip 2 sts, work a Double V st of [2dc, 1ch, 2dc] into ch sp at center of V st, *1ch, skip next V st, work a Double V st into sp at center of next V st; rep from * leaving last loop of last dc of last Double V st on hook and working it together with 1dc into top of tch, turn.

3rd row: 3ch, work a V st into each sp to end finishing with 1dc into top of tch, turn.

4th row: 3ch, 1dc into first st, *1ch, skip next V st, work a Double V st into sp at center of next V st; rep from * until 1 V st remains, 1ch, skip V st, 2dc into top of tch, turn.

5th row: As 3rd row.

Rep 2nd, 3rd, 4th and 5th rows.

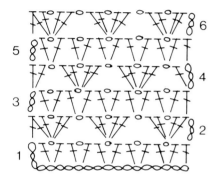

Empress Stitch

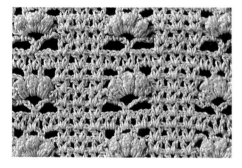

Multiple of 18 sts + 1.
(add 3 for base chain)

Notes
For description of Popcorn see page 14.
Popcorns occur on both right and wrong side rows alternately. Be sure to push them all out on the right side of the fabric as you complete them.

1st row (wrong side): 1dc into 4th ch from hook, *skip 2ch, work a V st of [1dc, 1ch, 1dc] into next ch; rep from * to last 3ch, skip 2ch, 2dc into last ch, turn.

2nd row: 3ch, 1dc into first st, V st into sp at center of next V st, *5ch, skip next V st, 1sc into sp at center of next V st, 5ch, skip next V st**, [V st into sp at center of next V st] 3 times; rep from * ending last rep at **, V st into sp at center of last V st, 2dc into top of tch, turn.

3rd row: 3ch, 1dc into first st, V st into sp at center of next V st, *[3ch, 1sc into next 5ch arch] twice, 3ch**, [V st into sp at center of next V st] 3 times; rep from * ending last rep at **, V st into sp at center of last V st, 2dc into top of tch, turn.

4th row: 3ch, 1dc into first st, V st into sp at center of next V st, *skip next 3ch arch, [5dc Popcorn, 2ch, 5dc Popcorn, 2ch, 5dc Popcorn] into next 3ch arch, skip next 3ch arch**, [V st into sp at center of next V st] 3 times; rep from * ending last rep at **, V st into sp at center of last V st, 2dc into top of tch, turn.

5th row: 3ch, 1dc into first st, V st into sp at center of next V st, *[3ch, 1sc into next 2ch sp] twice, 3ch**, [V st into sp at center of next V st] 3 times; rep from * ending last rep at **, V st into sp at center of last V st, 2dc into top of tch, turn.

6th row: 3ch, 1dc into first st, V st into sp at center of next V st, *[V st into 2nd ch of next 3ch arch] 3 times**, [V st into sp at center of next V st] 3 times; rep from * ending last rep at **, V st into sp at center of last V st, 2dc into top of tch, turn.

Rep 2nd, 3rd, 4th, 5th and 6th rows.

Noughts and Crosses Stitch

Multiple of 2 sts + 1.
(add 3 for base chain)

Note: For description of crossed stitches see page 12 (Crossed Stitch II).

1st row (right side): 1dc into 6th ch from hook, *1ch, skip 1ch, 1dc into next ch; rep from * to end, turn.

2nd row: 3ch, skip next ch sp, work 2 crossed stitches as follows: 1dc forward into next ch sp, 1dc back into ch sp just skipped going behind forward dc so as not to catch it, *1dc forward into next unoccupied ch sp, 1dc back into previous ch sp going behind forward dc as before; rep from * to end when last forward dc occupies tch, 1dc into next ch, turn.

3rd row: 1ch (counts as 1sc), 1sc into first st, 1sc into next and each st to end working last st into top of tch, turn.

4th row: 4ch (counts as 1dc and 1ch), skip 2 sts, 1dc into next st, *1ch, skip 1 st, 1dc

into next st; rep from * ending last rep in tch, turn.

Rep 2nd, 3rd and 4th rows.

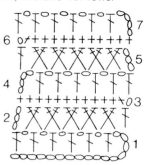

Fantail Stitch

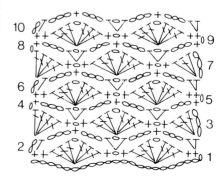

Multiple of 10 sts + 1.
(add 1 for base chain)

1st row (right side): 1sc into 2nd ch from hook, 1sc into next ch, *skip 3ch, work a Fan of [3dc, 1ch, 3dc] into next ch, skip 3ch, 1sc into next ch**, 1ch, skip 1ch, 1sc into next ch; rep from * ending last rep at **, 1sc into last ch, turn.

2nd row: 2ch (count as 1hdc), 1hdc into first st, *3ch, 1sc into ch sp at center of next Fan, 3ch**, work a V st of [1hdc, 1ch, 1hdc] into next sp; rep from * ending last rep at **, 2hdc into last sc, skip tch, turn.

3rd row: 3ch, 3dc into first st, *1sc into next 3ch arch, 1ch, 1sc into next arch**, work a Fan into sp at center of next V st; rep from * ending last rep at **, 4dc into top of tch, turn.

4th row: 1ch, 1sc into first st, *3ch, V st into next sp, 3ch, 1sc into sp at center of next Fan; rep from * ending last rep into top of tch, turn.

5th row: 1ch, 1sc into first st, *1sc into next arch, Fan into sp at center of next V st, 1sc into next arch**, 1ch; rep from * ending last rep at **, 1sc into last sc, skip tch, turn.

Rep 2nd, 3rd, 4th and 5th rows.

Openwork and Lace Patterns

Flying Shell Stitch

Multiple of 4 sts + 1.

(add 1 for base chain)

Note: For description of dc2tog see page 10.

1st row (right side): Work a Flying Shell (called FS) of [1sc, 3ch, 3dc] into 2nd ch from hook, *skip 3ch, 1FS into next ch; rep from * to last 4ch, skip 3ch, 1sc into last ch, turn.

2nd row: 3ch, 1dc into first st, *skip 3 sts, 1sc into top of 3ch**, work a V st of [1dc, 1ch, 1dc] into next sc; rep from * ending last rep at **, 2dc into last sc, skip tch, turn.

3rd row: 3ch, 3dc into first st, skip next st, *1FS into next sc, skip next V st; rep from * ending 1sc into last sc, 3ch, dc2tog over last dc and top of tch, turn.

4th row: 1ch (counts as 1sc), *V st into next sc, skip 3 sts, 1sc into top of 3ch; rep from * to end, turn.

5th row: 1ch, FS into first st, *skip next V st, FS into next sc; rep from * ending skip last V st, 1sc into tch, turn.

Rep 2nd, 3rd, 4th and 5th rows.

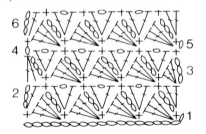

Picot V Stitch

Multiple of 3 sts + 1.

(add 2 for base chain)

1st row (right side): Skip 3ch (count as 1dc), 1dc into next ch, skip 1ch, 1dc into next ch, work a picot of [3ch, insert hook down through top of dc just made and work a sl st], 1dc into same ch as last dc, *skip 2ch, [1dc, picot, 1dc] into next ch; rep from * to last 3ch, skip 2ch, 1dc into last ch, turn.

2nd row: 3ch (count as 1dc), 1dc into first st, *skip 1dc and picot, [1dc, picot, 1dc] into next dc; rep from * to last 2 sts, skip next dc, 1dc into top of tch, turn.

Rep 2nd row.

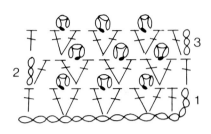

Pebble Lace Stitch

Multiple of 4 sts + 3.

(add 1 for base chain)

Notes

For description of tr7tog see page 10.

Close tr7tog clusters with 1ch drawn tightly, (this does not count as part of following ch loop).

Clusters always occur on wrong side rows. Be sure to push them all out to the back (right side) of the fabric as you complete them.

1st row (wrong side): 1sc into 2nd ch from hook, *2ch, skip 1ch, work tr7tog into next ch, 2ch, skip 1ch, 1sc into next ch; rep from * to last 2ch, 2ch, skip 1ch, 1hdc into last ch, turn.

2nd row: 1ch, 1sc into first st, *3ch, 1sc into next cluster; rep from * ending 1ch, 1hdc into last sc, skip tch, turn.

3rd row: 4ch, skip first hdc and ch, 1sc into next sc, *2ch, tr7tog into 2nd of next 3ch, 2ch, 1sc into next sc; rep from * to end, skip tch, turn.

4th row: 3ch, skip first st and 2ch, 1sc into next cluster, *3ch, 1sc into next cluster; rep from * ending 3ch, 1sc into last 4ch arch, turn.

5th row: 1ch, 1sc into first st, *2ch, tr7tog into 2nd of next 3ch, 2ch, 1sc into next sc; rep from * ending 2ch, skip 1ch, 1hdc into next ch of tch, turn.

Rep 2nd, 3rd, 4th and 5th rows.

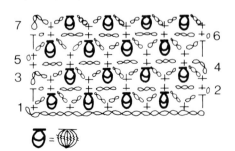

Plain Trellis Stitch

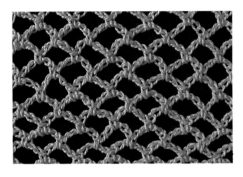

Multiple of 4 sts + 3.

(add 3 for base chain)

1st row: 1sc into 6th ch from hook, *5ch, skip 3ch, 1sc into next ch; rep from * to end, turn.

2nd row: *5ch, 1sc into next 5ch arch; rep from * to end, turn.

Rep 2nd row.

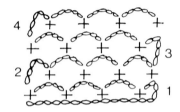

Picot Trellis Stitch

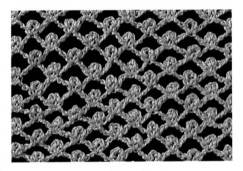

Multiple of 5 sts + 1.

(add 1 for base chain)

1st row: 1sc into 2nd ch from hook, *5ch, skip 4ch, 1sc into next ch; rep from * to end, turn.

2nd row: *5ch, work a picot of [1sc, 3ch, 1sc] into 3rd ch of next 5ch arch; rep from * ending 2ch, 1dc into last sc, skip tch, turn.

3rd row: 1ch, 1sc into first st, *5ch, skip picot, picot into 3rd ch of next 5ch arch; rep from * ending 5ch, skip picot, 1sc into tch arch, turn.

Rep 2nd and 3rd rows.

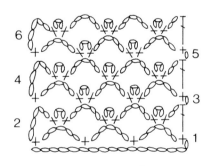

○ Chain   ● Slip stitch   + Single crochet   T Half double crochet   ⊤ Double crochet   ⧧ Treble   ⧦ Double treble

Block Trellis Stitch

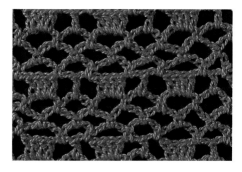

Multiple of 8 sts + 5.
(add 1 for base chain)

1st row (right side): 1sc into 2nd ch from hook, *5ch, skip 3ch, 1sc into next ch; rep from * to end, turn.

2nd row: *5ch, 1sc into next 5ch arch; rep from * ending 2ch, 1dc into last sc, skip tch, turn.

3rd row: 3ch (count as 1dc), 1dc into first st, 2ch, 1dc into next 5ch arch, *2ch, 4dc into next arch, 2ch, 1dc into next arch; rep from * to end, turn.

4th row: *5ch, 1sc into next 2ch sp; rep from * ending 2ch, 1dc into top of tch, turn.

5th row: 1ch, 1sc into first st, *5ch, 1sc into next 5ch arch; rep from * to end, turn.

Rep 2nd, 3rd, 4th and 5th rows.

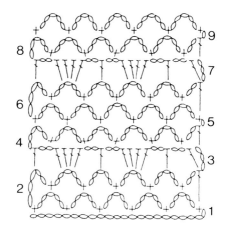

Bullion Trellis Stitch

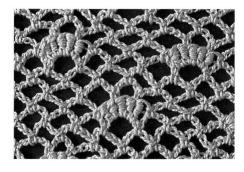

Multiple of 16 sts + 5.
(add 1 for base chain)

Note: For description of Bullion st see page 14. Make Bullion sts with [yo] 7 times.

Base row (right side): 1sc into 2nd ch from hook, *[5ch, skip 3ch, 1sc into next ch] twice, skip 3ch, work 5 Bullion sts into next ch, skip 3ch, 1sc into next ch; rep from * to last 4ch, 5ch, skip 3ch, 1sc into last ch, turn.

Commence Pattern

1st row: 5ch, 1sc into next 5ch arch, *5ch, 1sc into 2nd of next 5 Bullion sts, 5ch, 1sc into 4th Bullion st of same group, [5ch, 1sc into next arch] twice; rep from * ending 2ch, 1dc into last sc, skip tch, turn.

2nd row: 1ch, 1sc into first st, *5ch, 1sc into next arch; rep from * to end, turn.

3rd row: *5ch, 1sc into next arch; rep from * ending 2ch, 1dc into last sc, skip tch, turn.

4th row: 1ch, 1sc into first st, skip 2ch sp, *5 Bullion sts into next 5ch arch, 1sc into next arch, [5ch, 1sc into next arch] twice; rep from * ending 5ch, 1sc into tch arch, turn.

5th row: 5ch, 1sc into next 5ch arch, *[5ch, 1sc into next arch] twice, 5ch, 1sc into 2nd of next 5 Bullion sts, 5ch, 1sc into 4th Bullion st of same group; rep from * ending 2ch, 1dc into last sc, skip tch, turn.

6th row: As 2nd row.

7th row: As 3rd row.

8th row: 1ch, 1sc into first st, *[5ch, 1sc into next 5ch arch] twice, 5 Bullion sts into next arch, 1sc into next arch; rep from * ending 5ch, 1sc into tch arch, turn.

Rep these 8 rows.

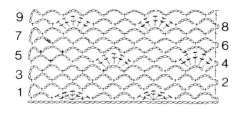

$\maltese$ = Bullion st with [yo] 7 times.

Shell Trellis Stitch

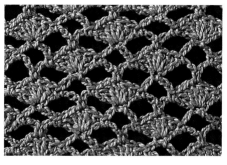

Multiple of 12 sts + 1.
(add 2 for base chain)

1st row (right side): 2dc into 3rd ch from hook, *skip 2ch, 1sc into next ch, 5ch, skip 5ch, 1sc into next ch, skip 2ch, 5dc into next ch; rep from * ending last rep with only 3dc into last ch, turn.

2nd row: 1ch, 1sc into first st, *5ch, 1sc into next 5ch arch, 5ch, 1sc into 3rd dc of next 5dc; rep from * ending last rep with 1sc into top of tch, turn.

3rd row: *5ch, 1sc into next 5ch arch, 5dc into next sc, 1sc into next arch; rep from * ending 2ch, 1dc into last sc, skip tch, turn.

4th row: 1ch, 1sc into first st, *5ch, 1sc into 3rd dc of next 5dc, 5ch, 1sc into next 5ch arch; rep from * to end, turn.

5th row: 3ch (count as 1dc), 2dc into first st, *1sc into next arch, 5ch, 1sc into next arch, 5dc into next sc; rep from * ending last rep with only 3dc into last sc, skip tch, turn.

Rep 2nd, 3rd, 4th and 5th rows.

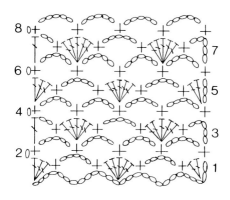

Puff Cluster Trellis Stitch

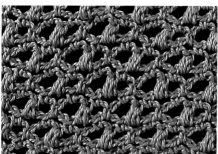

Multiple of 6 sts + 2.
(add 3 for base chain)

Note: For description of hdc3tog see page 10.

1st row (right side): 1sc into 5th ch from hook, *3ch, skip 2ch, 1sc into next ch; rep from * to end, turn.

2nd row: 3ch, 1sc into next 3ch arch, *3ch, hdc3tog into next arch, 3ch, 1sc into next arch; rep from * to end, turn.

3rd row: *3ch, 1sc into next 3ch arch; rep from * to end, turn.

4th row: *3ch, hdc3tog into next 3ch arch, 3ch, 1sc into next arch; rep from * ending 3ch, hdc3tog into tch arch, turn.

5th row: As 3rd row.

Rep 2nd, 3rd, 4th and 5th rows.

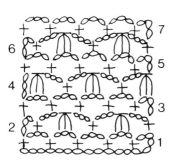

Openwork and Lace Patterns

Fan Trellis Stitch

Multiple of 12 sts + 11.
(add 1 for base chain)

1st row (wrong side): 1sc into 2nd ch from hook, *5ch, skip 3ch, 1sc into next ch; rep from * to last 2ch, 2ch, skip 1ch, 1dc into last ch, turn.

2nd row: 1ch, 1sc into first st, skip 2ch sp, *7dc into next 5ch arch, 1sc into next arch**, 5ch, 1sc into next arch; rep from * ending last rep at **, 2ch, 1tr into last sc, skip tch, turn.

3rd row: 1ch, 1sc into first st, *5ch, 1sc into 2nd of next 7dc, 5ch, 1sc into 6th dc of same group**, 5ch, 1sc into next 5ch arch; rep from * ending last rep at **, 2ch, 1tr into last sc, skip tch, turn.

Rep 2nd and 3rd rows.

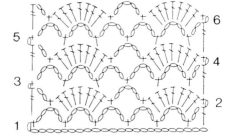

Floral Trellis Stitch

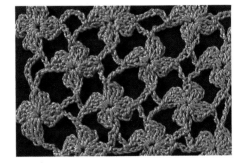

Any number of Flower Units.

1st row (right side): 7ch, *sl st into 4th ch from hook, 3ch, into ring just formed work a Base Flower Unit of [2dc, 3ch, sl st, 3ch, 2dc]**, 10ch; rep from * ending last rep at ** when fabric is required width, then keep same side facing and turn so as to be able to work along underside of Base Flower Units.

2nd row (right side): *3ch, sl st into ch ring at center of Flower, 3ch, [2dc, 3ch, sl st — center Petal completed, 3ch, 2dc] all into same ring, skip 2ch of base chain which connects Units, sl st into next 7ch, skip 2ch,

sl st into next ch; rep from * into next and each Base Flower Unit to end, turn. **Note:** Check that each Base Flower Unit is not twisted before you work into it.

3rd row: 11ch, sl st into 4th ch from hook, 3ch, 2dc into ring just formed, 3ch, sl st into top of 3ch of center Petal of last Flower made in previous row (see diagram), *10ch, sl st into 4th ch from hook, 3ch, 2dc into ring just formed, sl st into 4th of next 7ch arch of previous row, 3ch, [sl st, 3ch, 2dc] into same ch ring as last 2dc, 3ch, sl st into top of 3ch of center Petal of next Flower in previous row; rep from * to end, turn.

4th row: 9ch, skip 2ch, sl st into next ch, *3ch, sl st into ch ring at center of Flower, 3ch, work [2dc, 3ch, sl st, 3ch, 2dc] into same ring, skip 2ch, sl st into next ch, 7ch, skip [3ch, sl st and next 2ch], sl st into next ch; rep from * ending 3ch, sl st into ch ring at center of last Flower, 3ch, 2dc into same ring, turn.

5th row: *10ch, sl st into 4th ch from hook, 3ch, 2dc into ring just formed, sl st into 4th ch of next arch of previous row, 3ch, [sl st, 3ch, 2dc] into same ch ring as last 2dc**, 3ch, sl st into top of 3ch of center Petal of next Flower in previous row; rep from * ending last rep at **, turn.

Rep 2nd, 3rd, 4th and 5th rows.

When fabric is required length, finishing after a 4th (right side) row (see asterisk on diagram), continue down left side to complete edge Flowers as follows: *3ch, [sl st, 3ch, 2dc, 3ch, sl st, 3ch, 2dc] all into ch ring at center of edge Flower, skip 3ch, sl st into next ch**, 6ch, sl st into last ch before center Petal of next edge Flower (see diagram); rep from * ending last rep at ** after last edge Flower.

Fasten off.

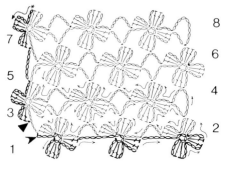

Double Trellis Stitch

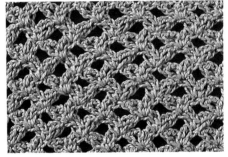

Multiple of 4 sts + 1.
(add 1 for base chain)

Note: For description of dc2tog see page 10.

1st row (right side): 1sc into 2nd ch from hook, *3ch, dc2tog inserting hook into same place as sc just made for first leg and then into following 4th ch for 2nd leg, (skipping 3ch between), 3ch, 1sc into same place as 2nd leg of cluster just made; rep from * to end, turn.

2nd row: 4ch, 1dc into top of next cluster (counts as edge cluster), 3ch, 1sc into same place as dc just made, *3ch, dc2tog inserting hook into same place as sc just made for first leg and then into next cluster for 2nd leg, 3ch, 1sc into same place as 2nd leg of cluster just made; rep from * ending 3ch, yo, insert hook into same place as sc just made, yo, draw loop through, yo, draw through 2 loops, [yo] twice, insert hook into last sc, yo, draw loop through, [yo, draw through 2 loops] twice, yo, draw through all 3 loops on hook, skip tch, turn.

3rd row: 1ch, 1sc into first st, *3ch, dc2tog inserting hook into same place as sc just made for first leg and then into next cluster for 2nd leg, 3ch, 1sc into same place as 2nd leg of cluster just made; rep from * to end, turn.

Rep 2nd and 3rd rows.

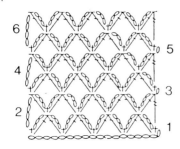

Diamond Shell Trellis Stitch

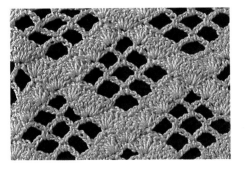

Multiple of 16 sts + 5.
(add 1 for base chain)

Base row (right side): 1sc into 2nd ch from hook, [5ch, skip 3ch, 1sc into next ch] twice, *skip 1ch, 5dc into next ch, skip 1ch, 1sc into next ch**, [5ch, skip 3ch, 1sc into next ch] 3 times; rep from * ending last rep at ** when 8ch remain, [5ch, skip 3ch, 1sc into next ch] twice, turn.

Commence Pattern

1st row: *[5ch, 1sc into next 5ch arch] twice, 5dc into next sc, 1sc into 3rd of next 5dc, 5dc into next sc, 1sc into next arch; rep from * ending 5ch, 1sc into next arch, 2ch, 1dc into last sc, skip tch, turn.

○ Chain ● Slip stitch + Single crochet T Half double crochet ⊺ Double crochet ⊧ Treble ⊧ Double treble

2nd row: 1ch, 1sc into first st, skip 2ch, *5ch, 1sc into next 5ch arch, 5dc into next sc, 1sc into 3rd of next 5dc, 5ch, 1sc into 3rd of next 5dc, 5dc into next sc, 1sc into next arch; rep from * ending 5ch, 1sc into tch arch, turn.

3rd row: 3ch (count as 1dc), 2dc into first st, *1sc into next 5ch arch, 5dc into next sc, 1sc into 3rd of next 5dc, 5ch, 1sc into next arch, 1sc into 3rd of next 5dc, 5dc into next sc; rep from * ending 1sc into next arch, 3dc into last sc, skip tch, turn.

4th row: 1ch, 1sc into first st, *5dc into next sc, 1sc into 3rd of next 5dc, [5ch, 1sc into next arch] twice, 5ch, 1sc into 3rd of next 5dc; rep from * ending 5dc into next sc, 1sc into top of tch, turn.

5th row: 3ch (count as 1dc), 2dc into first st, *1sc into 3rd of next 5dc, 5dc into next sc, 1sc into next arch, [5ch, 1sc into next arch] twice, 5dc into next sc; rep from * ending 1sc into 3rd of next 5dc, 3dc into last sc, skip tch, turn.

6th row: 1ch, 1sc into first st, *5ch, 1sc into 3rd of next 5dc, 5dc into next sc, 1sc into next arch, 5ch, 1sc into next arch, 5dc into next sc, 1sc into 3rd of next 5dc; rep from * ending 5ch, 1sc into top of tch, turn.

7th row: *5ch, 1sc into next 5ch arch, 5ch, 1sc into 3rd of next 5dc, 5dc into next sc, 1sc into next arch, 5dc into next sc, 1sc into 3rd of next 5dc; rep from * ending 5ch, 1sc into next arch, 2ch, 1dc into last sc, skip tch, turn.

8th row: 1ch, 1sc into first st, skip 2ch, 5ch, 1sc into next 5ch arch, 5ch, 1sc into 3rd of next 5dc, *5dc into next sc, 1sc into 3rd of next 5dc, [5ch, 1sc into next arch] twice**, 5ch, 1sc into 3rd of next 5dc; rep from * ending last rep at ** in tch arch, turn.

Rep these 8 rows.

Ruled Lattice

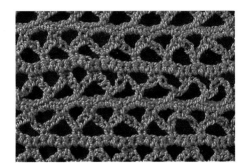

Multiple of 4 sts + 1.
(add 1 for base chain)

1st row (right side): 1sc into 2nd ch from hook, 1sc into each ch to end, turn.

2nd row: 7ch, skip first 2 sts, 1sc into next st, *7ch, skip 3 sts, 1sc into next st; rep from * to last 2 sts, 3ch, skip 1 st, 1dc into last st, skip tch, turn.

3rd row: 1ch, 1sc into first st, *3ch, 1sc into next 7ch arch; rep from * to end, turn.

4th row: 1ch, 1sc into first st, *3sc into next 3ch arch, 1sc into next sc; rep from * to end, skip tch, turn.

Rep 2nd, 3rd and 4th rows.

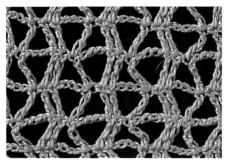

Doubled Lattice Stitch

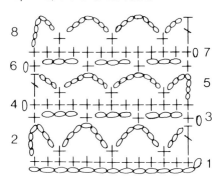

Multiple of 6 sts + 2.
(add 3 for base chain)

Note: For description of tr2tog see page 10.
1st row (right side): Skip 6ch, 1tr into next ch (counts as edge cluster), 4ch, 1tr into same ch as tr just made, *tr2tog inserting hook into next ch for first leg and then into following 5th ch for 2nd leg (skipping 4ch between), 4ch, 1tr into same ch as 2nd leg of cluster just made; rep from * to last 4ch, tr2tog inserting hook into next ch for first leg and into last ch for 2nd leg, (skipping 2ch between), turn.

2nd row: 6ch (count as 1tr and 2ch), 1tr into first st, *tr2tog inserting hook into next tr for first leg and then into next cluster for 2nd leg**, 4ch, 1tr into same place as 2nd leg of cluster just made; rep from * ending last rep at ** when 2nd leg is in edge cluster, 2ch, 1tr into same place, turn.

3rd row: 4ch, skip 2ch, 1tr into next cluster (counts as edge cluster), *4ch, 1tr into same place as tr just made**, tr2tog inserting hook into next tr for first leg and then into next cluster for 2nd leg; rep from * ending last rep at **, tr2tog inserting hook into next tr for first leg and then into following 3rd ch for 2nd leg, turn.

Rep 2nd and 3rd rows.

Crown Puff Lattice

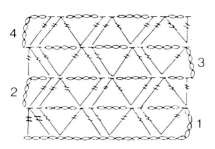

Multiple of 6 sts + 1.
(add 2 for base chain)

Note: For description of sc2tog and sc3tog (see page 10) and for hdc5tog see page 14.
1st row (right side): 1hdc into 3rd ch from hook, *1sc into next ch, sc3tog over next 3ch, 1sc into next ch, [1hdc, 1dc, 1hdc] into next ch; rep from * omitting 1hdc at end of last rep, turn.

2nd row: 3ch (count as 1dc), skip first 3 sts, *[1tr, 3ch, 1tr] into next sc cluster, skip 2 sts**, work hdc5tog into next dc; rep from * ending last rep at **, 1dc into top of tch, turn.

3rd row: 1ch, skip 1 st, 1sc into next tr (all counts as sc cluster), *[1sc, 1hdc, 1dc, 1hdc, 1sc] into next 3ch arch**, sc3tog over next 3 sts; rep from * ending last rep at **, sc2tog over last st and top of tch, turn.

4th row: 5ch (count as 1tr and 1ch), 1tr into first st, *skip 2 sts, hdc5tog into next dc, skip 2 sts**, [1tr, 3ch, 1tr] into next sc cluster; rep from * ending last rep at **, [1tr, 1ch, 1tr] into top of tch, turn.

5th row: 3ch (count as 1dc), 1hdc into first st, 1sc into next ch sp, *sc3tog over next 3 sts**, [1sc, 1hdc, 1dc, 1hdc, 1sc] into next 3ch arch; rep from * ending last rep at **, 1sc into next ch of tch, [1hdc, 1dc] into next ch, turn.

Rep 2nd, 3rd, 4th and 5th rows.

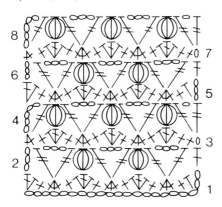

Openwork and Lace Patterns

Crow's Foot Lattice

Multiple of 6 sts + 1.
(add 4 for base chain)

1st row (wrong side): Skip 4ch (count as 1tr and 1ch), 1dc into next ch, 1ch, skip 2ch, 1sc into next ch, *1ch, skip 2ch, work [1dc, 1ch, 1tr, 1ch, 1dc] into next ch, 1ch, skip 2ch, 1sc into next ch; rep from * to last 3ch, 1ch, skip 2ch, [1dc, 1ch, 1tr] into last ch, turn.

2nd row: 1ch, 1sc into first st, *1ch, skip 2 sps, 1tr into next sc, 1ch, 1dc into base of tr just made, 1ch, skip 2 sps, 1sc into next tr; rep from * ending last rep in tch, turn.

3rd row: 1ch, 1sc into first st, *1ch, skip sp, work [1dc, 1ch, 1tr, 1ch, 1dc] into next sp, 1ch, skip sp, 1sc into next sc; rep from * to end, turn.

4th row: 4ch (count as 1tr), 1dc into 4th ch from hook, *1ch, skip 2 sps, 1sc into next tr, 1ch, 1tr into next sc**, 1ch, 1dc into base of tr just made; rep from * ending last rep at **, 1dc into base of tr just made, turn.

5th row: 5ch (count as 1tr and 1ch), 1dc into first st, 1ch, skip sp, 1dc into next sc, *1ch, skip sp, work [1dc, 1ch, 1tr, 1ch, 1dc] into next sp, 1ch, skip sp, 1sc into next sc; rep from * ending 1ch, skip sp, [1dc, 1ch, 1tr] into top of tch, turn.

Rep 2nd, 3rd, 4th and 5th rows.

Open Fan Stitch

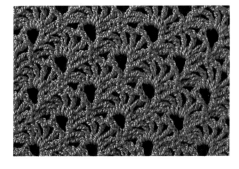

Multiple of 10 sts + 6.
(add 1 for base chain)

1st row (right side): 1sc into 2nd ch from hook, *1ch, skip 4ch, into next ch work a Fan of 1tr, [2ch, 1tr] 4 times, then 1ch, skip 4ch, 1sc into next ch; rep from * to last 5ch, 1ch, skip 4ch, into last ch work [1tr, 2ch] twice and 1tr, turn.

2nd row: 1ch, 1sc into first st, *3ch, skip next 2ch sp, 1dc into next sp**, 2ch, skip next tr, sc and tr and work 1dc into first 2ch sp of next Fan, 3ch, work 1sc into center tr of Fan; rep from * ending last rep at **, 1ch, 1tr into last sc, skip tch, turn.

3rd row: 7ch (count as 1tr and 2ch), skip first tr, work [1tr, 2ch, 1tr] into next 1ch sp, 1ch, skip 3ch sp, 1sc into next sc, *1ch, skip next 3ch sp, work a Fan into next 2ch sp, 1ch, skip next 3ch sp, 1sc into next sc; rep from * to end, skip tch, turn.

4th row: 6ch (count as 1tr and 1ch), skip first tr, work 1dc into next 2ch sp, 3ch, 1sc into center tr of Fan, *3ch, skip next 2ch sp, 1dc into next 2ch sp, 2ch, skip next tr, sc and tr, work 1dc into next 2ch sp, 3ch, 1sc into center tr of Fan; rep from * ending last rep in 3rd ch of tch, turn.

5th row: 1ch, *1sc into sc, 1ch, skip next 3ch sp, Fan into next 2ch sp, 1ch, skip next 3ch sp; rep from * to last sc, 1sc into sc, 1ch, skip next 3ch sp, work [1tr, 2ch] twice and 1tr all into top of tch, turn.

Rep 2nd, 3rd, 4th and 5th rows.

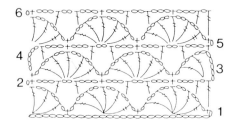

Open Shell and Picot Stitch

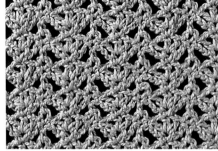

Multiple of 7 sts.
(add 1 for base chain)

1st row (right side): 1sc into 2nd ch from hook, *skip 2ch, work a Shell of [1dc, 1ch, 1dc, 1ch, 1dc] into next ch, skip 2ch, 1sc into next ch**, 3ch, 1sc into next ch; rep from * ending last rep at ** in last ch, turn.

2nd row: 7ch (count as 1tr and 3ch), *work a Picot of [1sc, 3ch, 1sc] into center dc of next Shell, 3ch**, 1dc into next 3ch arch; rep from * ending last rep at **, 1tr into last

sc, skip tch, turn.

3rd row: 1ch, 1sc into first st, *skip next 3ch sp, Shell into center of next Picot, skip next 3ch sp**, Picot into next dc; rep from * ending last rep at **, 1sc into next ch of tch, turn.

Rep 2nd and 3rd rows.

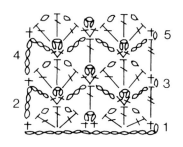

Ridged String Network

Multiple of 4 sts + 1.
(add 1 for base chain)

1st row (right side): 1sc into 2nd ch from hook, *3ch, skip 3ch, 1sc into next ch; rep from * to end, turn.

2nd row: 1ch, working into back loop only of each st work 1sc into first st, *3ch, skip 3ch, 1sc into next sc; rep from * to end, skip tch, turn.

Rep 2nd row.

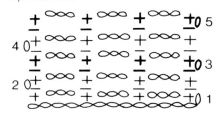

Double Picot String Network

◦ Chain ● Slip stitch + Single crochet T Half double crochet ⊤ Double crochet ‡ Treble ‡ Double treble

Multiple of 6 sts + 5.
(add 1 for base chain)

1st row (wrong side): 1sc into 2nd ch from hook, *3ch, skip 4ch, work a picot of [1sc, 3ch, 1sc] into next ch; rep from * to last 5ch, 3ch, skip 4ch, 1sc into last ch, turn.

2nd row: 1ch, 1sc into first st, *3ch, skip 3ch, 2 picots into next 3ch arch; rep from * ending 3ch, skip 3ch, 1sc into last sc, turn.

3rd row: 6ch (count as 1dc and 3ch), skip 3ch, *1sc into next picot arch, 3ch, 1sc into next picot arch, 3ch, skip 3ch; rep from * ending 1dc into last sc, skip tch, turn.

Rep 2nd and 3rd rows.

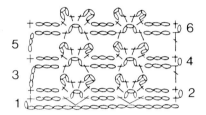

Zigzag Double String Network

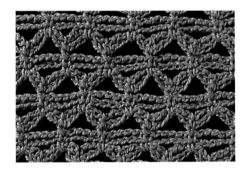

Multiple of 6 sts + 1.
(add 1 for base chain)

Base row (right side): 1sc into 2nd ch from hook, *5ch, skip 5ch, 1sc into next ch; rep from * to end, turn.

Commence Pattern

1st row: 1ch, 1sc into first st, *5ch, skip 5ch, 1sc into next sc; rep from * to end, skip tch, turn.

2nd row: 1ch, 1sc into first st, *7ch, skip 5ch, 1sc into next sc; rep from * to end, skip tch, turn.

3rd row: 1ch, 1sc into first st, *7ch, skip 7ch, 1sc into next sc; rep from * to end, skip tch, turn.

4th row: 5ch (count as 1dc and 2ch), inserting hook under the 7ch arch made in the 2nd row, work 1sc thus binding the arches of the 2nd and 3rd rows together, *5ch, 1sc under next pair of arches as before; rep from * ending 2ch, 1dc into last sc, skip tch, turn.

5th row: 1ch, 1sc into first st, 2ch, skip 2ch, 1sc into next sc, *5ch, skip 5ch, 1sc into next sc; rep from * ending 2ch, skip next 2ch of tch, 1sc into next ch, turn.

6th row: 6ch (count as 1dc and 3ch), skip 2ch, 1sc into next sc, *7ch, skip 5ch, 1sc into next sc; rep from * ending 3ch, skip 2ch, 1dc into last sc, skip tch, turn.

7th row: 1ch, 1sc into first st, 3ch, skip 3ch,

1sc into next sc, *7ch, skip 7ch, 1sc into next sc; rep from * ending 3ch, skip next 3ch of tch, 1sc into next ch, turn.

8th row: 1ch, 1sc into first st, *5ch, 1sc under next pair of arches together; rep from * ending last rep with 1sc into last sc, skip tch, turn.

Rep these 8 rows.

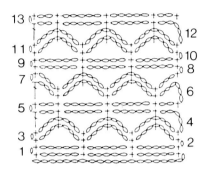

Zigzag Popcorn Network

Multiple of 10 sts + 1.
(add 5 for base chain)

Note: For description of 5dc popcorn see page 14. Popcorns occur on both right and wrong side rows. Be sure to push them all out on the right side of the fabric as you complete them.

1st row (right side): 1sc into 9th ch from hook, 1sc into each of next 2ch, *3ch, skip 3ch, 5dc popcorn into next ch, 3ch, skip 3ch, 1sc into each of next 3ch; rep from * to last 4ch, 3ch, skip 3ch, 1dc into last ch, turn.

2nd row: 1ch, 1sc into first st, *1sc into next arch, 3ch, 5dc popcorn into 2nd of next 3sc, 3ch**, 1sc into next arch, 1sc into next popcorn; rep from * ending last rep at **, skip 2ch of tch arch, 1sc into each of next 2ch, turn.

3rd row: 6ch (count as 1dc and 3ch), *1sc into next arch, 1sc into next popcorn, 1sc into next arch, 3ch**, 5dc popcorn into 2nd of next 3sc, 3ch; rep from * ending last rep at **, 1dc into last sc, skip tch, turn.

Rep 2nd and 3rd rows.

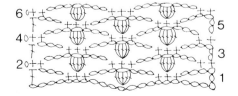

Boxed Shell Stitch

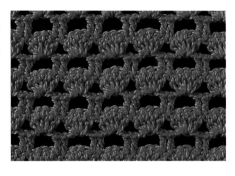

Multiple of 5 sts + 2.
(add 2 for base chain)

1st row (right side): Skip 3ch (count as 1dc), 1dc into next ch, *3ch, skip 3ch, 1dc into each of next 2ch; rep from * to end, turn.

2nd row: 3ch (count as 1dc), skip first st, *5dc into 2nd ch of next 3ch arch; rep from * ending 1dc into top of tch, turn.

3rd row: 3ch (count as 1dc), skip first st, 1dc into next dc, *3ch, skip 3dc, 1dc into each of next 2dc; rep from * to end, turn.

Rep 2nd and 3rd rows.

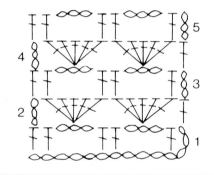

Boxed Block Stitch

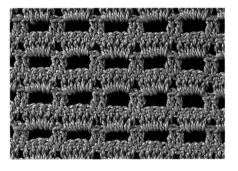

Worked as Boxed Shell Stitch, except that on 2nd and every alternate row 5dc are worked under 3ch arch instead of into actual st, thus making a block rather than a shell.

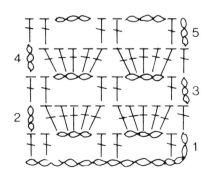

Openwork and Lace Patterns

Norman Arch Stitch

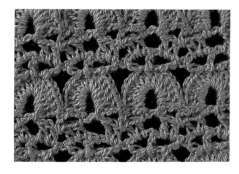

Multiple of 9 sts + 1.
(add 1 for base chain)

1st row (wrong side): 1sc into 2nd ch from hook, *3ch, skip 3ch, 1sc into next ch, 7ch, 1sc into next ch, 3ch, skip 3ch, 1sc into next ch; rep from * to end, turn.

2nd row: 1ch, 1sc into first sc, *skip 3ch, work 13dc into next 7ch arch, skip 3ch, 1sc into next sc; rep from * to end, skip tch, turn.

3rd row: 5ch (count as 1dtr), skip first sc and next 5dc, *[1dc into next dc, 3ch] twice, 1dc into next dc**, skip [next 5dc, 1sc and 5dc]; rep from * ending last rep at **, skip next 5dc, 1dtr into last sc, skip tch, turn.

4th row: 3ch (count as 1dc), skip first st and next dc, *1dc into next ch, 1ch, skip 1ch, 1dc into next ch, 3ch, skip 1dc, 1dc into next ch, 1ch, skip 1ch, 1dc into next ch**, skip next 2dc; rep from * ending last rep at **, skip next dc, 1dc into top of tch, turn.

5th row: 6ch (count as 1dc and 3ch), *skip next 1ch sp, work [1sc, 7ch, 1sc] into next 3ch sp, 3ch, skip next 1ch sp**, 1dc between next 2dc; rep from * ending last rep at **, 1dc into top of tch, turn.

Rep 2nd, 3rd, 4th and 5th rows.

Double Arch Ground

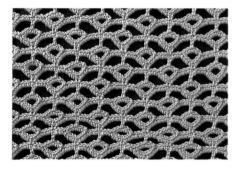

Multiple of 10 sts + 1.
(add 8 for base chain)

1st row (wrong side): 1sc into 14th ch from hook, *5ch, skip 4ch, 1dc into next ch**, 5ch, skip 4ch, 1sc into next ch; rep from * ending last rep at **, turn.

2nd row: 1ch, 1sc into first dc, *6sc into next 5ch arch, 1sc into next sc, 3sc into beginning of next 5ch arch, work a 'back double' of [4ch, then without turning work, skip 6 previous sc and work a sl st back into previous sc, now work 5sc in the normal direction into 4ch arch just worked], 3sc into remaining part of 5ch arch**, 1sc into next dc; rep from * ending last rep at **, 1sc into next ch, turn.

3rd row: 1ch, 1sc into first st, *5ch, 1dc into 3rd of 5sc of next 'back double', 5ch, 1sc into sc over dc of previous row; rep from * ending last rep in last sc, turn.

4th row: 1ch, 1sc into first st, 3sc into beginning of next 5ch arch, turn, 2ch, skip 3 previous sc, work 1dc into first sc, 1ch, turn, 1sc into dc, 2sc into 2ch arch, 3sc into remaining part of 5ch arch, *1sc into next dc, 6sc into next 5ch arch, 1sc into next sc**, 3sc into beginning of 5ch arch, 1 'back double' as before, 3sc into remaining part of 5ch arch; rep from * ending last rep at ** in last sc, 5ch, skip 3 previous sc, sl st back into next sc, 3sc in normal direction into beginning of 5ch arch, turn.

5th row: 8ch, *1sc into sc over dc of previous row, 5ch**, 1dc into 3rd of 5sc of next 'back double', 5ch; rep from * ending last rep at ** 1dc into last sc, skip tch, turn.

Rep 2nd, 3rd, 4th and 5th rows.

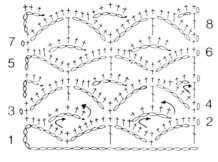

Coronet Ground

Multiple of 8 sts.
(add 1 for base chain)

1st row (right side): Skip 1ch, *1sc into each of next 4ch, work a picot of [3ch, insert hook down through top of last sc made and work sl st to close], 1sc into each of next 4ch, work 9ch then without turning skip 7 previous sc, work a sl st back into previous sc, then working in the normal direction work 7sc into 9ch arch, work a Coronet of [5ch, sl st into 5th ch from hook, 7ch, sl st into 7th ch from hook, 5ch, sl st into 5th ch from hook], work 7sc into arch; rep from * ending sl st into last sc, turn.

2nd row: 11ch (count as 1ttr and 4ch), *1sc into 7ch arch at center of next Coronet, 7ch; rep from * ending 1sc into 7ch arch at center of last Coronet, 2ch, 1ttr into last sc, skip tch, turn.

3rd row: 1ch, 1sc into first st, 1sc into each of next 2ch and next sc, turn, 4ch, skip 3sc, 1tr into last sc, turn, 8ch, sl st into 7th ch from hook, 5ch, sl st into 5th ch from hook (½ Coronet worked), 7sc into next 4ch arch, *1sc into each of next 4ch, 3ch Picot, 1sc into each of next 3ch, 1sc into next sc, work 9ch, skip 7 previous sc, sl st back into previous sc, work 7sc into 9ch arch, work a Coronet as before, then 7sc into 9ch loop; rep from * ending 1sc into each of next 4ch of tch arch, 9ch, skip previous 3sc, sl st into previous sc, work 7sc into 9ch arch, work a ½ Coronet of 5ch, sl st into 5th ch from hook, 1sc into 9ch arch, 3ch, 1tr into last sc, turn.

4th row: 1 ch, 1sc into top of 3ch, *7ch, 1sc into 7ch arch at center of next Coronet; rep from * ending last rep in 8ch arch of ½ Coronet, turn.

5th row: 1ch, 1sc into first st, 1sc into each of next 3ch, *3ch Picot, 1sc into each of next 3ch, 1sc into next sc, 9ch, skip 7 previous sc, sl st back into previous sc, work 7sc, Coronet and 7sc into arch**, 1sc into each of next 4ch; rep from * ending last rep at **, sl st into last sc, turn.

Rep 2nd, 3rd, 4th and 5th rows.

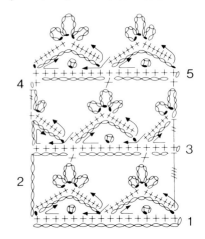

Shell and V Stitch

Multiple of 8 sts + 1.
(add 2 for base chain)

1st row (right side): Skip 2ch (count as 1dc), 2dc into next ch, *skip 3ch, work a V st of

◦ Chain ● Slip stitch + Single crochet T Half double crochet ┬ Double crochet ╪ Treble ╪ Double treble

[1dc, 1ch, 1dc] into next ch, skip 3ch**, 5dc into next ch; rep from * ending last rep at **, 3dc into last ch, turn.

2nd row: 3ch (count as 1dc), 1dc into first st, *5dc into sp at center of next V st**, V st into 3rd of next 5dc; rep from * ending last rep at **, 2dc into top of tch, turn.

Rep 2nd row.

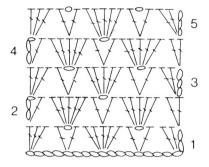

Fan and V Stitch

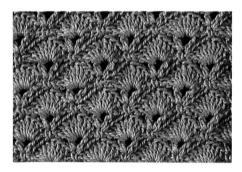

Multiple of 8 sts + 1.
(add 1 for base chain)

1st row (right side): 1sc into 2nd ch from hook, *skip 3ch, 9dc into next ch, skip 3ch, 1sc into next ch; rep from * to end, turn.

2nd row: 3ch (count as 1dc), 1dc into first st, *5ch, skip 9dc group, work a V st of [1dc, 1ch, 1dc] into next sc; rep from * ending 5ch, skip last 9dc group, 2dc into last sc, skip tch, turn.

3rd row: 3ch (count as 1dc), 4dc into first st, *working over next 5ch so as to enclose it, work 1sc into 5th dc of group in row below**, 9dc into sp at center of next V st; rep from * ending last rep at **, 5dc into top of tch, turn.

4th row: 3ch, skip 5dc, V st into next sc, *5ch, skip 9dc group, V st into next sc; rep from * ending 2ch, sl st to top of tch, turn.

5th row: 1ch, 1sc over sl st into first st of row below, *9dc into sp at center of next V st, working over next 5ch so as to enclose it work 1sc into 5th dc of group in row below; rep from * to end, turn.

Rep 2nd, 3rd, 4th and 5th rows.
End with a wrong side row working [2ch, sl st to 5th dc of group, 2ch] in place of 5ch between the V sts.

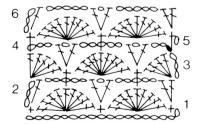

Peacock Fan Stitch

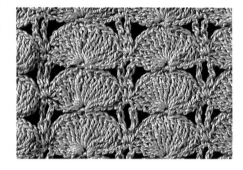

Multiple of 12 sts + 1.
(add 1 for base chain)

1st row (right side): 1sc into 2nd ch from hook, *skip 5ch, 13dtr into next ch, skip 5ch, 1sc into next ch; rep from * to end, turn.

2nd row: 5ch (count as 1dtr), 1dtr into first st, *4ch, skip 6dtr, 1sc into next dtr, 4ch, skip 6dtr**, work [1dtr, 1ch, 1dtr] into next sc; rep from * ending last rep at **, 2dtr into last sc, skip tch, turn.

3rd row: 1ch, 1sc into first st, *skip [1dtr and 4ch], 13dtr into next sc, skip [4ch and 1dtr], 1sc into next ch; rep from * to end, turn.

Rep 2nd and 3rd rows.

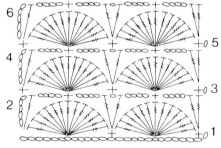

Block and Offset Shell Stitch

Multiple of 11 sts + 4.
(add 2 for base chain)

1st row (right side): Skip 3ch (count as 1dc), 1dc into each of next 4ch, *skip 2ch, 5dc into next ch, 2ch, skip 3ch, 1dc into each of next 5ch; rep from * to end, turn.

2nd row: 3ch (count as 1dc), skip first st, 1dc into each of next 4 sts, *skip 2ch, 5dc into next dc, 2ch, skip 4dc, 1dc into each of next 5 sts; rep from * to end, turn.

Rep 2nd row.

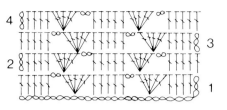

Soft Fan Stitch

Multiple of 10 sts + 1.
(add 1 for base chain)

Note: For description of Crossed Stitches see page 12 (Cross Stitch II); for hdc3tog see page 14 (Puff Stitch).

1st row (wrong side): 1sc into 2nd ch from hook, *3ch, work 2 crossed dcs as follows: skip 5ch, 1dc into next ch, 5ch, inserting hook behind dc just made work 1dc into 4th of 5ch just skipped, then 3ch, skip 3ch, 1sc into next ch; rep from * to end, turn.

2nd row: 3ch (count as 1dc), skip first st, *skip next 3ch sp, work a group of 11dc into next 5ch arch, skip next 3ch sp, work hdc3tog into next sc, 1ch; rep from * omitting hdc3tog and 1ch at end of last rep and working 1dc into last sc, skip tch, turn.

3rd row: 2ch, skip first 2 dc, 1hdc into next dc, 4ch, 1hdc into top of hdc just made, *3ch, skip 3dc, 1sc into next dc, 3ch**, work 2 crossed dcs as follows: 1dc into 2nd dc of next 11dc group, 5ch, going behind dc just made work 1dc into 10th dc of previous 11dc group; rep from * ending last rep at **, 1dc into top of tch, 2ch, going behind dc just made work 1dc into 10th dc of previous 11dc group, turn.

4th row: 3ch (count as 1dc), skip first st, 5dc into next 2ch sp, *skip next 3ch sp, work hdc3tog into next sc, 1ch, skip next 3ch sp**, 11dc into next 5ch arch; rep from * ending last rep at **, 6dc into top of tch, turn.

5th row: 1ch, 1sc into first st, 3ch, 1dc into 2nd dc of next 11dc group, 5ch, going behind dc just made work 1dc into 5th dc of previous 6dc group, *3ch, skip 3dc, 1sc into next dc**, 3ch, 1dc into 2nd dc of next dc group, 5ch, going behind dc just made work 1dc into 10th dc of previous dc group; rep from * ending last rep at ** in top of tch, turn.

Rep 2nd, 3rd, 4th and 5th rows.

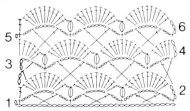

Openwork and Lace Patterns

Hotcross Bun Stitch

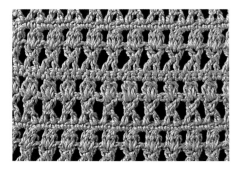

Multiple of 3 sts + 2.
(add 1 for base chain)

Special Abbreviation

TrX (treble 'X' shape — worked over 3 sts) = [yo] twice, insert hook into next st, yo, draw loop through, yo, draw through 2 loops, skip next st, insert hook into next st, yo, draw loop through, [yo, draw through 2 loops] 4 times, 1ch, yo, insert hook half way down st just made where lower 'legs' join, yo, draw loop through, [yo, draw through 2 loops] twice (see also page 12 'X' Shapes).

Note: For description of dc3tog see page 14.

1st row (wrong side): 1sc into 2nd ch from hook, 1sc into next and each ch to end, turn.

2nd row: 4ch (count as 1tr), skip first st, *TrX over next 3 sts; rep from * ending 1tr into last st, skip tch, turn.

3rd row: 4ch (count as 1dc and 1ch), *work dc3tog into next 1ch sp**, 2ch; rep from * ending last rep at **, 1ch, 1dc into top of tch, turn.

4th row: 1ch, 1sc into first st, 1sc into next ch, *1sc into next cluster, 1sc into each of next 2ch; rep from * to end, turn.

Rep 2nd, 3rd and 4th rows.

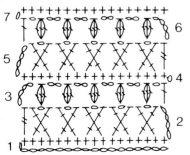

Hearts and Diamonds Stitch

Multiple of 10 sts + 7.
(add 5 for base chain)

Special Abbreviation

Diamond = 4 rows inside a main row worked as follows: Turn, **1st row:** 1ch, 1sc into first sc, 1sc into each of next 3ch, turn. **Next row:** 1ch, 1sc into each of next 4sc, skip tch, turn. Rep the last row twice more.

1st row (wrong side): 1sc into 9th ch from hook, *2ch, skip 4ch, work a Heart of [3dc, 1ch, 3dc] into next ch, 2ch, skip 4ch, 1sc into next ch; rep from * to last 3ch, 2ch, skip 2ch, 1dc into last ch, turn.

2nd row: 6ch, skip first st and next 2ch, 1sc into next sc, work a Diamond, *skip 2ch, 1 Heart into ch sp at center of next Heart, 3ch, skip 2ch, 1sc into next sc, work Diamond; rep from * ending skip 2ch, 1dc into next ch of tch, turn.

3rd row: 5ch (count as 1dc and 2ch), *1sc into top corner of next Diamond, 2ch**, 1 Heart into sp at center of next Heart, 2ch; rep from * ending last rep at **, 1dc into 3rd ch of tch, turn.

Rep 2nd and 3rd rows.

Tread Pattern Stitch

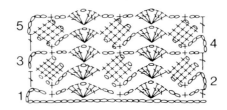

Multiple of 8 sts + 3.
(add 2 for base chain)

1st row (right side): Skip 3ch (count as 1dc), 1dc into each of next 2ch, *skip 2ch, 1dc into next ch, 3ch, work a block of 3dc evenly spaced into side of dc just made, skip 2ch, 1dc into each of next 3ch; rep from * to end, turn.

2nd row: 3ch (count as 1dc), skip first st, 1dc into each of next 2dc, *2ch, 1sc into top of 3ch at corner of next block, 2ch, skip dc which forms base of same block, 1dc into each of next 3dc; rep from * ending last rep in top of tch, turn.

3rd row: 3ch (count as 1dc), skip first st, 1dc into each of next 2dc, *skip 2ch, 1dc into next sc, 3ch, 3dc evenly spaced into side of dc just made, skip 2ch, 1dc into each of next 3dc; rep from * ending last rep in top of tch, turn.

Rep 2nd and 3rd rows.

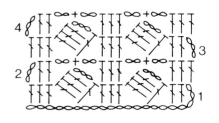

Butterfly Lace

Multiple of 12 sts + 3.
(add 1 for base chain)

Note: For description of dc2tog see page 10.

1st row (right side): 1sc into 2nd ch from hook, 2ch, skip 1ch, 1sc into next ch, *skip 3ch, work [3tr, 4ch, 1sc] into next ch, 2ch, skip 1ch, work [1sc, 4ch, 3tr] into next ch, skip 3ch, 1sc into next ch, 2ch, skip 1ch, 1sc into next ch; rep from * to end, turn.

2nd row: 4ch (count as 1dc and 1ch), skip first sc, 1dc into next 2ch sp, *1ch, skip 3tr, 1sc into top of 4ch, 2ch, work dc2tog into next 2ch sp, 2ch, skip 3ch, 1sc into next ch, 1ch**, work [1dc, 1ch, 1dc] into next sp; rep from * ending last rep at **, 1dc into last sp, 1ch, 1dc into last sc, skip tch, turn.

3rd row: 1ch, 1sc into first st, 2ch, skip [1ch and 1dc], 1sc into next ch, *work [3tr, 4ch, 1sc] into next 2ch sp, 2ch, skip next cluster, work [1sc, 4ch, 3tr] into next 2ch sp, 1sc into next 1ch sp, 2ch, skip 1ch, 1sc into next 1ch sp; rep from * ending last rep in 3rd ch of tch, turn.

Rep 2nd and 3rd rows.

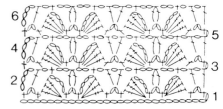

Cluster Lace Stitch

○ Chain ● Slip stitch + Single crochet T Half double crochet ⊤ Double crochet ‡ Treble ⧣ Double treble

Multiple of 8 sts + 1.
(add 1 for base chain)

Note: For description of dc2tog, dc3tog and dc4tog see pages 10 and 14 (Bobble).

1st row (right side): 1sc into 2nd ch from hook, 1sc into next ch, *4ch, work dc4tog over next 5ch as follows: leaving last loop of each st on hook work 1dc into each of next 2ch, skip 1ch, 1dc into each of next 2ch, yo and draw through all 5 loops on hook, 4ch, 1sc into next ch**, 1ch, skip 1ch, 1sc into next ch; rep from * ending last rep at **, 1sc into last ch, turn.

2nd row: 3ch (count as 1dc), 1dc into first st, *3ch, 1sc into top of next 4ch, 1ch, skip cluster, 1sc into top of next 4ch, 3ch, skip 1sc**, dc3tog into next 1ch sp; rep from * ending last rep at **, dc2tog into last sc, skip tch, turn.

3rd row: 1ch, 1sc into first st, *1sc into next ch, 4ch, dc4tog as follows: leaving last loop of each st on hook work 1dc into each of next 2ch, skip [1sc, 1ch and 1sc], 1dc into each of next 2ch, yo and draw through all 5 loops on hook, 4ch, 1sc into next ch**, 1ch, skip cluster; rep from * ending last rep at **, 1sc into top of tch, turn.

Rep 2nd and 3rd rows.

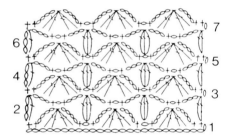

Triple Picot V Stitch

Multiple of 11 sts + 7.
(add 3 for base chain)

1st row (right side): 1dc into 4th ch from hook, *3ch, skip 3ch, 1sc into next ch**, work a picot of [3ch, 1sc into next ch] 3 times, 3ch, skip 3ch, [1dc, 2ch, 1dc] into next ch; rep from * ending last rep at ** when 2ch remain, 3ch, 1sc into next ch, 1ch, 1hdc into last ch, turn.

2nd row: 4ch (count as 1dc and 1ch), 1dc into first st, *3ch, skip 1 Picot and 3ch**, into next 2ch sp work 1sc, [3ch, 1sc] 3 times, then 3ch, skip 3ch and 1 Picot, [1dc, 2ch, 1dc] into next Picot; rep from * ending last rep at **, work [1sc, 3ch, 1sc] into top of tch, 1ch, 1hdc into next ch, turn.

Rep 2nd row.

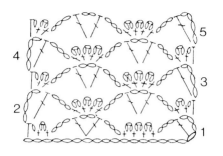

Lacy Wave Stitch

Multiple of 11 sts + 1.
(add 1 for base chain)

1st row (right side): 1sc into 2nd ch from hook, *2ch, skip 2ch, 1dc into each of next 2ch, 2ch, skip 2ch, 1sc into each of next 5ch; rep from * to end, turn.

2nd row: 5ch (count as 1dc and 2ch), 1dc into first st, *[1ch, skip 1 st, 1dc into next st] twice, 1ch, 1dc into next 2ch sp, skip 2dc**, 5dc into next 2ch sp, 2ch, 1dc into next st; rep from * ending last rep at **, 4dc into last 2ch sp, 1dc into last sc, skip tch, turn.

3rd row: 5ch (count as 1dc and 2ch), 1dc into first st, *[1ch, skip 1 st, 1dc into next st] twice, 1ch, skip 1 st, 1dc into next ch, skip [1dc, 1ch, 1dc, 1ch and 1dc], 5dc into next 2ch sp**, 2ch, 1dc into next st; rep from * ending last rep at ** in tch, turn.

Rep 3rd row.

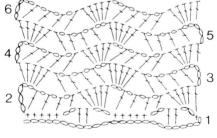

Alternative V Stitch

Multiple of 9 sts + 1.
(add 2 for base chain)

1st row: 2dc into 5th ch from hook, *1ch, 2dc into next ch, skip 3ch, work [1dc, 2ch, 1dc] into next ch**, skip 3ch, 2dc into next ch; rep from * ending last rep at ** when 2ch remain, skip 1ch, 1dc into last ch, turn.

2nd row: 3ch (count as 1dc), skip first st, *work [2dc, 1ch, 2dc] into next 2ch sp, work [1dc, 2ch, 1dc] into next 1ch sp; rep from * ending 1dc into top of tch, turn.

Rep 2nd row.

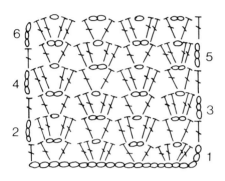

Shell Filigree Stitch

Multiple of 5 sts + 1.
(add 2 for base chain)

1st row (wrong side): 2dc into 3rd ch from hook, *1ch, skip 4ch, 5dc into next ch; rep from * working only 3dc at end of last rep, turn.

2nd row: 1ch, 1sc into first st, *2ch, skip 2dc, work a Picot V st of [1dc, 3ch, insert hook down through top of dc just made and work a sl st to close, 1dc] into next 1ch sp, 2ch, skip 2dc, 1sc into next dc; rep from * ending last rep in top of tch, turn.

3rd row: 3ch (count as 1dc), 2dc into first sc, *1ch, skip 2ch, Picot V st and 2ch, work 5dc into next sc; rep from * finishing with only 3dc at end of last rep, skip tch, turn.

Rep 2nd and 3rd rows.

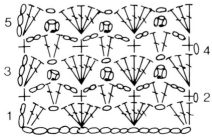

Openwork and Lace Patterns

Arched Lace Stitch

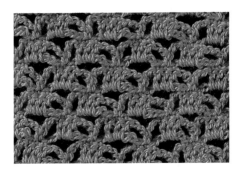

Multiple of 8 sts + 1.
(add 1 for base chain)

1st row (right side): 1sc into 2nd ch from hook, 1sc into next ch, *5ch, skip 5ch, 1sc into each of next 3ch; rep from * omitting 1sc at end of last rep, turn.

2nd row: 1ch, 1sc into first st, *3ch, skip next sc, 3dc into next 5ch arch, 3ch, skip 1sc, 1sc into next sc; rep from * to end, skip tch, turn.

3rd row: 6ch (count as 1tr and 2ch), skip 3ch, *1sc into each of next 3dc**, 5ch, skip [3ch, 1sc and 3ch]; rep from * ending last rep at **, 2ch, skip 3ch, 1tr into last sc, skip tch, turn.

4th row: 3ch (count as 1dc), skip first st, 1dc into 2ch sp, *3ch, skip next sc, 1sc into next sc, 3ch, skip 1sc**, 3dc into next 5ch arch; rep from * ending last rep at **, skip 1ch, 1dc into each of next 2ch of tch, turn.

5th row: 1ch, 1sc into first st, 1sc into next st, *5ch, skip [3ch, 1sc and 3ch], 1sc into each of next 3dc; rep from * to end, omitting 1sc at end of last rep, turn.

Rep 2nd, 3rd, 4th and 5th rows.

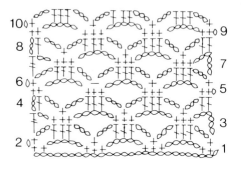

Chain Lace Stitch

Multiple of 10 sts + 1.
(add 7 for base chain)

Special Abbreviation

TP (Triple Picot) = work 1sc, [7ch, 1sc] 3 times all into same place.

1st row (right side): TP into 12th ch from hook, *4ch, skip 4ch, 1dc into next ch**, 4ch, skip 4ch, TP into next ch; rep from * ending last rep at ** in last ch, turn.

2nd row: 1ch, 1sc into first st, *1ch, 1sc into first arch of next TP, [3ch, 1sc into next arch of same TP] twice, 1ch, skip 4ch, 1sc into next dc; rep from * to end placing last sc into arch of tch, turn.

3rd row: 8ch, work [1sc, 7ch, 1sc] into first sc, *4ch, skip [1ch, 1sc and 3ch], 1dc into next sc, 4ch, skip [3ch, 1sc and 1ch]**, TP into next sc; rep from * ending last rep at **, work [1sc, 7ch, 1sc, 3ch and 1tr] into last sc, skip tch, turn.

4th row: 1ch, 1sc into first st, 3ch, 1sc into next 7ch arch, *1ch, skip 4ch, 1sc into next dc, 1ch, 1sc into first arch of next TP**, [3ch, 1sc into next arch of same TP] twice; rep from * ending last rep at **, 3ch, 1sc into tch arch, turn.

5th row: 7ch, skip [3ch, 1sc and 1ch], *TP into next sc, 4ch, skip [1ch, 1sc and 3ch], 1dc into next sc**, 4ch, skip [3ch, 1sc and 1ch]; rep from * ending last rep at **, turn.

Rep 2nd, 3rd, 4th and 5th rows.

Wavy Lace Stitch

Multiple of 12 sts + 1.
(add 4 for base chain)

Base row (right side): 1sc into 7th ch from hook, *3ch, skip 3ch, 1dc into next ch**, [3ch, skip 3ch, 1sc into next ch] twice; rep from * ending last rep at **, 3ch, skip 3ch, 1sc into next ch, 1ch, skip 1ch, 1dc into last ch, turn.

Commence Pattern

1st row: 4ch (count as 1tr), [1tr, 1ch, 1tr] all into next 1ch sp, *3ch, skip 3ch, 1sc into next dc, 3ch, skip 3ch**, work 1tr, [1ch, 1tr] 3 times all into next 3ch arch; rep from * ending last rep at **, 1tr into next ch, 1ch, 2tr into next ch of tch, turn.

2nd row: 4ch (count as 1dc and 1ch), skip first 2tr, 1sc into 1ch sp, *3ch, skip [1tr and 3ch], 1sc into next sc, 3ch, skip [3ch and

1tr], 1sc into next ch sp**, 4ch, skip next sp, 1sc into next sp; rep from * ending last rep at **, 1ch, skip 1tr, 1dc into top of tch, turn.

3rd row: 1ch, 1sc into first st, skip 1ch, *[3ch, 1sc into next 3ch arch] twice, 3ch, 1sc into next 4ch arch; rep from * to end, turn.

4th row: 1ch, 1sc into first st, *3ch, skip 3ch, work 1tr, [1ch, 1tr] 3 times into next 3ch arch, 3ch, skip 3ch, 1sc into next sc; rep from * to end, skip tch, turn.

5th row: 1ch, 1sc into first st, *3ch, skip [3ch and 1tr], 1sc into next ch sp, 4ch, skip next sp, 1sc into next sp, 3ch, skip [1tr and 3ch], 1sc into next sc; rep from * to end, skip tch, turn.

6th row: 5ch (count as 1tr and 1ch), *1sc into next 3ch arch, 3ch, 1sc into next 4ch arch, 3ch, 1sc into next arch**, 3ch; rep from * ending last rep at **, 1ch, 1tr into last sc, skip tch, turn.

Rep these 6 rows.

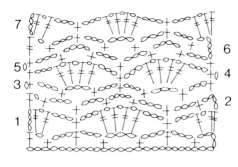

Petal Stitch

Multiple of 8 sts + 1.
(add 1 for base chain)

1st row (wrong side): 1sc into 2nd ch from hook, *2ch, skip 3ch, 4tr into next ch, 2ch, skip 3ch, 1sc into next ch; rep from * to end, turn.

2nd row: 1ch, 1sc into first st, *3ch, skip 2ch and 1tr, 1sc into next tr, 3ch, skip 2tr and 2ch, 1sc into next sc; rep from * to end, skip tch, turn.

3rd row: 4ch (count as 1tr), 1tr into first st, *2ch, skip 3ch, 1sc into next sc, 2ch, skip 3ch, 4tr into next sc; rep from * to end omitting 1tr at end of last rep, skip tch, turn.

4th row: 1ch, 1sc into first st, *3ch, skip 2ch and 2tr, 1sc into next sc, 3ch, skip 2ch and 1tr, 1sc into next tr; rep from * ending last rep in top of tch, turn.

5th row: 1ch, 1sc into first st, *2ch, skip 3ch, 4tr into next sc, 2ch, skip 3ch, 1sc into next sc; rep from * to end, skip tch, turn.

Rep 2nd, 3rd, 4th and 5th rows.

◦ Chain ● Slip stitch + Single crochet T Half double crochet ╤ Double crochet ╪ Treble ⹅ Double treble

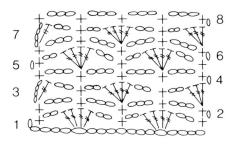

hook, *4ch, skip 5ch, 5dc into next ch; rep from * working only 3dc at end of last rep, turn.

2nd row: 2ch (count as 1dc), skip first 3 sts, *work [3dc, 3ch, 3dc] into next 4ch arch**, skip next 5dc; rep from * ending last rep at **, skip 2dc, 1dc into top of tch, turn.

3rd row: 6ch (count as 1dtr and 1ch), *5dc into next 3ch arch**, 4ch; rep from * ending last rep at **, 1ch, 1dtr into top of tch, turn.

4th row: 5ch (count as 1tr and 1ch), 3dc into next 1ch sp, *skip 5dc, work [3dc, 3ch, 3dc] into next 4ch arch; rep from * ending skip 5dc, work [3dc, 1ch, 1tr] into tch, turn.

5th row: 3ch (count as 1dc), 2dc into next 1ch sp, *4ch, 5dc into next 3ch arch; rep from * ending 4ch, 3dc into tch, turn.

Rep 2nd, 3rd, 4th and 5th rows.

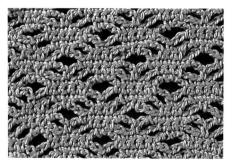

Diamond Lace Stitch

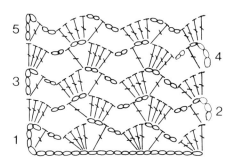

Multiple of 8 sts + 1.
(add 1 for base chain)

Base row (right side): 1sc into 2nd ch from hook, 1sc into each of next 2ch, *5ch, skip 3ch**, 1sc into each of next 5ch; rep from * ending last rep at **, 1sc into each of last 3ch, turn.

Commence Pattern

1st row: 1ch, 1sc into each of first 2 sts, *3ch, skip 1sc, 1sc into next 5ch arch, 3ch, skip 1sc**, 1sc into each of next 3sc; rep from * ending last rep at **, 1sc into each of last 2sc, skip tch, turn.

2nd row: 1ch, 1sc into first st, *3ch, skip 1sc, 1sc into next 3ch sp, 1sc into next sc, 1sc into next 3ch sp, 3ch, skip 1sc, 1sc into next sc; rep from * to end, skip tch, turn.

3rd row: 5ch (count as 1dc and 2ch), *1sc into next 3ch sp, 1sc into each of next 3sc, 1sc into next 3ch sp**, 5ch; rep from * ending last rep at **, 2ch, 1dc into last sc, skip tch, turn.

4th row: 1ch, 1sc into first st, *3ch, skip 2ch

and 1sc, 1sc into each of next 3sc, 3ch, skip 1sc, 1sc into next 5ch arch; rep from * ending last rep in tch, turn.

5th row: 1ch, 1sc into first st, *1sc into next 3ch sp, 3ch, skip 1sc, 1sc into next sc, 3ch, skip 1sc, 1sc into next 3ch sp, 1sc into next sc; rep from * to end, skip tch, turn.

6th row: 1ch, 1sc into each of first 2 sts, *1sc into next 3ch sp, 5ch, 1sc into next 3ch sp**, 1sc into each of next 3sc; rep from * ending last rep at **, 1sc into each of last 2sc, skip tch, turn.

Rep these 6 rows.

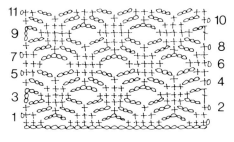

Picot Fan Stitch

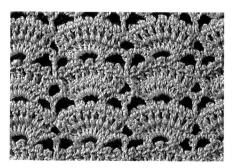

Multiple of 12 sts + 1.
(add 1 for base chain)

1st row (right side): 1sc into 2nd ch from hook, *5ch, skip 3ch, 1sc into next ch; rep from * to end, turn.

2nd row: 5ch (count as 1dc and 2ch), *1sc into next 5ch arch, 8dc into next arch, 1sc into next arch**, 5ch; rep from * ending last rep at ** in last arch, 2ch, 1dc into last sc, skip tch, turn.

3rd row: 1ch, 1sc into first st, skip 2ch and 1sc, *work a picot of [1dc into next dc, 3ch, insert hook down through top of dc just made and sl st to close] 7 times, 1dc into next dc, 1sc into next arch; rep from * to end, turn.

4th row: 8ch, skip 2 picots, *1sc into next picot, 5ch, skip 1 picot, 1sc into next picot, 5ch, skip 2 picots, 1dc into next sc**, 5ch, skip 2 picots; rep from * ending last rep at **, skip tch, turn.

Rep 2nd, 3rd and 4th rows.

Webbed Lace Stitch

Multiple of 7 sts.
(add 4 for base chain)

1st row: 1dc into 5th ch from hook, *2ch, skip 5ch, 4dc into next ch**, 2ch, 1dc into next ch; rep from * ending last rep at ** in last ch, turn.

2nd row: 4ch, 1dc into first st, *2ch, skip [3dc, 2ch and 1dc]**, work [4dc, 2ch, 1dc] into next 2ch sp; rep from * ending last rep at **, 4dc into tch, turn.

Rep 2nd row.

Acrobatic Stitch

Multiple of 6 sts + 1.
(add 2 for base chain)
1st row (right side): 2dc into 3rd ch from

Openwork and Lace Patterns

Crazy Diamond Stitch

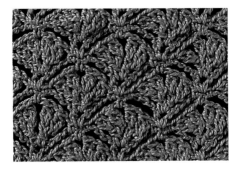

Multiple of 12 sts + 1.
(add 1 for base chain)

Special Abbreviation

CRC (Crazy Cluster) = [yo] 3 times, insert hook as indicated, yo, draw loop through, [yo, draw through 2 loops] 3 times, (2 loops on hook), yo, insert hook into center left side of dtr in progress, yo, draw loop through, yo, draw through 2 loops, (3 loops on hook), yo, draw through all loops on hook, 1ch, [yo] twice, insert hook into lower left side of original dtr, yo, draw loop through, [yo, draw through 2 loops] twice, (2 loops on hook), yo, insert hook into center left side of tr in progress, yo, draw loop through, yo, draw through 2 loops, (3 loops on hook), yo, draw through all loops on hook.

1st row (right side): 1sc into 2nd ch from hook, *1sc into next ch, 1ch, skip 4ch, work [1CRC, 2ch, 1CRC] into next ch, 1ch, skip 4ch, 1sc into next ch**, 1ch, skip 1ch; rep from * ending last rep at **, 1sc into last ch, turn.

2nd row: 3ch (count as 1dc), 1dc into first st, *4ch, 1sc into 2ch sp between next 2CRCs, 4ch**, work a V st of [1dc, 1ch, 1dc] into ch sp between next 2sc; rep from * ending last rep at **, 2dc into last sc, skip tch, turn.

3rd row: 6ch (count as 1ttr), 1CRC into first st, *1ch, 1sc into next 4ch sp, 1ch, 1sc into next 4ch sp, 1ch**, work [1CRC, 2ch, 1CRC] into sp at center of next V st; rep from * ending last rep at **, work [1CRC, 1ttr] into top of tch, turn.

4th row: 1ch, 1sc into first st, *4ch, V st into sp between next 2sc, 4ch, 1sc into 2ch sp between next 2CRCs; rep from * ending last rep in top of tch, turn.

5th row: 1ch, 1sc into first st, *1sc into next 4ch sp, 1ch, work [1CRC, 2ch, 1CRC] into sp at center of next V st, 1ch, 1sc into next 4ch sp**, 1ch; rep from * ending last rep at **, 1sc into last sc, skip tch, turn.
Rep 2nd, 3rd, 4th and 5th rows.

Christmas Tree and Bauble Stitch

Multiple of 10 sts + 6.
(add 2 for base chain)

Special Abbreviation

Note: For description of trtog see page 10; for rf and rb see page 11 (Raised Stitches).

Tree = work 1ttr as indicated, 1ch, 1dtr into base of stem of previous ttr, 1ch, 1tr into base of stem of previous dtr, 1ch, 1dc into base of stem of previous tr, 2ch, 1hdc into stem of previous dc, 1ch, 1dc into stem of previous tr in same place as previous dc, 1ch, 1tr into stem of previous dtr in same place as previous tr, 1ch, 1dtr into stem of previous ttr in same place as previous dtr.

Base row (right side): Skip 2ch (count as 1dc), 3dc into next ch, *skip 4ch, 1sc into next ch**, skip 4ch, 7dc into next ch; rep from * ending last rep at ** in last ch, turn.

Commence Pattern

1st row: 8ch, 1hdc into 3rd ch from hook, 1ch, skip 1ch, 1dc into next ch, 1ch, 1tr into next ch, 1ch, 1dtr into next ch, 1ch, skip 1ch, 1sc and 3dc, 1sc into next st, *1ch, skip 3dc, work 1 Tree into next sc, 1ch, skip 3dc, 1sc into next st; rep from * to end, turn.

2nd row: 4ch (count as 1tr), skip first st, tr4tog/rb round stems of next 4 branches of Tree, *4ch, 1sc into next 2ch sp**, 4ch, tr8tog/rb round stems of 4 remaining branches of same Tree and first 4 branches of next Tree; rep from * ending last rep at ** in tch, turn.

3rd row: 1ch, 1sc into first st, *skip 4ch, 7dc into loop which closed next cluster, skip 4ch, 1sc into next sc; rep from * ending skip 4ch, 4dc into loop which closed half cluster at edge, turn.

4th row: 1ch, 1sc into first st, *1ch, skip 3dc**, Tree into next sc, 1ch, skip 3dc, 1sc into next st; rep from * ending last rep at **, work first half of Tree into last sc, omitting 2ch at top center and ending 1ch, 1hdc into stem of previous dc, turn.

5th row: 1ch, 1sc into first st, *4ch, tr8tog/rf round stems of 4 branches of first Half Tree and first 4 branches of next Tree, 4ch, 1sc into next 2ch sp; rep from * ending 4ch, tr5tog/rf round stems of 4 remaining branches of last Tree and last sc, skip tch, turn.

6th row: 3ch (count as 1dc), 3dc into first st, *skip 4ch, 1sc into next sc**, skip 4ch, 7dc into loop which closed next cluster; rep from * ending last rep at ** in last sc, skip tch, turn.

Rep these 6 rows.

Clover Fan Stitch

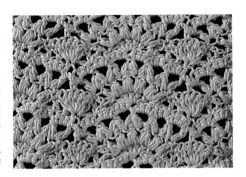

Multiple of 18 sts + 1.
(add 1 for base chain)

Special Abbreviation

CVC (Clover Cluster) = [yo, insert hook, yo, draw loop through loosely] twice as indicated for first leg, (5 loops on hook), and twice more as indicated for 2nd leg, (9 loops on hook), *yo, draw through all except last loop, yo, draw through remaining 2 loops.

Note: For CVC with 1 leg only, omit 2nd leg and complete as given from * to end.

1st row (wrong side): 1sc into 2nd ch from hook, *skip 2ch, 5dc into next ch, skip 2ch, 1sc into next ch; rep from * to end, turn.

2nd row: 3ch (count as 1dc), 2dc into first st, *skip 2dc, 1sc into next dc, 1ch, skip 2dc, work CVC with 1 leg only into next dc, [2ch, 1CVC inserting hook into same place as previous CVC for first leg and into next dc for 2nd leg] 4 times, 2ch, work CVC with 1 leg only into same place as 2nd leg of previous CVC, 1ch, skip 1sc and 2dc, 1sc into next dc, skip 2dc, 5dc into next sc; rep from * ending last rep with only 3dc into last sc, skip tch, turn.

3rd row: 1ch, 1sc into first st, *skip 2dc, 1sc and 1ch, work CVC with 1 leg only into next CVC, [2ch, 1CVC inserting hook into same place as previous CVC for first leg and into next CVC for 2nd leg, skipping 2ch between] 5 times, 2ch, work CVC with 1 leg only into same place as 2nd leg of previous CVC, skip 1ch, 1sc and 2dc, 1sc into next st; rep from * to end, turn.

4th row: 1ch, 1sc into first st, 1sc into each st and each ch to end, skip tch, turn.

5th row: 1ch, 1sc into first st, *skip 3sc, 5dc into next sc, [skip 2sc, 1sc into next sc, skip 2sc, 5dc into next sc] twice, skip 3sc, 1sc into next sc; rep from * to end, skip tch, turn.

○ Chain   ● Slip stitch   + Single crochet   T Half double crochet   ┼ Double crochet   ‡ Treble   ‡ Double treble

Rep 2nd, 3rd, 4th and 5th rows.

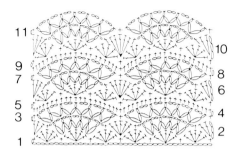

Open Pineapple Stitch

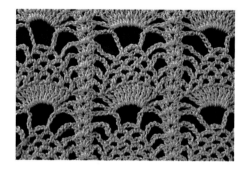

Multiple of 15 sts + 1.
(add 2 for base chain)

Special Abbreviation
DV Stitch = Double V Stitch.

Base row (right side): Skip 2ch (count as 1dc), 2dc into next ch, *7ch, skip 5ch, 1sc into next ch, 3ch, skip 2ch, 1sc into next ch, 7ch, skip 5ch**, work a DV st of [2dc, 1ch, 2dc] into next ch; rep from * ending last rep at **, 3dc into last ch, turn.

Commence Pattern
1st row: 3ch (count as 1dc), 2dc into first st, *3ch, 1sc into 7ch arch, 5ch, skip 3ch, 1sc into next 7ch arch, 3ch**, DV st into sp at center of DV st; rep from * ending last rep at **, 3dc into top of tch, turn.

2nd row: 3ch (count as 1dc), 2dc into first st, *skip 3ch, 11tr into next 5ch arch, skip 3ch**, DV st into next sp; rep from * ending last rep at **, 3dc into top of tch, turn.

3rd row: 3ch (count as 1dc), 2dc into first st, *2ch, skip 2dc, 1sc into next tr, [3ch, skip 1tr, 1sc into next tr] 5 times, 2ch, skip 2dc**, DV st into next sp; rep from * ending last rep at **, 3dc into top of tch, turn.

4th row: 3ch (count as 1dc), 2dc into first st, *3ch, skip 2ch, 1sc into next 3ch arch, [3ch, 1sc into next 3ch arch] 4 times, 3ch, skip 2ch**, DV st into next sp; rep from * ending last rep at **, 3dc into top of tch, turn.

5th row: 3ch (count as 1dc), 2dc into first st, *4ch, skip 3ch, 1sc into next 3ch arch, [3ch, 1sc into next 3ch arch] 3 times, 4ch, skip 3ch**, DV st into next sp; rep from * ending last rep at **, 3dc into top of tch, turn.

6th row: 3ch (count as 1dc), 2dc into first

st, *5ch, skip 4ch, 1sc into next 3ch arch, [3ch, 1sc into next 3ch arch] twice, 5ch, skip 4ch**, DV st into next sp; rep from * ending last rep at **, 3dc into top of tch, turn.

7th row: 3ch (count as 1dc), 2dc into first st, *7ch, skip 5ch, 1sc into next 3ch arch, 3ch, 1sc into next 3ch arch, 7ch, skip 5ch**, DV st into next sp; rep from * ending last rep at **, 3dc into top of tch, turn.
Rep these 7 rows.

Strawberry Lace Stitch

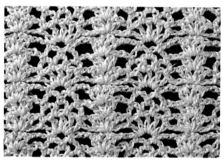

Multiple of 12 sts + 7.
(add 1 for base chain)

1st row (right side): 1sc into 2nd ch from hook, *3ch, skip 5ch, into next ch work a 5 group of 1dc, [1ch, 1dc] 4 times, 3ch, skip 5ch, 1sc into next ch; rep from * ending 3ch, skip 5ch, into last ch work 1dc, [1ch, 1dc] twice, turn.

2nd row: [3ch, 1sc into next ch sp] twice, *1ch, skip 3ch, work a DV st of [2dc, 1ch, 2dc] into next sc, 1ch, skip 3ch, 1sc into next ch sp, [3ch, 1sc into next sp] 3 times; rep from * ending 1ch, skip 3ch, 3dc into last sc, skip tch, turn.

3rd row: 3ch (count as 1dc), 2dc into first st, *2ch, skip 1ch, 1sc into next 3ch arch**, [3ch, 1sc into next 3ch arch] twice, 2ch, skip 1ch, DV st into next ch sp; rep from * ending last rep at **, 3ch, 1sc into tch, turn.

4th row: 4ch, 1sc into next 3ch arch, *3ch, skip 2ch, DV st into next ch sp, 3ch, skip 2ch, 1sc into next 3ch arch, 3ch, 1sc into next 3ch arch; rep from * ending 3ch, skip 2ch, 3dc into top of tch, turn.

5th row: 1ch, 1sc into first st, *3ch, skip 3ch, 5 group into next 3ch arch, 3ch, skip 3ch, 1sc into next ch sp; rep from * ending 3ch, skip 3ch, into tch work 1dc, [1ch, 1dc] twice, turn.

Rep 2nd, 3rd, 4th and 5th rows.

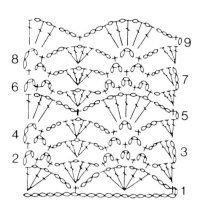

Open Crescent

Multiple of 18 sts + 1.
(add 1 for base chain)

1st row (wrong side): 1sc into 2nd ch from hook, *3ch, skip 2ch, 1sc into next ch, [5ch, skip 3ch, 1sc into next ch] 3 times, 3ch, skip 2ch, 1sc into next ch; rep from * to end, turn.

2nd row: 3ch (count as 1dc), 1dc into first st, *3ch, skip 3ch, 1sc into next arch, 9dc into next arch, 1sc into next arch, 3ch, skip 3ch, 3dc into next sc; rep from * working only 2dc at end of last rep, skip tch, turn.

3rd row: 1ch, 1sc into each of first 2 sts, *1ch, skip 3ch and 1sc, 1dc into next dc, [1ch, 1dc into next dc] 8 times, 1ch, skip 1sc and 3ch, 1sc into each of next 3 sts; rep from * omitting 1sc at end of last rep, turn.

4th row: 1ch, 1sc into first st, *skip 1sc and 1ch, 1dc into next dc, [1ch, skip 1ch, 1dc into next dc] 3 times, 1ch, skip 1ch, work [1dc, 1ch, 1dc] into next dc, [1ch, skip 1ch, 1dc into next dc] 4 times (Crescent completed), skip 1ch and 1sc, 1sc into next sc; rep from * to end, skip tch, turn.

5th row: 6ch (count as 1dc and 3ch), *1sc into 3rd dc of next Crescent, 5ch, skip 1ch and 1dc, 1sc into next ch, 5ch, skip 1dc, 1ch and 1dc, 1sc into next ch, 5ch, skip 1dc and 1ch, 1sc into next dc, 3ch, skip remaining sts of same Crescent, 1dc into next sc, 3ch; rep from * omitting 3ch at end of last rep, skip tch, turn.

Rep 2nd, 3rd, 4th and 5th rows.

Openwork and Lace Patterns

Broomstick Lace

Multiple of 4 sts.
(add 1 for base chain)

Note: For description of Lace Loop see page 13.

1st row (right side): 1sc into 2nd ch from hook, 1sc into next and each ch to end, turn.

2nd row: 1ch, 1sc into first st, 1sc into next and each st to end, skip tch, turn.

3rd row: *1ch, draw loop on hook up to approx height of dtr, keeping loop on hook and not allowing it to change size through yarn slippage, insert hook into next st, yo, draw loop through; rep from * to end keeping all lace loops on hook. (Hint: slip some sts off handle end of hook if they become too numerous.) At end remove all except last lace loop from hook, yo, draw loop through, insert hook under back thread and work 1sc as for Solomon's Knot (see page 13), to lock last lace loop, turn.

4th row: *Always inserting hook through next 4 lace loops together work 4sc; rep from * to end, turn.

Rep 2nd, 3rd and 4th rows.

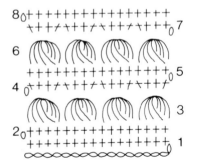

Crossed Lace Loop Stitch

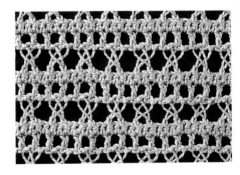

Multiple of 2 sts + 1.
(add 3 for base chain)

Note: For description of Lace Loop see page 13.

1st row (right side): 1dc into 6th ch from hook, *1ch, skip 1ch, 1dc into next ch; rep from * to end, turn.

2nd row: 1ch, 1sc into first st, *1sc into next ch, 1sc into next dc; rep from * ending 1sc into each of next 2ch of tch, turn.

3rd row: *1ch, draw loop on hook up to approx height of tr, keeping loop on hook and not allowing it to change size through yarn slippage, insert hook into next st, yo, draw loop through, sl st into next st; rep from * to end keeping all lace loops on hook. (Hint: slip some off handle end of hook, if they become too numerous.) At end remove all except last lace loop from hook, yo, draw loop through, insert hook under back thread as though for Solomon's Knot (see page 13), but make sl st to lock last lace loop, turn.

4th row: *1ch, skip 1 lace loop, sl st into top of next loop, 1ch, bring forward loop just skipped and sl st into top of it; rep from * ending sl st into top of last loop, turn.

5th row: 4ch (count as 1dc and 1ch), skip 1ch, 1dc into next sl st, *1ch, skip 1ch, 1dc into next sl st; rep from * to end, turn.

Rep 2nd, 3rd, 4th and 5th rows.

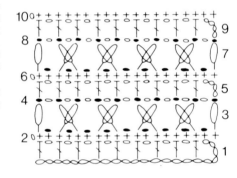

Little Pyramid Stitch

Multiple of 4 sts + 1.
(add 1 for base chain)

1st row (right side): 1sc into 2nd ch from hook, *work a Pyramid of [6ch, 1sc into 3rd ch from hook, 1dc into each of next 3ch], skip 3ch, 1sc into next ch; rep from * to end, turn.

2nd row: 6ch (count as 1dtr and 1ch), *1sc into ch at tip of next Pyramid, 3ch; rep from * ending 1sc into ch at tip of last Pyramid, 1ch, 1dtr into last sc, skip tch, turn.

3rd row: 10ch, skip 1ch, 1sc into next sc, *work Pyramid, skip 3ch, 1sc into next sc; rep from * ending 5ch, skip 1ch, 1dtr into

next ch of tch, turn.

4th row: 1ch, 1sc into first st, *3ch, 1sc into ch at tip of next Pyramid; rep from * ending last rep in center of 10tch, turn.

5th row: 1ch, 1sc into first st, *work Pyramid, skip 3ch, 1sc into next sc; rep from * to end, skip tch, turn.

Rep 2nd, 3rd, 4th and 5th rows.

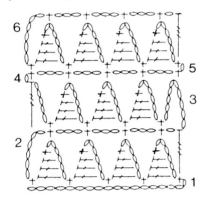

Chevron Lattice

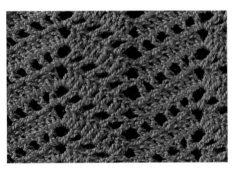

Multiple of 20 sts + 11.
(add 3 for base chain)

Special Abbreviation (see also page 10)

Dc cluster: leaving last loop of each dc on hook work 1dc into next ch, skip 3ch, and work 1dc into next ch, then yo and draw through all 3 loops on hook.

1st row (wrong side): 1dc into 6th ch from hook, *[1ch, skip 1ch, 1dc into next ch] 3 times, 1ch, skip 1ch**, work [1dc, 3ch, 1dc] into next ch, [1ch, skip 1ch, 1dc into next ch] 3 times, 1ch, skip 1ch, work a dc cluster over next 1dc, 3ch and 1dc; rep from * ending last rep at **, work [1dc, 1ch, 1dc] into last ch, turn.

2nd row: 3ch (count as 1dc), 2dc into first st, *1dc into next ch sp, [1dc into next dc, 1dc into next ch sp] 3 times**, leaving last loop of each dc on hook work 1dc into next dc, skip dc cluster, work 1dc into next dc and complete as dc cluster, [1dc into next ch sp, 1dc into next dc] 3 times, 1dc into next ch, work [1dc, 3ch, 1dc] into next ch; rep from * ending last rep at **, work dc cluster over next 2 dcs, skip tch, turn.

3rd row: 3ch, skip first 2 sts, 1dc into next st, *[1ch, skip 1dc, 1dc into next dc] 3 times**, 1ch, skip 1ch, work [1dc, 3ch, 1dc] into next ch, 1ch, skip 1ch, [1dc into next dc, 1ch, skip 1dc] 3 times, leaving last loop of each dc on hook work 1dc into next dc, skip 1dc, dc cluster and 1dc, work 1dc into next dc and complete as dc cluster; rep from * ending last rep at **, 1ch, skip 1dc, work [1dc, 1ch, 1dc] into top of tch, turn.

Rep 2nd and 3rd rows.

○ Chain   ● Slip stitch   + Single crochet   T Half double crochet   ╪ Double crochet   ╪ Treble   ╪ Double treble

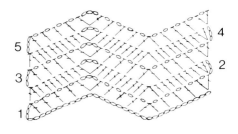

Solomon's Knot

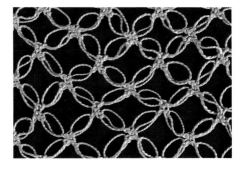

Multiple of 2 Solomon's Knots + 1.
(add 2 Solomon's Knots for base 'chain')

Special Abbreviations (also see page 13)

ESK (Edge Solomon's Knot): these form the base 'chain' and edges of the fabric and are only two-thirds the length of MSK's.

MSK (Main Solomon's Knot): These form the main fabric and are half as long again as ESK's.

Base 'chain': 2ch, 1sc into 2nd ch from hook, now make a multiple of 2ESK's (say, 2cm), ending with 1MSK (say, 3cm).

1st row: 1sc into sc between 3rd and 4th loops from hook, *2MSK, skip 2 loops, 1sc into next sc; rep from * to end, turn.

2nd row: 2ESK and 1MSK, 1sc into sc between 4th and 5th loops from hook, *2MSK, skip 2 loops, 1sc into next sc; rep from * ending in top of ESK, turn.

Rep 2nd row.

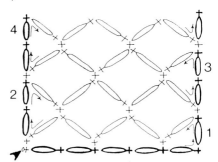

Lacewing Network

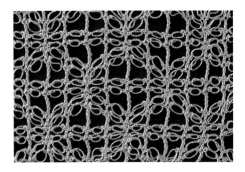

Multiple of 16 sts + 1.
(add 1 for base chain)

Special Abbreviation (also see page 13)

SK (Solomon's Knot): loop approx 1.5cm.

Note: You may need to experiment with the number of ch in the base chain and length of loop, or even make the base 'chain' itself out of Knots.

Base row (right side): 1sc into 2nd ch from hook, *1SK, skip 3ch, 1tr into next ch, 1SK, skip 3ch, 1ttr into next ch, 1SK, skip 3ch, 1tr into next ch, 1SK, skip 3ch, 1sc into next ch; rep from * to end, turn.

Commence Pattern

1st row: 3ch, 1sc into 2nd ch from hook, *1SK, skip SK, 1dc into next st; rep from * to end, turn.

2nd row: 6ch, 1sc into 2nd ch from hook, *1SK, skip SK, 1tr into next st, 1SK, skip SK, 1sc into next st, 1SK, skip SK, 1tr into next st, 1SK, skip SK, 1 ttr into next st; rep from * to end, turn.

Rep the last 2 rows once then work 1st row again.

6th row: 1ch, 1sc into first st, *1SK, skip SK, 1tr into next st, 1SK, skip SK, 1 ttr into next st, 1SK skip SK, 1tr into next st, 1SK, skip SK, 1sc into next st; rep from * to end, turn.

7th row: As 1st row.

8th row: As 6th row.

Rep these 8 rows.

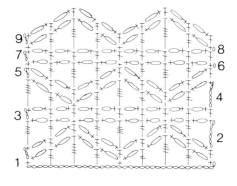

Embossed Flower Network

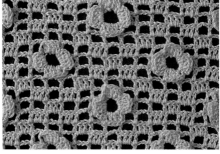

Multiple of 24 sts + 4.
(add 4 for base chain)

Note: When working Embossed Flower always treat the various stitches and threads which form the four sides of the space as if they were the base ring of a Motif, i.e. always insert hook through center of this 'ring' to make stitches.

Base row (right side): 1dc into 8th ch from hook, *2ch, skip 2ch, 1dc into each of next 4ch, [2ch, skip 2ch, 1dc into next ch] 3 times, 1dc into each of next 3ch, [2ch, skip 2ch, 1dc into next ch] twice; rep from * to end, turn.

Commence Pattern

1st row: 5ch (count as 1dc and 2ch), skip 2ch, 1dc into next st, *2dc into next 2ch sp, 1dc into next st, [2ch, skip 2 sts, 1dc into next st] twice, 2dc into next sp, 1dc into next st, [2ch, skip 2 sts, 1dc into next st] twice, 2dc into next sp, 1dc into next st, 2ch, skip 2ch, 1dc into next st; rep from * to end, turn.

2nd row: 3ch (count as 1dc), skip first st, 2dc into next 2ch sp, 1dc into next st, *[2ch, skip 2 sts, 1dc into next st] twice, 2dc into next sp, 1dc into next st, 2ch, skip 2dc, 1dc into next st. Now work Embossed Flower round space just completed, (see note above); with right side facing and working around anticlockwise, work 1sc into corner (top left), down left side work **3ch, 3dc, 3ch, 1sc into next corner** (bottom left), rep from ** to ** 3 more times, omitting sc at end of last rep and ending sl st to first sc, sl st to last dc made of main fabric. Continue working main fabric as follows: 2dc into next 2ch sp, 1dc into next st, [2ch, skip 2 sts, 1dc into next st] twice, 2dc into next 2ch sp, 1dc into next st; rep from * ending last rep in 3rd ch of tch, turn.

3rd row: As 1st row.

4th row: 5ch (count as 1dc and 2ch), skip 2ch, 1dc into next st, *2ch, skip 2 sts, 1dc into next st, 2dc into next 2ch sp, 1dc into next st, [2ch, skip 2 sts, 1dc into next st] 3 times, 2dc into next sp, 1dc into next st, [2ch, skip 2 sts, 1dc into next st] twice; rep from * ending last rep in 3rd ch of tch, turn.

5th row: 3ch (count as 1dc), skip first st, 2dc into next 2ch sp, 1dc into next st, *[2ch, skip 2 sts, 1dc into next st] twice, [2dc into next sp, 1dc into next st, 2ch, skip 2 sts, 1dc into next st] twice, 2ch, skip 2ch, 1dc into next st, 2dc into next sp, 1dc into next st; rep from * ending last rep in 3rd ch of tch, turn.

6th row: 5ch (count as 1dc and 2ch), skip first 3 sts, 1dc into next st. Now work Embossed Flower round space just completed as in 3rd row. Continue working main fabric as follows: *2dc into next 2ch sp, 1dc into next st, [2ch, skip 2 sts, 1dc into next st] twice, 2dc into next sp, 1dc into next st, [2ch, skip 2 sts, 1dc into next st] twice, 2dc into next sp, 1dc into next st, 2ch, skip 2 sts, 1dc into next st. Now work Embossed Flower round space just completed as before; rep from * ending last rep of main fabric in top of tch, turn.

7th row: As 5th row.

8th row: As 4th row.

Rep these 8 rows.

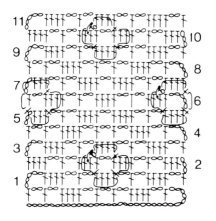

Motifs

Royal Square

Note: For description of dtr2tog and dtr3tog see page 10.

Base ring: 16ch, join with sl st.

1st round: 1ch, 24sc into ring, sl st to first sc, (24 sts).

2nd round: 1ch, 1sc into same place as 1ch, *4ch, dtr2tog over next 2 sts, into top of cluster just made work set of 3 leaves as follows: [8ch, 1 quad tr, 7ch, 1sc, 8ch, 1 quin tr, 8ch, 1sc, 7ch, 1 quad tr, 7ch, sl st], 4ch, 1sc into next st of 1st round, 7ch, skip 2 sts, 1sc into next st; rep from * 3 more times, omitting sc at end of last rep, sl st to first sc. Fasten off.

3rd round: Rejoin yarn at tip of 2nd Leaf of next set, in top of 8ch before quin tr work 1ch, 1sc into same place, *2ch, skip quin tr, 1sc into next ch, 5ch, into tip of 3rd Leaf of same set work in same way 1sc just before and 1sc just after quad tr, 7ch, into tip of 1st Leaf of next set work 1sc just before and 1sc just after quad tr, 5ch, into tip of 2nd Leaf of same set work 1sc just before quin tr; rep from * 3 more times, omitting sc at end of last rep, sl st to first sc.

4th round: 1ch, 1sc in same place as 1ch, *3sc into next 2ch sp, 1sc into next sc, 1sc into each of next 5ch, 1sc into each of next 2sc, 1sc into each of next 7ch, 1sc into each of next 2sc, 1sc into each of next 5ch, 1sc into next sc; rep from * 3 more times, omitting sc at end of last rep, sl st to first sc.

5th round: Sl st into each of next 2sc to corner, 4ch (count as 1dc and 1ch), 1dc into same place as 4ch, *[1ch, skip 1st st, 1dc into next st] 13 times to next corner**, [1ch, 1dc] twice all into same place as last dc; rep from * twice more and from * to ** again, ending 1ch, sl st to 3rd of 4ch.

6th round: 4ch (count as 1dc and 1ch), 1dc into same place as 4ch, *[1ch, 1dc into next ch sp] 15 times, 1ch**, [1dc, 1ch, 1dc, 1ch, 1dc] all into next corner st; rep from * twice and from * to ** again, ending 1dc into corner st, 1ch, sl st to 3rd of 4ch.

7th round: 3ch (count as 1dc), 1dc into same place as 3ch, *1ch, [1dc into next ch sp, 1dc into next dc, 1ch, skip 1ch, 1dc into next dc, 1dc into next ch sp, 1ch, skip 1dc] 5 times, 1dc into next ch sp, 1dc into next dc, 1ch, skip 1ch, 1dc into next dc, 1dc into next ch sp, 1ch**, 3dc into corner st; rep from * twice and from * to ** again, ending 1dc into corner st, sl st to top of 3ch.

8th round: 4ch (count as 1dc and 1ch), 1dc into same place as 4ch, *1dc into next dc, [1ch, skip 1ch, 1dc into each of next 2 sts] 13 times to next corner, 1ch**, [1dc, 1ch, 1dc] into same place as last dc; rep from * twice and from * to ** again, ending sl st to 3rd of 4ch.

9th round: 1ch, 2sc into same place as 1ch, 1sc into each ch sp and each dc all round, except 3sc into st at each of next 3 corners and ending 1sc into first corner, sl st to first sc.

10th round: 5ch, dtr2tog all into same place as 5ch (counts as dtr3tog), 2ch, dtr3tog all into same place as last cluster, *5ch, skip 4 sts, dtr3tog all into next st, [5ch, skip 5 sts, dtr3tog all into next st] 6 times, 5ch, skip 4 sts**, [dtr3tog, 2ch, dtr3tog] all into next corner st; rep from * twice and from * to ** again, ending sl st to top of first cluster.

11th round: Sl st to next ch, 8ch, 1sc into 5th ch from hook, 1dc into same 2ch sp, work a picot of [5ch, 1sc into 5th ch from hook], *1dc into next cluster, [picot, skip 2ch, 1dc into next ch, picot, skip 2ch, 1dc into next cluster] 8 times, picot**, [1dc, picot] twice into 2ch sp at corner; rep from * twice more and from * to ** again, ending sl st to 3rd of 8ch.
Fasten off.

Pineapple Square

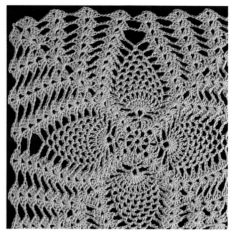

Base ring: 4ch, join with sl st.

1st round: 4ch (count as 1dc and 1ch), [1dc into ring, 1ch] 7 times, sl st to 3rd of 4ch.

2nd round: 5ch (count as 1dc and 2ch), *3dc into next ch sp, 1ch**, 3dc into next sp, 2ch; rep from * twice more and from * to ** again, 2dc into next sp, sl st to 3rd of 5ch.

3rd round: Sl st into next ch, 5ch (count as 1dc and 2ch), 3dc into next sp, *1ch, 1sc into next sp, 1ch**, work a V st of [3dc, 2ch, 3dc] into next 2ch sp; rep from * twice more and from * to ** again, 2dc into next sp, sl st to 3rd of 5ch.

4th round: Sl st into next ch, 5ch (count as 1dc and 2ch), 3dc into next ch sp, *1ch, skip 1ch, work [1dc, 2ch, 1dc] into next sc, 1ch, skip 1ch**, V st into next 2ch sp; rep from * twice more and from * to ** again, 2dc into next sp, sl st to 3rd of 5ch.

5th round: Sl st into next ch, 5ch (count as 1dc and 2ch), 3dc into next sp, *2ch, skip 1ch, 10dc into next 2ch sp, 2ch, skip 1ch**, V st into next sp; rep from * twice more and from * to ** again, 2dc into next sp, sl st to 3rd of 5ch.

6th round: Sl st into next ch, 5ch (count as 1dc and 2ch), 3dc into next sp, *2ch, skip 2ch, 1dc into next dc, [1ch, 1dc into next dc] 9 times, 2ch, skip 2ch**, V st into next

○ Chain ● Slip stitch + Single crochet T Half double crochet ╪ Double crochet ╪ Treble ╪ Double treble

sp; rep from * twice more and from * to ** again, 2dc into next sp, sl st to 3rd of 5ch.

7th round: Sl st into next ch, 5ch (count as 1dc and 2ch), V st into next sp, *2ch, skip 2ch, 1sc into next sp, [3ch, 1sc into next sp] 8 times, 2ch, skip 2ch**, work [V st, 2ch, 3dc] into next sp; rep from * twice more and from * to ** again, 2dc into next sp, sl st to 3rd of 5ch.

8th round: Sl st into each of next 2ch, 5ch (count as 1dc and 2ch), skip 3dc, *V st into next sp, 2ch, skip 2ch, 1sc into next 3ch arch, [3ch, 1sc into next sp] 7 times, 2ch, skip 2ch**, V st into next sp, 2ch; rep from * twice more and from * to ** again, work [3dc, 2ch, 2dc] into next sp, sl st to 3rd of 5ch.

9th round: Sl st into next ch, 5ch (count as 1dc and 2ch), 3dc into next sp, *V st into next sp, 2ch, skip 2ch, 1sc into next 3ch arch, [3ch, 1sc into next 3ch arch] 6 times, 2ch, skip 2ch, V st into next sp**, V st into next sp; rep from * twice more and from * to ** again, 2dc into next sp, sl st to 3rd of 5ch.

10th round: Sl st into next ch, 5ch (count as 1dc and 2ch), V st into next sp, *2ch, V st into next sp, 2ch, skip 2ch, 1sc into next 3ch arch, [3ch, 1sc into next 3ch arch] 5 times, 2ch, skip 2ch, V st into next sp, 2ch**, work [V st, 2ch, 3dc] into next sp; rep from * twice more and from * to ** again, 2dc into next sp, sl st to 3rd of 5ch.

11th round: Sl st into each of next 2ch, 5ch (count as 1dc and 2ch), skip 3dc, *[V st into next sp, 2ch, skip 2ch] twice, 1sc into next 3ch arch, [3ch, 1sc into next 3ch arch] 4 times, [2ch, skip 2ch, V st into next sp] twice**, 2ch; rep from * twice more and from * to ** again omitting 1dc at end of last rep and ending sl st to 3rd of 5ch.

12th round: Sl st into next ch, 5ch (count as 1dc and 2ch), 3dc into next sp, *[V st into next sp, 2ch, skip 2ch] twice, 1sc into next 3ch arch, [3ch, 1sc into next 3ch arch] 3 times, [2ch, skip 2ch, V st into next sp] twice**, V st into next sp; rep from * twice more and from * to ** again, 2dc into next sp, sl st to 3rd of 5ch.

13th round: Sl st into next ch, 5ch (count as 1dc and 2ch), V st into next sp, *2ch, [V st into next sp, 2ch, skip 2ch] twice, 1sc into next 3ch arch, [3ch, 1sc into next 3ch arch] twice, [2ch, skip 2ch, V st into next sp] twice, 2ch**, work [V st, 2ch, 3dc] into next sp; rep from * twice more and from * to ** again, 2dc into next sp, sl st to 3rd of 5ch.

14th round: Sl st into each of next 2ch, 5ch (count as 1dc and 2ch), skip 3dc, *[V st into next sp, 2ch, skip 2ch] 3 times, 1sc into next 3ch arch, 3ch, 1sc into next 3ch arch, [2ch, skip 2ch, V st into next sp] 3 times**, 2ch; rep from * twice more and from * to ** again omitting 1dc at end of last rep and ending sl st to 3rd of 5ch.

15th round: Sl st into next ch, 5ch (count as 1dc and 2ch), 3dc into next sp, *[V st into next sp, 2ch, skip 2ch] twice, V st into next sp, 3ch, skip 2ch, 1sc into next 3ch arch, 3ch, skip 2ch, V st into next sp, [2ch, skip 2ch, V st into next sp] twice**, V st into next sp; rep from * twice more and from * to ** again, 2dc into next sp, sl st to 3rd of 5ch.

16th round: Sl st into next ch, 5ch (count as 1dc and 2ch), V st into next sp, *2ch, [V st into next sp, 2ch, skip 2ch] twice, V st into next sp, 2ch, skip 3ch, 1sc and 3ch, [V st into next sp, 2ch, skip 2ch] twice, V st into next sp, 2ch**, work [V st, 2ch, 3dc] into next sp, rep from * twice more and from * to ** again, 2dc into next sp, sl st to 3rd of 5ch.

17th round: Sl st into each of next 2ch, 5ch (count as 1dc and 2ch), skip 3dc, *V st into next sp, [2ch, skip 2ch, V st into next sp] 3 times, V st into next sp, [2ch, skip 2ch, V st into next sp] 3 times**, 2ch; rep from * twice more and from * to ** again omitting 1dc at end of last rep and ending sl st to 3rd of 5ch. Fasten off.

Trefoil Motif

Leaf (make 3 alike)
Base chain: 17ch.

1st row (right side): Skip 2ch (count as 1sc), 1sc into each ch to last ch, work 3sc into last ch for point, then work back along underside of base chain with 1sc into each ch to end, turn.

2nd row: 1ch (counts as 1sc), skip 1 st, 1sc into each st up to st at center of point, work 3sc into center st, 1sc into each st to last 3 sts and tch, turn.

3rd, 4th, 5th, 6th and 7th rows: As 2nd row.

Fasten off.

Stem

Make 22ch (or as required), sl st to center Leaf (2nd) as diagram, work back along base chain in sc and at same time join in side Leaves (1st and 3rd) at, say, 6th and 7th sts as follows: *insert hook through 1st Leaf and base chain, make 1sc, sl st to 3rd Leaf to match; rep from * once more. Continue to end of base chain in sc.

Fasten off.

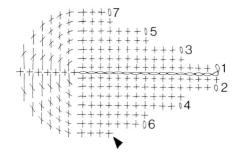

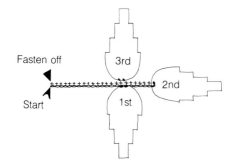

Motifs

Bachelor's Buttonhole

Base ring: Using A, 4ch, join with sl st.
Special Abbreviations (see also page 15)
Ldc (Linked double crochet) = insert hook down through horizontal loop round stem of last st made, yo, draw loop through; insert hook as indicated to make st and complete normally.

Note: At beginning of round to make first Ldc treat 2nd ch of starting ch as horizontal loop.

Ldtr (Linked Double Treble) = insert hook down through uppermost of 3 horizontal loops round stem of last st made, yo, draw loop through, [insert hook down through next lower horizontal loop, yo, draw loop through] twice; insert hook as indicated to make st and complete normally.

Note: at beginning of round to make first Ldtr treat 2nd, 3rd and 4th chs of starting ch as horizontal loops.

1st round: 3ch (count as 1dc), 5Ldc into ring, sl st to top of 3ch. (6 sts).

2nd round: 5ch (count as 1dtr), 1Ldtr into first st, [2Ldtr into next st] 5 times, sl st to top of 5ch. (12 sts). Fasten off A.

3rd round: Using B, 1ch, 1sc into each st all round, sl st to first sc.

4th round: As 3rd round.

5th round: 1ch, 2sc into first st, 3sc into each st all round, 1sc into same place as first 2sc, sl st to first sc. (36 sts).

6th round: 3ch (count as 1dc), 2dc into first st, 3dc into each st all round, sl st to top of 3ch, 108 sts. Turn.

7th round (wrong side): 1ch, 1sc into first st, 5ch, *1sc into next st, 5ch; rep from * all round, ending sl st to first sc. (108 arches). Fasten off.

Stem: Rejoin A at underside of flower head into base ring, make 20ch (or as required), 1sc into 2nd ch from hook, 1sc into next and each ch, sl st to opposite side of base ring; now work back down stem in sl st, twisting stem as you go to create interest. Fasten off.

Lace Triangle

Base ring: Wrap yarn round finger.
1st round: 1ch, 12sc into ring, sl st to first sc.

2nd round: 10ch (count as 1dc and 7ch arch), skip first 2sc, *1dc into next sc, 3ch, skip 1sc, 1dc into next sc, 7ch, skip 1sc; rep from * once, 1dc into next sc, 3ch, skip last sc, sl st to 3rd of 10ch.

3rd round: 3ch (count as 1dc), into next ch arch work [3dc, 7ch, 4dc], *3dc into next ch arch, [4dc, 7ch, 4dc] into next ch arch; rep from * once, 3dc into last ch arch, sl st to top of 3ch.

4th round: 6ch (count as 1dc and 3ch arch), *[4dc, 5ch, 4dc] into next 7ch arch, 3ch, skip 2dc, 1dc into next dc, 3ch, skip 2dc, 1sc into next dc, 3ch**, skip 2dc, 1dc into next dc, 3ch; rep from * once and from * to ** again, sl st to 3rd of 6ch. Fasten off.

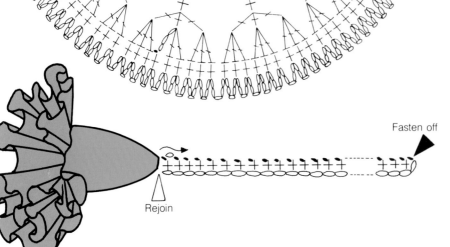

○ Chain   ● Slip stitch   + Single crochet   T Half double crochet   ‡ Double crochet   ‡ Treble   ‡ Double treble

Viola

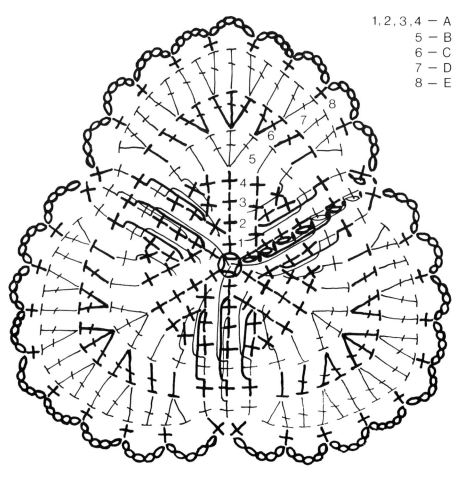

Base ring: Using A, 4ch, join with sl st.

Special Abbreviation

Ssc (Spike single crochet) = insert hook lower than usual (as indicated), yo, draw loop through and up to height of current row, yo, draw through both loops on hook (see also page 10).

1st round: 1ch, 6sc into ring, sl st to first sc. (6 sts).

2nd round: 1ch, 2sc into each sc, sl st to first sc. (12 sts).

3rd round: 1ch, 1sc into first st, [2sc into next st, 1sc into next st] 5 times, 2sc into last st, sl st to first sc. (18 sts).

4th round: 1ch, 1sc into first st, [2sc into next st, 1sc into each of next 2 sts] 5 times, 2sc into next st, 1sc into last st, sl st to first sc. (24 sts). Fasten off.

5th round: Using B join into same place, 1ch, then starting in same st as 1ch work *1Ssc inserting hook into base ring, [1Ssc over next st inserting hook to left of last sc, but 1 round higher] twice, 1hdc into next st, 3dc into next st, 1hdc into next st, 1Ssc over next st inserting hook through top of 2nd round, 1Ssc over next st inserting hook through top of 1st round; rep from * twice, sl st to first Ssc. Fasten off.

6th round: Using C join into same place, 1ch, then starting in same st as 1ch work *1Ssc inserting hook between threads of previous Ssc and through top of 1st round, 1Ssc over next st inserting hook between threads of previous Ssc and through top of 2nd round, 1hdc into next st, 1dc into next st, 2dc into next st, 3dc into next st, 2dc into next st, 1dc into next st, 1hdc into next st, 1Ssc over next st inserting hook between threads of 2nd of 5 previous Sscs and 1 round higher; rep from * twice, sl st to first Ssc. Fasten off.

7th round: Using D join into same place, 1ch, starting in same st as 1ch *1Ssc inserting hook between threads of previous Sscs and through top of 2nd round, 1sc into next st, [1hdc, 1dc] into next st, [1dc into next st, 2dc into next st] 4 times, 1dc into next st, [1dc, 1hdc] into next st, 1sc into next st; rep from * twice, sl st to first Ssc. Fasten off.

8th round: Using E join into next st, 1ch, 1sc into same st as 1ch, *[5ch, skip next st, 1sc into next st] 9 times, skip next st**, 1sc into next st; rep from * and from * to ** again, sl st to first sc. Fasten off.

Popcorn Trefoil

Note: For description of Popcorn see page 14; for dc2tog see page 10.

Base ring: Using A, 5ch, join with sl st.

1st round: 1ch, 6sc into ring, sl st to first sc. Fasten off.

2nd round: Using B, 1ch, 1sc into same place as 1ch, *3ch, 5dc Popcorn into next st, 3ch**, 1sc into next st; rep from * and from * to ** again, sl st into first sc.

3rd round: 1ch, 1sc into same place as 1ch, *4ch, 1sc into next 3ch arch, dc2tog inserting hook into same ch arch for first leg and into next ch arch for 2nd leg, 2dc into same ch arch, 4ch**, 1sc into next sc; rep from * and from * to ** again, sl st to first sc. Fasten off.

4th round: Using C join into corner cluster, 1ch, 1sc into same place as 1ch, *2ch, skip 2dc, going behind ch arches of 3rd round work [3dc into next ch arch of 2nd round] twice, 2ch, skip 2dc**, 1sc into corner cluster; rep from * and from * to ** again, sl st to first sc. Fasten off.

5th round: Using B join into last 2ch arch of 4th round, 1ch, *[1sc, 1hdc, 1dc] into 2ch arch, 1ch, 1dc into next sc, 1ch, [1dc, 1hdc, 1sc] into next 2ch arch, 1sc into each of next 6dc; rep from * twice, sl st to first sc. Fasten off.

6th round: Using A join into same place, 1ch, 1sc into same place as 1ch, 3ch, 1sc into each of next 2 sts, 3ch, *2sc into next ch sp, 3ch, 3sc into dc at corner, 3ch, 2sc into next ch sp, 3ch**, [1sc into each of next 2 sts, 3ch] 6 times; rep from * and from * to ** again, [1sc into each of next 2 sts, 3ch] 4 times, 1sc into next st, sl st to first sc. Fasten off.

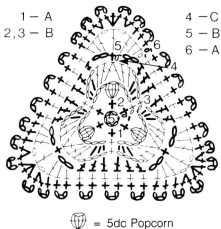

⬡ = 5dc Popcorn

Motifs

Traditional Square I

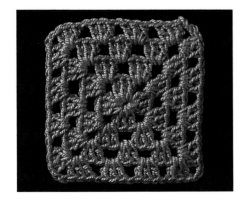

Base ring: 4ch, join with sl st.

1st round: 5ch (count as 1dc and 2ch), [3dc into ring, 2ch] 3 times, 2dc into ring, sl st to 3rd of 5ch.

2nd round: Sl st into next ch, 5ch (count as 1dc and 2ch), 3dc into same sp, *1ch, skip 3dc, [3dc, 2ch, 3dc] into next sp; rep from * twice, 1ch, skip 3 sts, 2dc into same sp as 5ch at beg of round, sl st to 3rd of 5ch.

3rd round: Sl st into next ch, 5ch (count as 1dc and 2ch), 3dc into same sp, *1ch, skip 3dc, 3dc into next sp, 1ch, skip 3dc**, [3dc, 2ch, 3dc] into next sp; rep from * twice and from * to ** again, 2dc into same sp as 5ch, sl st to 3rd of 5ch.

4th round: Sl st into next ch, 5ch (count as 1dc and 2ch), 3dc into same sp, *[1ch, skip 3dc, 3dc into next sp] twice, 1ch, skip 3dc**, [3dc, 2ch, 3dc] into next sp; rep from * twice and from * to ** again, 2dc into same sp as 5ch, sl st to 3rd of 5ch.

Fasten off.

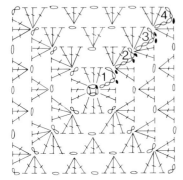

Traditional Square II

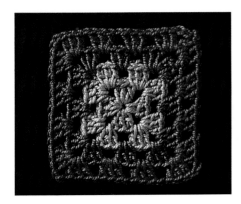

Worked as Traditional Square I.
Work 1 round each in colors A, B, C and D.

Double Crochet Square I

Base ring: 4ch, join with sl st.

1st round: 5ch (count as 1dc and 2ch), [3dc into ring, 2ch] 3 times, 2dc into ring, sl st to 3rd of 5ch. (4 groups of 3dc).

2nd round: Sl st into next ch, 7ch (count as 1dc and 4ch), *2dc into same arch, 1dc into each dc across side of square**, 2dc into next arch, 4ch; rep from * twice and from * to ** again, 1dc into same arch as 7ch, sl st to 3rd of 7ch (4 groups of 7dc).

3rd round: As 2nd round. (4 groups of 11dc).

4th round: As 2nd round. (4 groups of 15dc).

Fasten off.

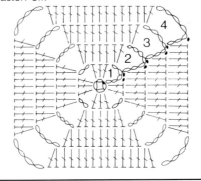

Double Crochet Square II

Worked as Double Crochet Square I.
Work 1 round each in colors A, B, C and D.

French Square

Note: For description of hdc3tog and hdc4tog see page 14 (Puff Stitch).

Base ring: 6ch, join with sl st.

1st round: 4ch (count as 1dc and 1ch), [1dc into ring, 1ch] 11 times, sl st to 3rd of 4ch. (12 spaces).

2nd round: Sl st into next ch, 3ch, work hdc3tog into same sp (counts as hdc4tog), *2ch, work hdc4tog into next sp, 3ch, 1tr into next dc, 3ch, work hdc4tog into next sp, 2ch**, hdc4tog into next sp; rep from * twice more and from * to ** again, sl st to top of first cluster.

3rd round: 1ch, 1sc into same place, *2ch, skip next 2ch sp, 4dc into next 3ch sp, 2ch, 1tr into next tr, 3ch, insert hook down through top of last tr and work sl st, 2ch, 4dc into next 3ch sp, 2ch, skip next 2ch sp, 1sc into next cluster; rep from * 3 more times, omitting sc at end, sl st to first sc.

Fasten off.

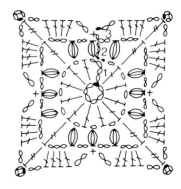

Italian Square

Note: For description of hdc3tog and hdc4tog see page 14 (Puff Stitch).

○ Chain ● Slip stitch + Single crochet T Half double crochet ⊤ Double crochet ‡ Treble ‡ Double treble

Base ring: 4ch, join with sl st.

1st round: 3ch (count as 1dc), 11dc into ring, sl st to top of 3ch. (12 sts).

2nd round: 3ch, work hdc3tog into same place as 3ch (counts as hdc4tog), *[1ch, work hdc4tog into next st] twice, 5ch**; hdc4tog into next st; rep from * twice more and from * to ** again, sl st to top of first cluster.

3rd round: Sl st into next sp, 3ch, work hdc3tog into same sp (counts as hdc4tog), *1ch, hdc4tog into next sp, 2ch, 5dc into next 5ch arch, 2ch**, hdc4tog into next sp; rep from * twice more and from * to ** again, sl st to top of first cluster.

4th round: Sl st into next sp, 3ch, work hdc3tog into same sp (counts as hdc4tog), *3ch, skip 2ch, [1dc into next dc, 1ch] twice, work [1dc, 1ch, 1dc, 1ch, 1dc] into next dc, [1ch, 1dc into next dc] twice, 3ch, skip 2ch**, work hdc4tog into next sp; rep from * twice more and again from * to **, sl st to top of first cluster.

5th round: 1ch, 1sc into each ch and each st all round, but working 3sc into 3rd of 5 dc at each corner, ending sl st to first sc.

Fasten off.

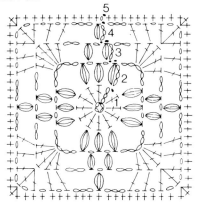

Christmas Rose Square

Note: For description of dc3tog and dc4tog see page 10.

Base ring: Using A, 6ch, join with sl st.

1st round: 5ch (count as 1dc and 2ch), [1dc into ring, 2ch] 7 times, sl st to 3rd of 5ch. (8 spaces).

2nd round: 3ch, work dc3tog into next sp (counts as dc4tog), [5ch, work dc4tog into next sp] 7 times, 5ch, sl st to top of first cluster. Fasten off.

3rd round: Using B join into same place, 1ch, 1sc into same place, *2ch, working over the 5ch arch so as to enclose it work 1dc into next dc of 1st round, 2ch, 1sc into top of next cluster; rep from * all round omitting sc at end, sl st to first sc.

4th round: Sl st into next ch, 1ch, 1sc into same place, *3ch, 1sc into next sp; rep from * all round omitting sc at end, sl st to first sc.

5th round: Sl st into next ch, 3ch (count as 1dc), [1dc, 2ch, 2dc] into same arch, *2ch, 1sc into next arch, [3ch, 1sc into next arch] twice, 2ch**, [2dc, 2ch, 2dc] into next arch; rep from * twice more and from * to ** again, sl st to top of 3ch.

Fasten off.

1,2 – A   3,4,5 – B

Baltic Square

Note: For description of Popcorn see page 14.

Base ring: 8ch, join with sl st.

1st round: 3ch, 4dc Popcorn into ring (counts as 5dc Popcorn), [5ch, 5dc Popcorn into ring] 3 times, 5ch, sl st to top of first Popcorn.

2nd round: 3ch (count as 1dc), *work [2dc, 2ch, 5dc Popcorn, 2ch, 2dc] into next 5ch arch**, 1dc into next Popcorn; rep from * twice more and from * to ** again, sl st to top of 3ch.

3rd round: 3ch (count as 1dc), 1dc into each of next 2 sts, *2dc into next sp, 2ch, 5dc Popcorn into next Popcorn, 2ch, 2dc into next sp**, 1dc into each of next 5dc; rep from * twice more and from * to ** again, 1dc into each of last 2dc, sl st to top of 3ch.

4th round: 3ch (count as 1dc), 1dc into each of next 4dc, *2dc into next sp, 2ch, 5dc

Popcorn into next Popcorn, 2ch, 2dc into next sp**, 1dc into each of next 9dc; rep from * twice more and from * to ** again, 1dc into each of last 4dc, sl st to top of 3ch.

Fasten off.

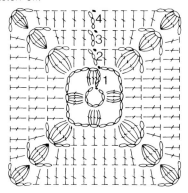

Cranesbill Lace Square

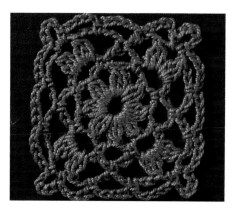

Note: For description of dc2tog and dc3tog see page 10.

Base ring: 6ch, join with sl st.

1st round: 3ch, dc2tog into ring (counts as dc3tog), [3ch, dc3tog into ring] 7 times, 3ch, sl st to top of first cluster.

2nd round: Sl st to center of next 3ch arch, 1ch, 1sc into same place, [5ch, 1sc into next arch] 7 times, 2ch, 1dc into first sc.

3rd round: *5ch, [dc3tog, 3ch, dc3tog] into next arch**, 5ch, 1sc into next arch; rep from * twice and from * to ** again, 2ch, 1dc into dc which closed 2nd round.

4th round: *5ch, 1sc into next arch, 5ch, [1sc, 5ch, 1sc] into corner 3ch arch, 5ch, 1sc into next 5ch arch; rep from * 3 times, ending last rep into dc which closed 3rd round, sl st to first ch.

Fasten off.

Motifs

Rose Square

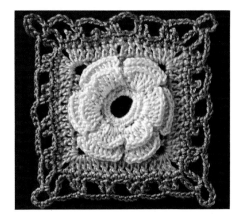

Base ring: Using A, 12ch, join with sl st.

1st round: 1ch, 18sc into ring, sl st to first sc. (18 sts).

2nd round: 1ch, beginning into same st as 1ch [1sc, 3ch, skip 2 sts] 6 times, sl st to first sc.

3rd round: 1ch, work a petal of [1sc, 3ch, 5dc, 3ch, 1sc] into each of next 6 3ch arches, sl st to first sc.

4th round: 1ch, [1sc between 2sc, 5ch behind petal of 3rd round] 6 times, sl st to first sc.

5th round: 1ch, work a petal of [1sc, 3ch, 7dc, 3ch, 1sc] into each of next 6 5ch arches, sl st to first sc. Fasten off.

6th round: Using B join between 2sc, 1ch, [1sc between 2sc, 6ch behind Petal of 5th round] 6 times, sl st to first sc.

7th round: Sl st into next ch, 3ch (count as 1dc), *[4dc, 2ch, 1dc] all into same arch,

6dc into next arch, [2dc, 2ch, 4dc] all into next arch**, 1dc into next arch; rep from * to **, sl st to top of 3ch.

8th round: 3ch (count as 1dc), 1dc into each dc all round with [3dc, 2ch, 3dc] into each 2ch corner sp, ending sl st to top of 3ch. Fasten off.

9th round: Using C join into same place, 1ch, 1sc into same st as 1ch, *1sc into next st, work a 3ch picot of [3ch, sl st down through top of last sc made] twice, 1sc into each of next 3 sts, work [3ch picot, 1sc into next st] twice, [1sc, 7ch, 1sc] into corner 2ch sp, [1sc into next st, 3ch picot] twice, 1sc into each of next 3 sts, [3ch picot, 1sc into next st] twice, 1sc into next st; rep from * 3 times omitting sc at end of last rep, sl st to first sc.

10th round: Sl st across to top of next 3ch picot, 1ch, 1sc into same picot, *5ch, skip next picot, 1sc into next picot, 5ch, [1sc, 7ch, 1sc] into corner 7ch arch, [5ch, skip next picot, 1sc into next picot] twice, 5ch, 1sc into next picot; rep from * 3 times omitting sc at end of last rep, sl st to first sc.

Fasten off.

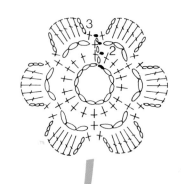

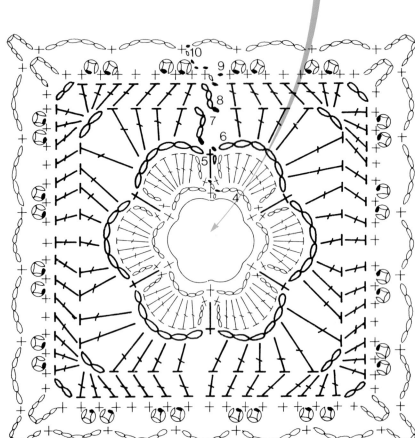

Popcorn Wheel Square

Note: For description of Popcorn see page 14.

Base ring: 6ch, join with sl st.

1st round: 3ch (count as 1dc), 4dc into ring and complete as for 5dc Popcorn, [3ch, 5dc Popcorn into ring] 7 times, 3ch, sl st to first Popcorn.

2nd round: 3ch (count as 1dc), 1dc into next 3ch arch, [9dc into next arch, 2dc into next arch] 3 times, 9dc into last arch, sl st to top of 3ch.

3rd round: 1ch, 1sc into same place as 1ch, 1sc into next st, *into next 9dc group work 1sc into each of first 3dc, skip 1dc, [1hdc, 4dc, 1hdc] into next dc, skip 1dc, 1sc into each of last 3dc**, 1sc into each of next 2 sts; rep from * twice and from * to ** again, sl st to first sc.

Fasten off.

= 5dc Popcorn

Floribunda

○ Chain ● Slip stitch + Single crochet T Half double crochet ‡ Double crochet ‡ Treble ‡ Double treble

Base ring: Using A, 6ch, join with sl st.

1st round: 1ch, 16sc into ring, sl st to first sc. (16 sts).

2nd round: 6ch (count as 1dc and 3ch arch), skip 2 sts, [1dc into next st, 3ch, skip 1 st] 7 times, sl st to 3rd of 6ch.

3rd round: 1ch, work a petal of [1sc, 1hdc, 5dc, 1hdc, 1sc] into each of next 8 3ch arches, sl st to first sc. Fasten off.

4th round: Using B join between 2sc, 1ch, [1sc between 2sc, 6ch behind petal of 3rd round] 8 times, sl st to first sc.

5th round: 1ch, work a petal of [1sc, 1hdc, 6dc, 1hdc, 1sc] into each of next 8 arches, sl st to first sc. Fasten off.

6th round: Using C join into 2nd dc of petal of 5th round, 1ch, 1sc into same place as 1ch, 6ch, skip 2dc, 1sc into next dc, [6ch, 1sc into 2nd dc of next petal, 6ch, skip 2dc, 1sc into next dc] 7 times, 3ch, 1dc into first sc.

7th round: 3ch (count as 1dc), 3dc into arch formed by dc which closed 6th round, *4ch, 1sc into next arch, [6ch, 1sc into next arch] twice, 4ch**, [4dc, 4ch] into next arch; rep from * twice and from * to ** again, ending [4dc, 4ch] into last ch arch, sl st to top of 3ch.
Fasten off.

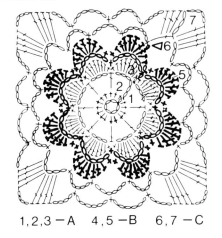

1,2,3 — A   4,5 — B   6,7 — C

Daisy Cluster Square

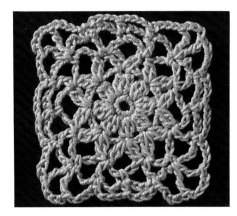

Note: For description of dc2tog and dc3tog see page 10.

Base ring: Wrap yarn round finger.

1st round: 1ch, 8sc into ring, sl st to first sc. (8 sts).

2nd round: 3ch, dc2tog into first st (counts as dc3tog), [3ch, dc3tog into next st] 7 times, 3ch, sl st to top of first cluster.

3rd round: 3ch, 1dc into first st (counts as dc2tog), *skip 3ch, [dc2tog, 5ch, dc2tog] all into next cluster; rep from * 6 times, dc2tog into next cluster, 5ch, sl st to top of 3ch.

4th round: Sl st into next cluster, 7ch (counts as 1dc and 4ch), [1sc into next 5ch arch, 4ch, skip 1 cluster, 1dc into next cluster, 4ch] 7 times, 1sc into next arch, 4ch, sl st to 3rd of 7ch.

5th round: 1ch, 1sc into same place as 1ch, *4ch, skip 4ch, [1tr, 4ch, 1tr] into next sc, 4ch, skip 4ch, 1sc into next dc, 4ch, skip 4ch, 1hdc into next sc, 4ch, skip 4ch, 1sc into next dc; rep from * 3 times, omitting sc at end of last rep, sl st to first sc.
Fasten off.

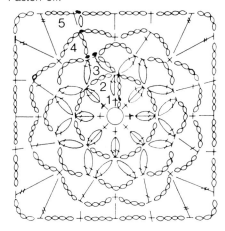

Sow Thistle Square

Note: For description of dc2tog and dc3tog see page 10.

Base ring: Using A, 4ch, join with sl st.

1st round: 4ch (count as 1dc and 1ch), [1dc, 1ch] 11 times into ring, sl st to 3rd of 4ch. Fasten off. (12 spaces).

2nd round: Using B join into sp, 3ch, dc2tog into same sp (counts as dc3tog), [3ch, dc3tog into next sp] 11 times, 3ch, sl st to top of first cluster. Fasten off.

3rd round: Using A join into 3ch arch, 1ch, 1sc into same arch, [5ch, 1sc into next arch] 11 times, 2ch, 1dc into first sc. Fasten off.

4th round: Using B join into same place, 1ch, 1sc into same place, *5ch, 1sc into next arch, 1ch, [5dc, 3ch, 5dc] into next arch, 1ch, 1sc into next arch; rep from * 3 times, omitting 1sc at end of last rep, sl st to first sc.
Fasten off.

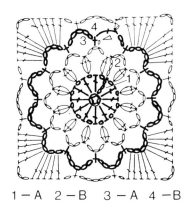

1 — A   2 — B   3 — A   4 — B

Daisy Wheel Square

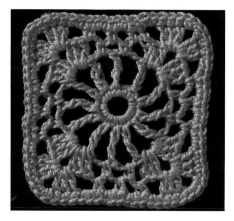

Base ring: 8ch, join with sl st.

1st round: 1ch, 12sc into ring, sl st to first sc. (12 sts).

2nd round: 6ch (count as 1tr and 2ch), skip 1 st, [1tr into next st, 2ch] 11 times, sl st to 4th of 6ch.

3rd round: 5ch (counts as 1dc and 2ch), *[1sc into next sp, 2ch] twice, [3dc, 2ch, 3dc] into next sp, 2ch; rep from * 3 times, omitting 1dc and 2ch at end of last rep, sl st to 3rd of 5ch.

4th round: 1ch, *[1sc into next sp, 2ch] 3 times, [3dc, 2ch, 3dc] into corner sp, 2ch; rep from * 3 times, sl st to first sc.

5th round: 1ch, work 2sc into each sp and 1sc into each st all round, but working 3sc into each corner sp, sl st to first sc.
Fasten off.

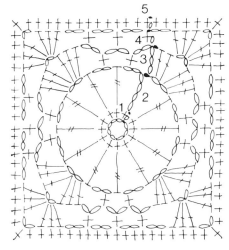

Motifs

Puff Stitch Square

Base ring: 8ch, join with sl st.

Special Abbreviation

Puff st = hdc5tog, (see page 14).

1st round: 2ch, hdc4tog into ring (counts as 1 Puff st), 2ch, work [Puff st, 2ch] 7 times into ring, sl st to first Puff st.

2nd round: 5ch (count as 1dc and 2ch), 1dc into same Puff st, *2ch, [Puff st into next sp, 2ch] twice**, work a V st of [1dc, 2ch, 1dc] into next Puff st; rep from * twice and from * to ** again, sl st to 3rd of 5ch.

3rd round: Sl st into next ch, 5ch (count as 1dc and 2ch), 1dc into same sp, *2ch, [Puff st into next sp, 2ch] 3 times**, V st into next sp at corner; rep from * twice and from * to ** again, sl st to 3rd of 5ch.

4th round: As for 3rd round, but work 4 Puff sts along each side of square.

5th round: As for 3rd round, but work 5 Puff sts along each side of square.

Fasten off.

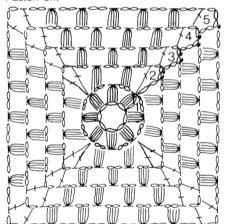

Spanish Square

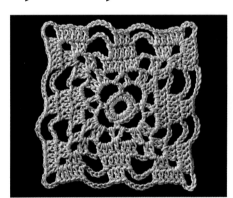

Note: For description of dc2tog see page 10.

Base ring: 8ch, join with sl st.

1st round: 1ch, 16sc into ring, sl st to first sc. (16 sts).

2nd round: 1ch, 1sc into same place as 1ch, [7ch, skip 3 sts, 1sc into next st] 3 times, 7ch, skip 3 sts, sl st to first sc.

3rd round: Sl st across to 3rd ch of next arch, 3ch (count as 1dc), 1dc into same place, *[3ch, 2dc] into same arch, 3ch, dc2tog inserting hook into same arch for first leg and into next arch for 2nd leg, 3ch, 2dc into same arch; rep from * 3 times, omitting 2dc at end of last rep, sl st to top of 3ch.

4th round: Sl st into next dc and next ch, 3ch (count as 1dc), 1dc into same place, *[3ch, 2dc] into same arch, 3ch, skip 2dc, 3dc into next 3ch, 1dc into next cluster, 3dc into next 3ch, 3ch, skip 2dc, 2dc into next arch; rep from * 3 times, omitting 2dc at end of last rep, sl st to top of 3ch.

5th round: Sl st into next dc and next ch, 3ch, 2dc into same place, *[3ch, 3dc] into same arch, 6ch, skip [2dc, 3ch, 1dc], 1dc into each of next 5dc, 6ch, skip [1dc, 3ch, 2dc], 3dc into next 3ch arch; rep from * 3 times, omitting 3dc at end of last rep, sl st to top of 3ch.

6th round: 3ch (count as 1dc), 1dc into each of next 2dc, *[3dc, 5ch, 3dc] into next 3ch arch, 1dc into each of next 3dc, 6ch, skip [6ch and 1dc], 1dc into each of next 3dc, 6ch, skip [1dc and 6ch], 1dc into each of next 3dc; rep from * 3 times, omitting 3dc at end of last rep, sl st to top of 3ch.

Fasten off.

Crystal Square

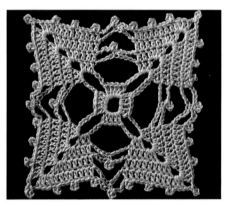

Base ring: 10ch, join with sl st.

1st round: 14ch, [5dc into ring, 11ch] 3 times, 4dc into ring, sl st to 3rd of 14ch.

2nd round: Sl st into each of next 5ch, 3ch (count as 1dc), [2dc, 3ch, 3dc] into same ch arch, *9ch, [3dc, 3ch, 3dc] into next arch; rep from * twice, 9ch, sl st to top of 3ch.

3rd round: 3ch (count as 1dc), 1dc into each of next 2dc, *[3dc, 3ch, 3dc] into 3ch sp, 1dc into each of next 3dc, 4ch, skip 4ch, 1sc into next ch, make a picot of [3ch, sl st down through top of last st], 4ch, skip 4ch**, 1dc into each of next 3dc; rep from * twice and from * to ** again, sl st to top of 3ch.

4th round: 3ch (count as 1dc), 1dc into each of next 5dc, *[3dc, 3ch, 3dc] into 3ch sp, 1dc into each of next 6dc, 9ch**, 1dc into each of next 6dc; rep from * twice and from * to ** again, sl st to top of 3ch.

5th round: 6ch, sl st to 4th ch from hook (counts as 1dc and picot), *[1dc into each of next 4dc, picot] twice, work [3dc, 5ch, sl st to 4th ch from hook, 1ch, 3dc] into 3ch sp, 1dc into next dc, picot, [1dc into each of next 4dc, picot] twice, 4ch, skip 4dc, 1sc into next ch, picot, 4ch, skip 4ch**, 1dc into next dc, picot; rep from * twice and from * to ** again, sl st to top of 3ch.

Fasten off.

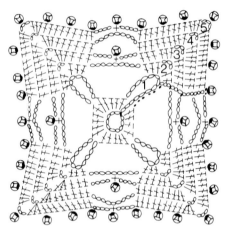

Moorish Medallion

Base ring: 6ch, join with sl st.

Special Abbreviation

Ssc (Spike single crochet) = insert hook 2 rounds below st indicated, i.e. into top of 1st round, yo, draw loop through and up to height of current round, yo, draw through both loops on hook (see also page 10).

1st round: 1ch, 16sc into ring, sl st to first sc. (16 sts).

2nd round: 1ch, 1sc into same place as 1ch, 1sc into next sc, *[1sc, 9ch, 1sc] into

○ Chain   ● Slip stitch   + Single crochet   T Half double crochet   ⊤ Double crochet   ⧧ Treble   ⧣ Double treble

next sc**, 1sc into each of next 3sc; rep from * twice and from * to ** again, 1sc into next sc, sl st to first sc.

3rd round: 1ch, 1sc into same place as 1ch, *skip next 2sc, work [2hdc, 17dc, 2hdc] into next 9ch arch, skip next 2sc, 1sc into next sc; rep from * 3 more times omitting 1sc at end of last rep and ending sl st to first sc.

4th round: 1ch, 1Ssc over first st, *5ch, skip 5 sts, 1sc into next st, 3ch, sl st into 3rd ch from hook, [5ch, skip 4 sts, 1sc into next st, 3ch, sl st into 3rd ch from hook] twice, 5ch, skip 5 sts, 1Ssc over next st; rep from * 3 times omitting Ssc at end of last rep and ending sl st to first Ssc.

Fasten off.

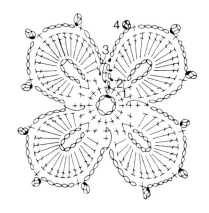

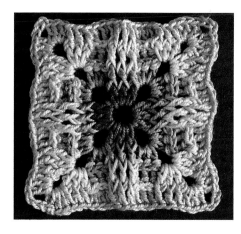

Russian Square

Note: For description of 1dc/rf and 1dc/rb see page 11.

Base ring: Using A, 8ch, join with sl st.

1st round: 6ch (count as 1dc and 3ch), [3dc into ring, 3ch] 3 times, 2dc into ring, sl st to 3rd of 6 ch. Fasten off.

2nd round: Using B join into a different corner sp, 3ch (count as 1dc), 2dc into same corner sp, *1dc/rf round each of next 3 sts**, [3dc, 3ch, 3dc] into next corner sp; rep from * twice more and from * to ** again, [3dc, 3ch] into last corner sp, sl st to top of 3 ch. Fasten off.

3rd round: Using C join into a different corner sp, 6ch (count as 1dc and 3ch), 3dc into same corner sp, *1dc/rb round each of next 3 sts, 1dc/rf round each of next 3 sts, 1dc/rb round each of next 3 sts**, [3dc, 3ch, 3dc] into next corner sp; rep from * twice more and from * to ** again, 2dc into last corner sp, sl st to 3rd of 6ch. Fasten off.

4th round: Using D join into a different corner sp, 3ch (count as 1dc), 2dc into same corner sp, *[1dc/rf round each of next 3 sts, 1dc/rb round each of next 3 sts] twice, 1dc/rf round each of next 3 sts**, [3dc, 3ch, 3dc] into next corner sp; rep from * twice more and from * to ** again, [3dc, 3ch] into last corner sp, sl st to top of 3ch.

Fasten off.

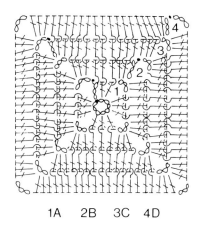

1A   2B   3C   4D

Frozen Star

Note: For description of dtr3tog, dtr4tog and tr3tog see page 10.

Base ring: 12ch, join with sl st.

1st round: 1ch, 24sc into ring, sl st to first sc. (24 sts).

2nd round: 6ch, dtr3tog over next 3 sts (counts as dtr4tog), [7ch, dtr4tog over same st as last leg of previous cluster and next 3 sts] 7 times, 7ch, sl st to top of first cluster.

3rd round: 1ch, 1sc into same place as 1ch, *[3ch, skip 1ch, 1sc into next ch] 3 times, 3ch, skip 1ch, 1sc into top of next cluster; rep from * 7 times, omitting sc at end of last rep, sl st to first sc.

4th round: Sl st to center of next 3ch arch, 1ch, 1sc into same arch, *3ch, 1sc into next arch; rep from * to end, omitting sc at end of last rep, sl st to first sc.

5th round: As 4th round.

6th round: Sl st to center of next 3ch arch, 1ch, 1sc into same arch, *[3ch, 1sc into next arch] 4 times, 3ch, skip next arch, work [tr3tog, 5ch, dtr4tog, 4ch, sl st to top of last cluster, 5ch, tr3tog] into next arch, 3ch, skip next arch, 1sc into next arch; rep from * 3 times, omitting sc at end of last rep, sl st to first sc.

Fasten off.

Spider Square

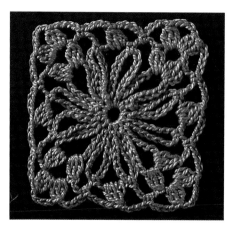

Note: For description of dc2tog and dc3tog see page 10.

Base ring: 6ch, join with sl st.

1st round: 1ch, [1sc into ring, 15ch] 12 times, sl st to first sc.

2nd round: Sl st along to center of next 15ch arch, 3ch, dc2tog into same arch (counts as dc3tog), *4ch, dc3tog into same arch, [4ch, 1sc into next arch] twice, 4ch, dc3tog into next arch; rep from * 3 times, omitting dc3tog at end of last rep, sl st to first cluster.

3rd round: Sl st into next arch, 3ch, dc2tog into same arch (counts as dc3tog), *4ch, dc3tog into same arch, [4ch, 1sc into next 4ch arch, 4ch, dc3tog into next 4ch arch] twice; rep from * 3 times, omitting dc3tog at end of last rep, sl st to first cluster.

Fasten off.

Motifs

Spiral Pentagram

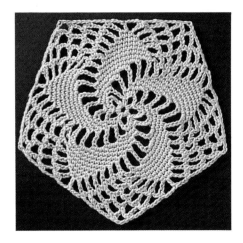

Base ring: 5ch, join with sl st.

1st round: [6ch, 1sc into ring] 5 times. (Hint: mark last sc of each round with contrasting thread.)

2nd round: [6ch, 3sc into next 6ch arch] 5 times.

3rd round: [6ch, 3sc into next 6ch arch, 1sc into each of next 2sc] 5 times. (5 blocks of 5sc each).

4th round: [6ch, 3sc into next 6ch arch, 1sc into each sc of next block except skip last sc] 5 times. (5 blocks of 7sc each).

Continue as given on 4th round for 3 more rounds finishing with 5 blocks of 13sc each.

8th round: *5ch, 1sc into center of next 6ch arch, 5ch, skip 1sc, 1sc into each sc of next block except last; rep from * 4 more times.

9th round: *[5ch, 1sc into next arch] twice, 5ch, skip 1sc, 1sc into each sc of next block except last sc; rep from * 4 more times.

Continue as given on 9th round for 3 more rounds, but work 1 more 5ch arch in each segment on each round at same time as number of sc in each block reduces, finishing with 6 arches and 3sc in each of 5 segments.

13th round: 5ch, 1sc into next arch, *[3ch, 1sc into next arch] 5 times, 3ch, 1dc into 2nd of next 3sc, 3ch, 1sc into next arch; rep from * 4 more times omitting sc at end of last rep, sl st to first sc.

Fasten off.

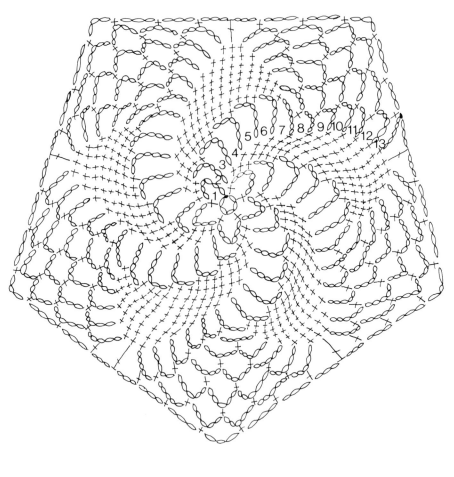

2-Color Star

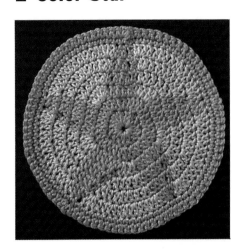

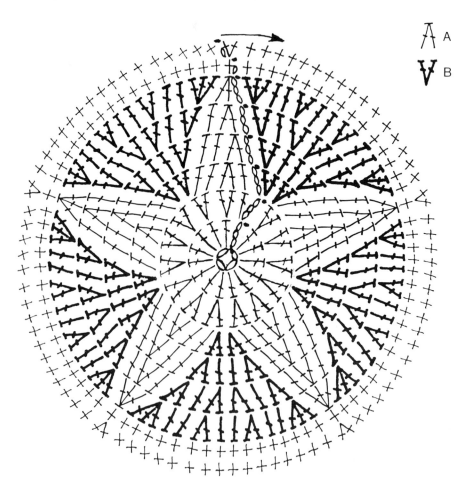

$\wedge$ A

$\vee$ B

---

80   ○ Chain   ● Slip stitch   + Single crochet   T Half double crochet   ⊤ Double crochet   ⊥ Treble   ⊥ Double treble

Note: For description of changing color see page 7; for dc2tog and dc3tog see page 10.

Base ring: Using A, 4ch, join with sl st.

1st round: 3ch (count as 1dc), 14dc into ring, sl st to top of 3ch. (15 sts).

2nd round: 3ch (count as 1dc), 1dc into same place as 3ch, 2dc into next and each dc all round, sl st to top of 3ch. (30 sts).

3rd round: 3ch (count as 1dc), *1dc into next st, dc2tog over next 2 sts, 1dc into each of next 2 sts, change to B, 2dc into same place as last dc with A, 2dc into next st, change to A**, 1dc into same place as last dc with B; rep from * 3 more times and from * to ** again, sl st to top of 3ch.

4th round: 3ch (count as 1dc), *dc2tog over next 2 sts, 1dc into each of next 2 sts, change to B, 2dc into next st, 1dc into each of next 2 sts, 2dc into next st, change to A**, 1dc into next st; rep from * 3 more times and from * to ** again, sl st to top of 3ch.

5th round: 3ch (count as 1dc), *dc2tog over next 2 sts, 1dc into next st, change to B, 2dc into next st, 1dc into next st, 2dc into each of next 2 sts, 1dc into next st, 2dc into next st, change to A**, 1dc into next st; rep from * 3 more times and from * to ** again, sl st to top of 3ch.

6th round: 3ch, *dc2tog over next 2 sts (counts as dc3tog), change to B, 3dc into next st, [1dc into each of next 2 sts, 2dc into next st] twice, 1dc into each of next 2 sts, 3dc into next st, change to A**, dc3tog over next 3 sts; rep from * 3 more times and from * to ** again, sl st to top of first cluster.

7th round: Continue using A only 1ch, 1sc into same place as 1ch, 1sc into next and each st all round, sl st to first sc, turn.

8th round (wrong side): 1ch, 2sc into same place as 1ch, 1sc into next and each st all round, except 2sc into each of 4 sts corresponding to remaining points of Star, ending sl st to first sc.

Fasten off.

from * to ** again, 1dc into last sp, 1ch, sl st to top of 3ch.

3rd round: 3ch (count as 1dc), 1dc/rb round each dc and 1 V st into each sp all round, ending with a sl st to top of 3ch. (6 groups of 6dc).

4th round: As 3rd round. (6 groups of 8dc).

5th round: As 3rd round. (6 groups of 10dc Fasten off.

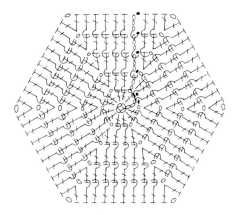

Ridged Hexagon II

Worked as Ridged Hexagon I.
Work 1 round each in colors A, B, C, D and E.

Ridged Hexagon I

Note: For description of dc/rb see page 11 (Raised Stitches).

Base ring: 4ch, join with sl st.

1st round: 3ch (count as 1dc), 1dc into ring, [1ch, 2dc into ring] 5 times, 1ch, sl st to top of 3ch. (6 spaces).

2nd round: Sl st into next dc and into next ch, 3ch (count as 1dc), *1dc/rb round each of next 2dc**, work a V st of [1dc, 1ch, 1dc] into next sp; rep from * 4 more times and

Traditional Hexagon I

Note: For description of dc2tog and dc3tog see page 10.

Base ring: 6ch, join with sl st.

1st round: 3ch, dc2tog into ring (counts as dc3tog), [3ch, dc3tog into ring] 5 times, 1ch, 1hdc into top of first cluster.

2nd round: 3ch, dc2tog into arch formed by hdc (counts as dc3tog), *3ch, work [dc3tog, 3ch, dc3tog] into next sp: rep from * 4 more times, 3ch, dc3tog into last sp, 1ch, 1hdc into top of first cluster.

3rd round: 3ch, dc2tog into arch formed by hdc (counts as dc3tog), *3ch, work [dc3tog, 3ch, dc3tog] into next sp**, 3ch, dc3tog into next sp; rep from * 4 more times and from * to ** again, 1ch, 1hdc into top of first cluster.

4th round: 3ch (counts as 1dc), 1dc into arch formed by hdc, *3ch, [3dc into next sp, [3dc, 2ch, 3dc] into next sp**, 3dc into next sp; rep from * 4 more times and from * to ** again, 1dc into next sp, sl st to top of 3ch.

5th round: 1ch, 1sc into same place, 1sc into each dc and each ch all round, ending sl st to first sc.

Fasten off.

Traditional Hexagon II

Worked as Traditional Hexagon I.
Work 1 round each in colors A, B, C, D and E.

Motifs

2-Color Popcorn Hexagon

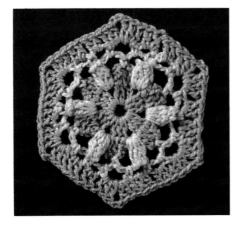

Note: For description of Popcorn see page 14.

Base ring: Using A, 6ch, join with sl st.

1st round: 3ch (count as 1dc), 2dc into ring, [2ch, 3dc into ring] 5 times, 2ch, sl st to top of 3ch. (6 spaces).

2nd round: 1ch, 1sc into same place, *2ch, 1dc into next dc, 2ch, 1sc into next dc, 1ch, sl st into each of next 2 ch, 1ch, 1sc into next dc; rep from * 5 more times omitting last sc and ending sl st to first sc. Fasten off.

3rd round: Using B, join into 2ch sp, 3ch, 4dc Popcorn into same sp (counts as 5dc Popcorn), *4ch, skip 1sc and 2ch, 1sc into next dc, 4ch, skip 2ch and 1sc, 5dc Popcorn into next sp; rep from * 5 more times omitting last Popcorn and ending sl st to top of first Popcorn.

4th round: 1ch, 1sc into same place, *[3ch, 1sc into next arch] twice, 3ch, 1sc into next Popcorn; rep from * 5 more times omitting last sc and ending sl st to first sc. Fasten off.

5th round: Using A, join into next ch, 3ch (count as 1dc), 1dc into same sp, *[3dc, 2ch, 3dc] into next sp**, 2dc into each of next 2 sps; rep from * 4 more times and from * to ** again, 2dc into next sp, sl st to top of 3ch.

Fasten off.

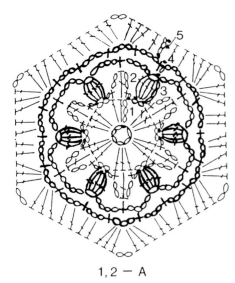

1, 2 — A
3, 4 — B
5 — A

Eastern Star

Base ring: 6ch, join with sl st.

1st round: 1ch, [1sc into ring, 3ch] 12 times, sl st to first sc.

2nd round: Sl st into each of next 2ch, 1ch, 1sc into same 3ch arch, [3ch, 1sc into next 3ch arch] 11 times, 1ch, 1hdc into top of first sc.

3rd round: *6ch, 1sc into next 3ch arch**, 3ch, 1sc into next 3ch arch; rep from * 4 more times and from * to ** again, 1ch, 1dc into hdc which closed previous round.

4th round: *[5dc, 2ch, 5dc] into next 6ch arch, 1sc into next 3ch arch; rep from * 5 more times ending last rep in dc which closed previous round, sl st into next st. Fasten off.

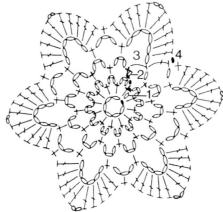

Water Wheel

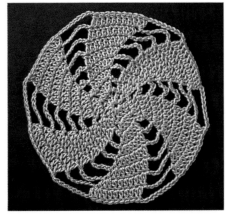

Note: For description of dc2tog see page 10.

Base ring: 4ch, join with sl st.

1st round: 3ch (count as 1dc), 1dc into ring, [2ch, 2dc into ring] 5 times, 2ch, sl st to top of 3ch.

2nd round: 3ch (count as 1dc), 2dc into same place as 3ch, 1dc into next dc, *3ch, skip 2ch, 3dc into next dc, 1dc into next dc; rep from * 4 more times, 3ch, skip 2ch, sl st to top of 3ch. (6 segments of 4dc and 3ch).

3rd round: 3ch (count as 1dc), 2dc into same place as 3ch, 1dc into next dc, dc2tog over next 2dc, *4ch, skip 2ch, 3dc into next dc, 1dc into next dc, dc2tog over next 2dc; rep from * 4 more times, 4ch, skip 3ch, sl st to top of 3ch.

4th round: 3ch (count as 1dc), 2dc into same place as 3ch, [1dc into next dc] twice, dc2tog over next 2dc, *5ch, skip 4ch, 3dc into next dc, [1dc into next dc] twice, dc2tog over next 2dc; rep from * 4 more times, 5ch, skip 4ch, sl st to top of 3ch.

5th round: 3ch (count as 1dc), 2dc into same place as 3ch, [1dc into next dc] 3 times, dc2tog over next 2dc, *6ch, skip 5ch, 3dc into next dc, [1dc into next dc] 3 times, dc2tog over next 2dc; rep from * 4 more times, 6ch, skip 5ch, sl st to top of 3ch.

6th, 7th and 8th rounds: As 5th round, but adding 1 more single dc in each dc block and 1 more ch in each ch arch on each round.

Fasten off.

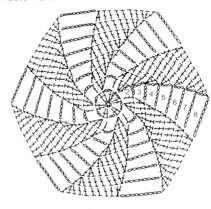

Little Gem

Note: For description of dc2tog and dc3tog see page 10; see also page 12 (Y Shapes).

Base ring: Using A, 5ch, join with sl st.

1st round: 4ch (count as 1tr), 2dc into 4th ch from hook, *3ch, 1tr into ring, 2dc into

---

82   ○ Chain ● Slip stitch + Single crochet ⊤ Half double crochet ╪ Double crochet ╪ Treble ╪ Double treble

base of stem of tr just made; rep from * 4 more times, 3ch, sl st to top of 4ch.

2nd round: 3ch, dc2tog over next 2dc (counts as dc3tog), *6ch, skip 3ch, dc3tog over next 3 sts; rep from * 5 more times omitting last dc3tog and ending sl st to top of first cluster. Fasten off.

3rd round: Using B join in to center of 3ch arch of 1st round, then so as to enclose 6ch arch of 2nd round work 1ch, 1sc into same place as 1ch, *5ch, 1dc into top of next cluster, 5ch, 1sc into 3ch arch of 1st round at same time enclosing 6ch arch of 2nd round; rep from * 5 more times omitting last sc and ending sl st into first sc. Fasten off.

4th round: Using C join in to same place, 1ch, 1sc into same place as 1ch, *5ch, skip 5ch, 3sc into next dc, 5ch, skip 5ch, 1sc into next sc; rep from * 5 more times omitting last sc and ending sl st into first sc.
Fasten off.

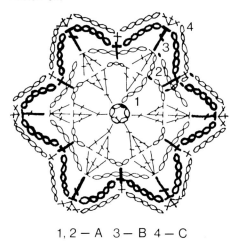

1, 2 – A 3 – B 4 – C

Snowflake

Base ring: 12ch, join with sl st.

1st round: 1ch, 24sc into ring, sl st to first sc. (24 sts).

2nd round: 1ch, 1sc into same place as 1ch, *1sc into next st, work a picot of [3ch, insert hook down through top of sc just made and work sl st]**, 1sc into next st; rep from * 10 times and from * to ** again, sl st to first sc.

3rd round: 8ch (count as 1tr and 4ch), skip Picot, [1tr into next sc between Picots, 4ch] 11 times, sl st to 4th of 8ch.

4th round: 1ch, [5sc into next 4ch arch] 12 times, sl st to first sc.

5th round: 1ch, *1sc into back loop only of each of next 5sc, 15ch, skip 5sc; rep from * 5 more times, sl st to first sc.

6th round: 1ch, *1sc into back loop only of each of next 5sc, 15sc into next 15ch arch; rep from * 5 more times, sl st to first sc.

7th round: Sl st into back loop only of next

st, 1ch, 1sc into same place as 1ch, 1sc into back loop only of each of next 2sc, *skip 1sc, [1sc into each of next 3sc, Picot] 4 times, 1sc into each of next 3sc, skip 1sc**, 1sc into back loop only of each of next 3sc; rep from * 4 more times and from * to ** again, sl st to first sc.
Fasten off.

Scallop Flower

Base ring: Using A, 6ch, join with sl st.

1st round: 3ch (count as 1dc), 17dc into ring, sl st to top of 3ch. (18 sts).

2nd round: 1ch, 1sc into same place as 1ch, *3ch, skip 2 sts, 1sc into next st; rep from * 5 more times omitting last sc and ending sl st to first sc. Fasten off.

3rd round: Using B join in to next ch, 1ch, *work a Petal of [1sc, 1hdc, 3dc, 1hdc, 1sc] into 3ch arch, sl st into next sc; rep from * 5 more times.

4th round: Sl st into each of next 4 sts to center dc of next Petal, 1ch, 1sc into same place as 1ch, *8ch, 1sc into center dc of next Petal; rep from * 5 more times omitting last sc and ending sl st to first sc. Fasten off.

5th round: Using A join in to next ch, 1ch, *work [1sc, 3hdc, 5dc, 3hdc, 1sc] into next arch; rep from * 5 more times, ending sl st into first sc.
Fasten off.

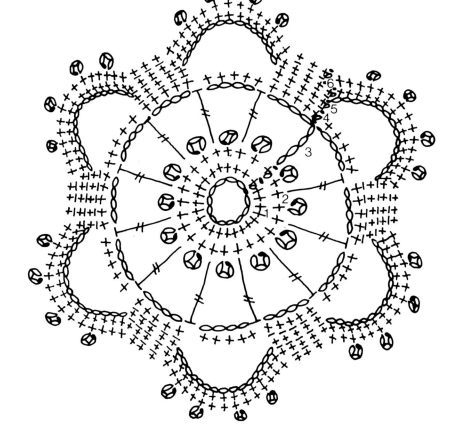

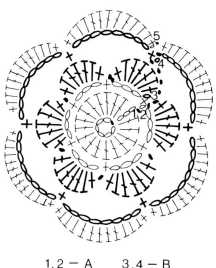

1, 2 – A   3, 4 – B
5 – A

83

Motifs

Ice Crystal

Note: For description of dc4tog and dc5tog see page 10.

Base ring: 6ch, join with sl st.

1st round: 1ch, 12sc into ring, sl st to first sc. (12 sts).

2nd round: 1ch, 1sc into same place as 1ch, [7ch, skip 1sc, 1sc into next sc] 5 times, 3ch, skip 1sc, 1tr into top of first sc.

3rd round: 3ch (count as 1dc), 4dc into arch formed by tr, [3ch, 5dc into next 7ch arch] 5 times, 3ch, sl st to top of 3ch.

4th round: 3ch (counts as 1dc), 1dc into each of next 4dc, *3ch, 1sc into next 3ch arch, 3ch**, 1dc into each of next 5dcs; rep from * 4 more times and from * to ** again, sl st to top of 3ch.

5th round: 3ch, dc4tog over next 4dcs (counts as dc5tog), *[5ch, 1sc into next 3ch arch] twice, 5ch**, dc5tog over next 5dcs; rep from * 4 more times and from * to ** again, sl st to first cluster.

6th round: Sl st into each of next 3ch, 1ch, 1sc into same place, *5ch, 1sc into next 5ch arch; rep from * all round omitting last sc and ending sl st to first sc.

7th round: Sl st into each of next 3ch, 1ch, 1sc into same place, *5ch, 1sc into next 5ch arch, 3ch, [5dc, 3ch, 5dc] into next arch, 3ch, 1sc into next arch; rep from * 5 more times omitting last sc and ending sl st to first sc.

Fasten off.

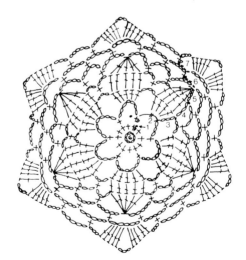

Rainbow Petal Motif

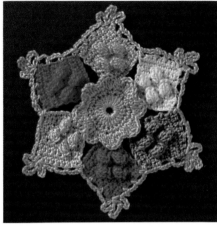

Note: For description of Popcorn see page 14; for sc2tog see page 10.

Center

Base ring: Using A (Blue), 6ch, join with sl st.

1st round: 3ch (count as 1dc), 23dc into ring, sl st to top of 3ch. (24 sts).

2nd round: 1ch, 1sc into same place as 1ch, 1sc into front loop only of next and each st all round, sl st to first sc.

3rd round: 1ch, 1sc into same place as 1ch, *work [1hdc, 1dc, 1tr] into next st, [1tr, 1dc, 1hdc] into next st, 1sc into next st; rep from * 7 more times, omitting sc at end of last rep, sl st to first st. Fasten off.

Star Blocks

Make 6 Star Blocks alike, 1 each in B (Red), C (Orange), D (Yellow), E (Green), F (Indigo) and G (Violet) as follows:

1st Block

Join yarn to back loop of any st in 1st round of Center and make 10ch, turn.

1st row (right side): Skip 2ch (count as 1sc), 1sc into next and each ch to end, turn. (9 sc).

2nd and every alt row: 1ch (counts as 1sc), skip first st, 1sc into next and each st to end working last st into tch, turn.

3rd row: Work as 2nd row but make a 5dc popcorn (to stand out on right side of fabric) on 5th st.

5th row: As 2nd row but making 5dc popcorns on the 3rd and 7th sts.

7th row: As 3rd row.

Work 2 more rows as 2nd row. (10 rows in all). Fasten off.

Remaining Blocks

Skip 3 sts of 1st round of Center and join new yarn into back loop of next st, then work as for 1st Block.

Edging

Making sure all parts of fabric are right side facing, join A at left corner of 1st Block, 1ch, sc2tog over same place as 1ch and right

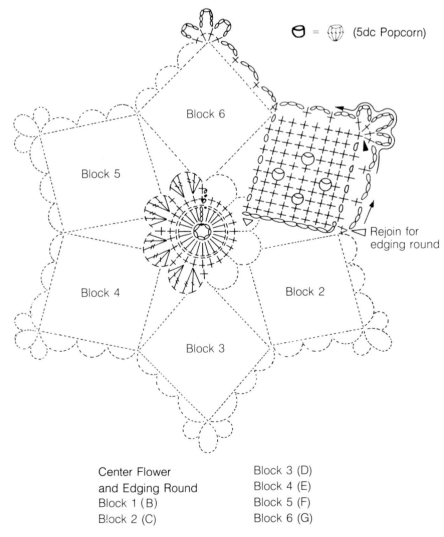

⊖ = (5dc Popcorn)

Center Flower
and Edging Round
Block 1 (B)
Block 2 (C)

Block 3 (D)
Block 4 (E)
Block 5 (F)
Block 6 (G)

○ Chain ● Slip stitch + Single crochet T Half double crochet ⌡ Double crochet ⌡ Treble ⌡ Double treble

corner of 2nd Block, *make 3 arches evenly spaced along edge of Block ending at top corner as follows: [3ch, 1sc into edge] 3 times, work [5ch, 1sc, 7ch, 1sc, 5ch, 1sc] into same corner, work 3 arches evenly spaced as before along next edge of same Block as follows: [3ch, 1sc into edge] twice, 3ch**, sc2tog over left corner of same Block and right corner of next Block; rep from * 4 more times and from * to ** again, sl st to first sc.

Fasten off.

Crystal Motif

Note: For description of sc3tog see page 10.

Base ring: Using A make 12ch, join with sl st.

1st round: 1ch, 1sc into ring, *work [7ch, 1sc, 4ch, 1dtr, 4ch, 1sc] into ring; rep from * 5 more times omitting sc at end of last rep, sl st to first sc. Fasten off.

2nd round: Join B into top of any dtr, 1ch, 1sc into same place as 1ch, *13ch, skip 7ch arch, 1sc into top of next dtr; rep from * 5 more times omitting sc at end of last rep, sl st to first sc.

3rd round: 1ch, 1sc into each of next 6ch, *3sc into next ch, 1sc into each of next 5ch**, sc3tog over [next ch, next sc and next ch], 1sc into each of next 5ch; rep from * 4 more times and from * to ** again, 1sc into next st, sl st to first sc.

4th round: 1ch, skip first st, 1sc into next st, *1sc into each of next 5 sts, 3sc into next st, 1sc into each of next 5sc**, sc3tog over next 3 sts; rep from * 4 more times and from * to ** again, 1sc into next st, sl st to first sc.

5th round: As 4th round. Fasten off.

6th round: Join C into same place, 1ch, 1sc into same place, *7ch, skip 6sc, work 1dtr, [5ch, 1dtr] 4 times into next sc at tip of star, 7ch, skip 6sc, 1sc into next sc cluster; rep from * 5 more times omitting sc at end of last rep, sl st to first sc.

Fasten off.

Mica Motif

Note: For description of dc3tog and dc4tog see page 10.

Base ring: 6ch, join with sl st.

1st round: 5ch (count as 1dc and 2ch), [1dc into ring, 2ch] 7 times, sl st to 3rd of 5ch. (8 spaces).

2nd round: 3ch (count as 1dc), [4dc into next sp, 1dc into next dc] 7 times, 4dc into next sp, sl st to top of 3ch. ·

3rd round: Sl st into next st, 3ch (count as 1dc), *1sc into each of next 2 sts, 1dc into next st, 5ch, skip 1 st**, 1dc into next st; rep from * 6 more times and from * to ** again, sl st to top of 3ch.

4th round: 3ch, dc3tog over next 3 sts (counts as dc4tog), *5ch, 1sc into next 5ch arch, 5ch**, dc4tog over next 4 sts; rep from * 6 more times and from * to ** again, sl st to top of first cluster.

5th round: 8ch (count as 1dc and 5ch), *1sc into next 5ch arch, 1sc into next sc, 1sc into next arch, 5ch**, 1dc into next cluster, 5ch; rep from * 6 more times and from * to ** again, sl st to 3rd of 8ch.

6th round: 10ch (count as 1dc and 7ch), skip 5ch, *1sc into 2nd of next 3sc, 7ch, skip 5ch**, 1dc into next dc, 7ch, skip 5ch; rep from * 6 more times and from * to ** again, sl st to 3rd of 10ch.

7th round: 6ch (count as 1dc and 3ch), 1dc into same place as 6ch, *[2ch, 1dc] 3 times into next 7ch arch, 1dc into next sc, [1dc, 2ch] 3 times into next 7ch arch**, work [1dc, 3ch, 1dc] into next dc; rep from * 6 more times and from * to ** again, sl st to 3rd of 6ch.

Fasten off.

1 — A

2, 3, 4, 5 — B

6 — C

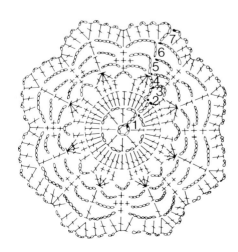

Motifs

Astrolabe Motif

Base ring: 4ch, join with sl st.

1st round: 4ch (count as 1dc and 1ch), [1dc into ring, 1ch] 7 times, sl st to 3rd of 4ch. (8 spaces).

2nd round: 1ch, 1sc into same place as 1ch, [3ch, skip 1ch, 1sc into next dc] 8 times omitting sc at end of last rep, sl st to first sc.

3rd round: Sl st into each of next 2ch, 1ch, 1sc into same place as 1ch, [6ch, 1sc into next 3ch arch] 8 times omitting sc at end of last rep, sl st to first sc.

4th round: Sl st into each of next 3ch, 1ch, 1sc into same place as 1ch, [6ch, 1sc into next arch] 8 times omitting sc at end of last rep, sl st to first sc.

5th round: 1ch, 1sc into same place as 1ch, *work [2dc, 4ch, 2dc] into next arch, 1sc into next sc; rep from * 7 more times omitting sc at end of last rep, sl st to first sc.

6th round: Sl st into each of next 2dc and next 2ch, 1ch, 1sc into same place as 1ch, [8ch, 1sc into next arch] 8 times omitting sc at end of last rep, sl st to first sc.

7th round: 1ch, *work a Wave of [1sc, 1hdc, 2dc, 1tr, 2dc, 1hdc, 1sc] into next arch; rep from * 7 more times, sl st to first sc.

8th round: Sl st into each of next 4 sts to tr, 1ch, 1sc into same place as 1ch, [11ch, 1sc into tr at center of next Wave] 8 times omitting sc at end of last rep, sl st to first sc.

9th round: 1ch, work [2sc, 2hdc, 2dc, 4tr, 2dc, 2hdc, 2sc] into next 11ch arch 8 times, sl st to first sc.
Fasten off.

Halley's Comet Motif

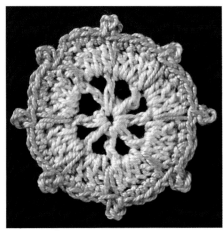

Special Abbreviation

Ssc (Spike single crochet) = insert hook below st indicated 1 row down, i.e. into top of 1st round, yo, draw loop through and up to height of current round, yo, draw through both loops on hook (see also page 10).

Base ring: Using A, 4ch, sl st to join.

1st round: 5ch (count as 1dc and 2ch), [1dc into ring, 2ch] 7 times, sl st to 3rd of 5ch. (8 spaces).

2nd round: 3ch (count as 1dc), 3dc into next sp, [1dc into next dc, 3dc into next sp] 7 times, sl st to top of 3ch. (32 sts). Fasten off.

3rd round: Join B into same place, 1ch, 1Ssc over first st, work a picot of [3ch, insert hook down through top of sc just made and work sl st to close], *1sc into next st, 2sc into next st, 1sc into next st**, 1Ssc over next st, picot; rep from * 6 more times and from * to ** again, sl st to first Ssc.
Fasten off.

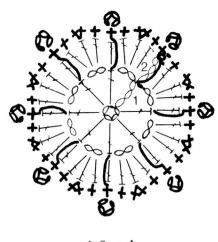

1, 2 — A

3 — B

Briar Rose

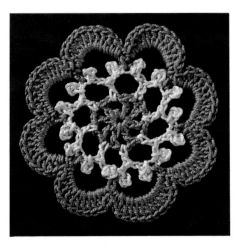

Base ring: Using A, 3ch, join with sl st.

1st round: 5ch (count as 1dc and 2ch), [1dc into ring, 2ch] 7 times, sl st to 3rd of 5ch. Fasten off. (8 spaces).

2nd round: Join B into a sp, 9ch, sl st into 4th ch from hook, 5ch, sl st into 4th ch from hook, 1ch, *1dc into next sp, work a picot of [5ch, sl st into 4th ch from hook] twice, 1ch; rep from * 6 more times, sl st to 3rd ch of starting ch. Fasten off.

3rd round: Join C into 1ch between 2 Picots, 1ch, 1sc into same place as 1ch, *7ch, skip [1 picot, 1dc and 1 picot], 1sc into next ch between picots; rep from * 7

○ Chain   ● Slip stitch   + Single crochet   T Half double crochet   ┴ Double crochet   ╪ Treble   ╪ Double treble

more times omitting sc at end of last rep, sl st to first sc.

4th round: Sl st into next ch, 1ch, *work [1sc, 1hdc, 9dc, 1hdc, 1sc] into next arch; rep from * 7 more times, sl st to first sc. Fasten off.

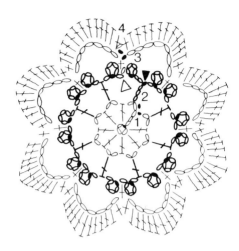

1 — A   2 — B

3, 4 — C

Galaxy Motif

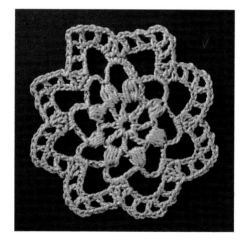

Note: For description of hdc4tog, hdc5tog, dc2tog, dc3tog see pages 14 and 10.
Base ring: 6ch, join with sl st.

1st round: 6ch (count as 1tr and 2ch), [1tr into ring, 2ch] 7 times, sl st to 4th of 6ch. (8 spaces).

2nd round: 2ch, work hdc4tog into next sp (counts as hdc5tog), work [7ch, hdc5tog into next sp] 7 times, 7ch, sl st to first cluster.

3rd round: Sl st into each of next 3ch, 1ch, 3sc into same arch, [9ch, 3sc into next arch] 7 times, 8ch, 1sc into first sc.

4th round: 3ch, dc2tog over next 1sc and next ch skipping sc between (counts as dc3tog), *2ch, skip 1ch, 1dc into next ch, 2ch, skip 1ch, work [1dc, 3ch, 1dc] into next ch, 2ch, skip 1ch, 1dc into next ch, 2ch, skip 1ch**, work dc3tog over [next ch, 2nd of next 3sc and next ch]; rep from * 6 more times and from * to ** again, sl st to top of first cluster.
Fasten off.

Sylvan Circles

Note: For description of dc2tog see page 10.

Base ring: 8ch, join with sl st.

1st round: 3ch (count as 1dc), 31dc into ring, sl st to top of 3ch. (32 sts).

2nd round: 3ch, 1dc into same place as 3ch (counts as dc2tog), 3ch, work dc2tog into same place as last cluster, *7ch, skip 3 sts, work [dc2tog, 3ch, dc2tog] into next st; rep from * 6 more times, 7ch, skip 3 sts, sl st to top of first cluster.

3rd round: Sl st into next ch, 3ch, 1dc into same place as 3ch (counts as dc2tog), 3ch, work dc2tog into same 3ch sp, *7ch, skip 7ch, work [dc2tog, 3ch, dc2tog] into next 3ch sp; rep from * 6 more times, 7ch, skip 7ch, sl st to top of first cluster.

4th round: Sl st into next ch, 3ch, 1dc into same place as 3ch (counts as dc2tog), 3ch, work dc2tog into same 3ch sp, *4ch, 1sc under 7ch arch of 2nd round so as to enclose 7ch arch of 3rd round, 4ch**, work [dc2tog, 3ch, dc2tog] into next 3ch sp; rep from * 6 more times and from * to ** again, sl st to top of first cluster.

5th round: Sl st into next ch, 3ch, 1dc into same place as 3ch (counts as dc2tog), 3ch, work dc2tog into same 3ch sp, *15ch, sl st into 12th ch from hook, 3ch, sl st to top of previous cluster, 6dc into 12ch ring, skip 4ch, sl st to next sc, 8dc into ring, skip 4ch, (inner half of Sylvan Circle completed)**, work [dc2tog, 3ch, dc2tog] into next 3ch sp; rep from * 6 more times and from * to ** again, sl st to top of first cluster.

6th round: *1ch, work [dc2tog, 6ch, sl st to 5th ch from hook, 1ch, dc2tog] into next 3ch sp, 1ch, sl st to top of next cluster, 16dc into 12ch ring (outer half of Sylvan Circle completed), sl st to top of next cluster; rep from * 7 times.

Fasten off.

Motifs

Flemish Motif

Base ring: 8ch, join with sl st.

1st round: 1ch, 16sc into ring, sl st to first sc. (16 sts).

2nd round: 12ch (count as 1tr and 8ch), skip first 2sc, [1tr into next sc, 8ch, skip 1sc] 7 times, sl st to 4th of 12 ch.

3rd round: 1ch, *into next 8 ch arch work [1sc, 1hdc, 1dc, 3tr, 4ch, insert hook down through top of tr just made and work a sl st to close, 2tr, 1dc, 1hdc, 1sc]; rep from * 7 more times, sl st to first sc.

Fasten off.

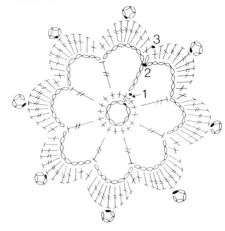

Barnacle Motif

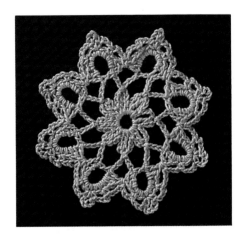

Base ring: 8ch, join with sl st.

1st round: 1ch, [1sc into ring, 3ch, 1tr into ring, 3ch] 8 times, sl st to first sc.

2nd round: Sl st into each of next 3ch and into tr, [12ch, 1dc into 9th ch from hook, 3ch, sl st to top of next tr] 8 times.

3rd round: Sl st into each of next 4ch, 3ch (count as 1dc), *work [1hdc, 7sc, 1hdc] into next 8ch arch, 1dc into next dc, skip last 3ch of same segment and first 3ch of next segment**, 1dc into next ch, (i.e. opposite side of same ch as dc of 2nd round); rep from * 6 more times and from * to ** again, sl st to top of 3ch.

4th round: 1ch, 1sc inserting hook under sl st which joined 3rd round, *3ch, skip [1hdc and 1sc], 1sc into next sc, 3ch, skip 1sc, work [1sc, 4ch, 1sc] into next sc, 3ch, skip 1sc, 1sc into next sc, 3ch, skip [1sc, 1hdc and 1dc]**, work 1sc between 2dc, skip 1dc; rep from * 6 more times and from * to ** again, sl st to first sc.

Fasten off.

Pulsar Motif

Base ring: 8ch, join with sl st.

1st round: 8ch, sl st into 6th ch from hook (counts as 1dc and picot), *4dc into ring, work a picot of [5ch, insert hook down through top of last dc made and work sl st to close]; rep from * 6 more times, 3dc into ring, sl st to 3rd of 8ch at beg of round. (8 picots).

2nd round: Sl st into each of next 2ch, 3ch (count as 1dc), work [1dc, 2ch, 2dc] into same picot, *4ch, work a DV st of [2dc, 2ch, 2dc] into next picot; rep from * 6 more times, 4ch, sl st to top of 3ch.

3rd round: Sl st into next dc and next ch, 3ch (count as 1dc), work [1dc, 2ch, 2dc] into same sp, *6ch, skip 4ch, DV st into next sp; rep from * 6 more times, 6ch, skip 4ch, sl

---

st to top of 3ch.

4th round: Sl st into next dc and next ch, 3ch (count as 1dc), work [1dc, 2ch, 2dc] into same sp, *8ch, skip 6ch, DV st into next sp; rep from * 6 more times, 8ch, skip 6ch, sl st to top of 3ch.

5th round: Sl st into next dc and next ch, 3ch (count as 1dc), 4dc into same sp, *1sc into each of next 8ch, 5dc into next sp; rep from * 6 more times, 1sc into each of next 8ch, sl st to top of 3ch.

Fasten off.

Amanda Whorl

Note: Segments are worked in 4 colors A, B, C and D used successively.

1st Segment

Base ring: Using A 12ch, join with sl st.

1st row (right side): 4ch (count as 1tr), [1tr into ring, 6ch, 1dc into top of tr just made, 1tr into ring] 3 times, 1tr into ring, 2ch, 10tr into ring, turn.

2nd row: Work a picot of [5ch, sl st to 5th ch from hook], ★skip first tr, 1sc into each of next 9tr, change to next color, turn.

2nd Segment

1ch, 1sc into same place as 1ch, 3ch, skip 3sc, 1sc into next sc, 9ch, sl st to first sc to complete joined base ring.

1st row: As given for 1st Segment.

2nd row: 2ch, 1sc into Picot of previous Segment, 3ch, sl st to first ch of row to complete Picot, continue as for 1st Segment from ★.

Work 5 more Segments as 2nd Segment using C, D, A, B and C.

8th Segment

Using D work as for previous Segments,

   ○ Chain   ● Slip stitch   + Single crochet   T Half double crochet   ⊤ Double crochet   ⧣ Treble   ⧢ Double treble

except also join to 1st Segment during 2nd row as follows: 2ch, 1sc into picot of 7th Segment, 1ch, 1sc into picot of 1st Segment, 2ch, sl st to first ch of row to complete picot, skip first tr, 1sc into each of next 5tr, sl st to 1st Segment, 1sc into each of next 4tr, sl st to 1st Segment. Fasten off.

Center Ring

Using A work inwards round center to make edging as follows: join into any sc, 1ch, 1sc into same place as 1ch, [1sc into next picot, 1sc into side of next sc] 7 times, 1sc into next picot, sl st to first sc.

Fasten off.

Celtic Motif

Base ring: Using A, 6ch, join with sl st.

1st round: Work a Leaf of [3ch, 2dc into ring, 3ch, sl st into ring] 4 times. Fasten off.

2nd round: Join B into same place, 6ch (count as 1dc and 3ch), skip next Leaf, *[1dc, 3ch, 1dc] into sl st, 3ch, skip next Leaf; rep from * twice more, 1dc into next sl st, 3ch, sl st to 3rd of 6ch.

3rd round: 1ch, 1sc into same place as 1ch, *work a Leaf of [3ch, 3dc into next 3ch sp, 3ch, 1sc into next dc]; rep from * 7 more times omitting sc at end of last rep, sl st to first sc. Fasten off.

4th round: Join C into same place, 1ch, 1sc into same place as 1ch, *4ch, skip next Leaf, 1sc into next sc; rep from * 7 more times omitting sc at end of last rep, sl st to first sc.

5th round: 3ch (count as 1dc), 4dc into next 4ch arch, [2ch, 5dc into next arch] 7 times, 2ch, sl st to top of 3ch.

6th round: 1ch, 1sc into same place as 1ch,

1sc into each of next 4dc, *into next 2ch sp work [1sc, 3ch, insert hook down through top of sc just made and work sl st to close, 1sc]**, 1sc into each of next 5dc; rep from * 6 more times and from * to ** again, sl st to first sc.

Fasten off.

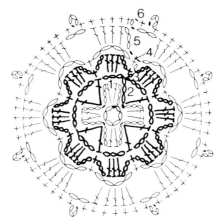

1 — A

2,3 — B

4,5,6 — C

Druid Motif

Note: For description of hdc2tog see page 14 (Puff Stitch).

Base ring: Using A, 6ch, join with sl st.

1st round: 2ch, 1hdc into ring (counts as hdc2tog), [3ch, hdc2tog into ring] 7 times, 3ch, sl st to first cluster.

2nd round: Sl st into each of next 2ch, 1ch, 1sc into same place as 1ch, [5ch, 1sc into next 3ch arch] 7 times, 5ch, sl st to first sc.

3rd round: 1ch, [5sc into next 5ch arch] 8 times, sl st to first sc. Fasten off.

4th round: Join B to 3rd of next 5sc, 1ch, 1sc into same place as 1ch, *7ch, skip 4sc, 1sc into next sc; rep from * 7 more times omitting sc at end of last rep, sl st to first sc.

5th round: 1ch, *[4sc, 3ch, 4sc] all into next 7ch arch; rep from * 7 more times, sl st to first sc.

Fasten off.

1,2,3 — A

4,5 — B

Starfish

Base ring: 5ch, join with sl st.

1st round: 7ch (count as 1tr and 3ch), [1tr into ring, 3ch] 7 times, sl st to 4th of 7ch. (8 spaces).

2nd round: 3ch (count as 1dc), [4dc into next sp, 1dc into next tr] 7 times, 4dc into next sp, sl st to top of 3ch. (40 sts).

3rd round: 1ch, 1sc into same place as 1ch, *6ch, 1sc into 2nd ch from hook, 1hdc into next ch, 1dc into next ch, 1tr into next ch, 1dtr into next ch, skip 4 sts, 1sc into next st; rep from * 7 more times omitting sc at end of last rep, sl st to first sc.

Fasten off.

Motifs

Curlicue Motif

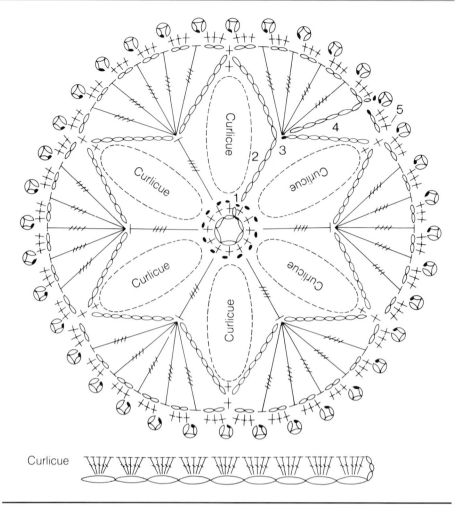

Curlicue

Base ring: 6ch, join with sl st.

1st round: 1ch, 12sc into ring, sl st to first sc. (12 sts).

2nd round: *Work a Curlicue of [12ch, 5dc into 4th ch from hook, 5dc into next and each ch ending sl st into same place as 12ch], sl st into each of next 2sc; rep from * 5 more times omitting 1 sl st at end of last rep.

3rd round: 14ch, *1sc into tip of next Curlicue, 8ch**, 1ttr into sc of 1st round between Curlicues, 8ch; rep from * 4 more times and from * to ** again, sl st to 6th ch of 14ch.

4th round: 8ch (count as 1ttr and 2ch), [1ttr, 2ch] 4 times into same place as 8ch, *skip 8ch, 1sc into next sc, 2ch, skip 8ch**, [1ttr, 2ch] 5 times into next ttr; rep from * 4 more times and from * to ** again, sl st to 6th ch of 8ch.

5th round: 1ch, *3sc into next 2ch sp, 3ch, insert hook down through top of sc just made and work sl st to close; rep from * into each 2ch sp all round, sl st to first sc.
Fasten off.

Lazy Wheel

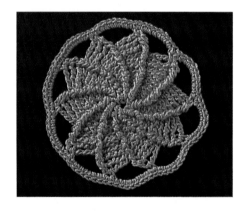

Note: For description of corded or reversed sc see page 15.

1st Segment

Make 17ch, sl st into 8th ch from hook, 1sc into next ch, 1hdc into next ch, 1dc into next ch, 2dc into next ch, 1dc into next ch, 2tr into next ch, 1tr into next ch, 2dtr into next ch, 1dtr into last ch. Do not turn, but work corded sc back from left to right inserting hook under front loop only of each st, ending sl st into ring.

2nd Segment

Working behind corded sc row into back loop only of next 9 sts of previous Segment work 1sc into first st, 1hdc into next st, 1dc into next st, 2dc into next st, 1dc into next st, 2tr into next st, 1tr into next st, 2dtr into next st, 1dtr into next st. Do not turn, but complete as for 1st Segment.

3rd to 10th Segments

Work as given for 2nd Segment. Fasten off leaving enough yarn to sew 10th Segment to 1st Segment on wrong side.

Edging

1st row (right side): Rejoin yarn at tip of any Segment in corded edge row, 1ch, 1sc into same place as 1ch, [7ch, 1sc into tip of next Segment] 9 times, 7ch, sl st to first sc.

2nd row: 1ch, 2sc into same place as 1ch, *7sc into next arch**, 2sc into next sc; rep from * 8 more times and from * to ** again, sl st to first sc.
Fasten off.

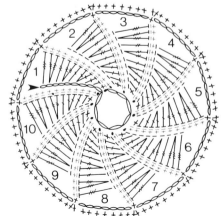

Granite Wheel

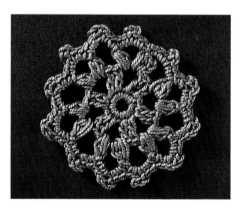

Note: For description of hdc2tog and hdc3tog see page 14 (Puff Stitch).

Base ring: 7ch, join with sl st.

1st round: 1ch, 12sc into ring, sl st to first sc. (12 sts).

2nd round: 3ch (count as 1dc), 1dc into next sc, *3ch, 1dc into each of next 2 sts; rep from * 4 more times, 3ch, sl st to top of 3ch.

3rd round: Sl st into next dc and next ch, 3ch, hdc2tog into same arch (counts as hdc3tog), 4ch, work hdc3tog into same arch, *4ch, work [hdc3tog, 4ch, hdc3tog] into next arch; rep from * 4 more times, 4ch, sl st to top of first cluster. (12 clusters).

4th round: 1ch, *work [2sc, 3ch, 2sc] into next arch; rep from * 11 more times, sl st to first sc.
Fasten off.

o Chain   ● Slip stitch   + Single crochet   T Half double crochet   ⟊ Double crochet   ⟊ Treble   ⟊ Double treble

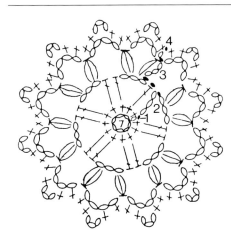

Base ring: Using A, 4ch, join with sl st.

1st round: 1ch, 1sc into ring, [4ch, 1dtr into ring, 4ch, 1sc into ring] 4 times omitting sc at end of last rep, sl st to first sc. Fasten off.

2nd round: Join B into same place, 11ch, skip 4ch, 1sc into next dtr, *7ch, skip 4ch**, 1tr into next sc, 7ch, skip 4ch, 1sc into next dtr; rep from * twice more and from * to ** again, sl st to 4th ch of 11ch. Fasten off.

3rd round: Join C into same place, 4ch (count as 1tr), 2tr into same place as 4ch, *1ch, 1sc into next arch, 1ch, work [2dtr, 2ch, 2dtr] into next sc, 1ch, 1sc into next arch, 1ch**, 3tr into next tr; rep from * twice more and from * to ** again, sl st to top of 4ch. Fasten off.

4th round: Rejoin B into same place, 1ch, 1sc into same place as 1ch, 1sc into next and each ch and each st all round, except 3sc into each 2ch sp at corners, ending sl st to first sc. Fasten off.

5th round: Rejoin A into next sc, 6ch (count as 1tr and 2ch), skip first 2sc, *1tr into next sc, 2ch, skip 1sc, 1dc into next sc, 2ch, skip 1sc, 1hdc into next sc, 2ch, skip 1sc, 1sc into next sc, 2ch, skip 1sc, 1hdc into next sc, 2ch, skip 1sc, 1dc into next sc, 2ch, skip 1sc, 1tr into next sc, 2ch, skip 1sc**, 1tr into next sc, 2ch, skip 1sc; rep from * twice more and from * to ** again, sl st to 4th ch of 6ch.

6th round: 1ch, into first st work a trefoil of [1sc, 5ch, 1sc, 7ch, 1sc, 5ch, 1sc], *[2sc into next 2ch sp, 1sc into next st] twice, work a picot of [3ch, insert hook down through top of sc just made and work sl st to close], [2sc into next 2ch sp, 1sc into next st] 4 times, picot, 2sc into next 2ch sp, 1sc into next st, 2sc into next 2ch sp**, trefoil into next st; rep from * twice more and from * to ** again, sl st to first sc.
Fasten off.

Spandrell Motif

1 — A
2 — B
3 — C
4 — B
5 — A

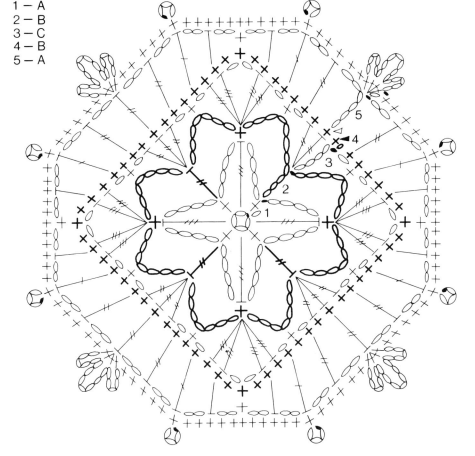

Sunflower Motif

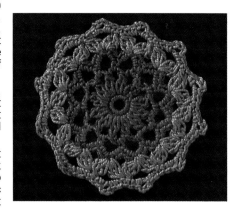

Note: For description of dc2tog and dc3tog see page 10.

Base ring: Using A, 8ch, join with sl st.

1st round: 1ch, 12sc into ring, sl st to first sc. (12 sts).

2nd round: 3ch, 1dc into same place as 3ch (counts as dc2tog), [3ch, dc2tog into next st] 11 times, 3ch, sl st to first cluster.

3rd round: Sl st into each of next 2ch, 1ch, 1sc into same place as 1ch, [4ch, 1sc into next 3ch arch] 11 times, 4ch, sl st to first sc.

4th round: 1ch, *[2sc, 3ch, 2sc] all into next 4ch arch; rep from * 11 more times, sl st to first sc. Fasten off.

5th round: Join B into next 3ch arch, 3ch, dc2tog into same arch (counts as dc3tog), 4ch, dc3tog all into same arch, *[dc3tog, 4ch, dc3tog] all into next 3ch arch; rep from * 10 more times, sl st to first cluster.

6th round: 1ch, 1sc into same place as 1ch, *[2sc, 3ch, 2sc] all into next 4ch arch, skip next cluster**, 1sc into next cluster; rep from * 10 more times and from * to ** again, sl st to first sc.
Fasten off.

1,2,3,4 — A

5,6 — B

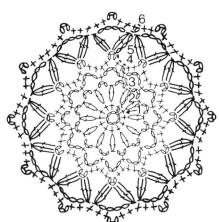

Edgings and Trimmings

When no instructions for a base chain are given the Edging is worked directly onto the edge of the fabric (crochet or otherwise). Those which do have such instructions are made separately and sewn on afterwards.

Shell Edging

Multiple of 4 sts + 1.

1st row (right side): 1sc, *skip 1 st or equivalent interval, 5dc into next st, skip 1 st, 1sc into next st; rep from *.

Chain Arch Edging

Multiple of 2 sts + 1.

1st row (right side): 1sc into each st or at equivalent intervals, turn.
2nd row: 1ch, 1sc into first st, *3ch, skip 1 st, 1sc into next st; rep from *.

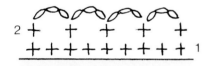

Double Chain Arch Edging

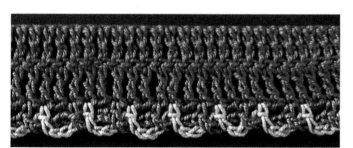

Multiple of 3 sts + 2.

1st row (right side): Using A, 1sc, *5ch, skip 2 sts or equivalent interval, 1sc into next st; rep from * ending with 1 st unworked. Fasten off, but do not turn.

2nd row (right side): Join B at right into 2nd st of fabric edge, picking up yarn and drawing through **below** 5ch arch of 1st row (so as not to enclose it) work 1sc into same place, *sl st above arch, 4ch, remove hook from working loop, insert below next arch, pick up working loop again, 1sc into next st picking up yarn and drawing through below arch as before; rep from *.

Note: Scs of 2nd row are always worked immediately to left of scs of 1st row into first of 2 skipped sts of original fabric edge or at equivalent intervals.

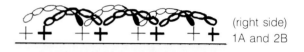

(right side)
1A and 2B

Corded Edging

Any number of sts.

Note: For description of corded or reversed sc see page 15.
1st row (right side): 1sc into each st or at equivalent intervals. Do not turn or fasten off.
2nd row: 1sc back into last st just worked, *1sc into next st to right; rep from *

Double Corded Edging

Any number of sts.

Note: For description of corded or reversed sc see page 15.
1st row (right side): 1sc into each st or at equivalent intervals. Do not turn or fasten off.
2nd row: *Inserting hook under front loop only of each st, 1sc into next st to right; rep from *. Fasten off, but do not turn.
3rd row: Rejoin yarn into left edge and work as 2nd row, but inserting hook under back loop only of each st of 1st row.

o Chain ● Slip stitch + Single crochet T Half double crochet ⸙ Double crochet ⸙ Treble ⹅ Double treble

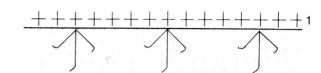

(right side) 3
(right side) 2
1 (right side)

ing up yarn, drawing through and up to height of edging row, insert hook into next st itself, yo, draw loop through, (5 loops on hook), ending yo, draw through all loops (see also page 10 — Spikes).

1st row (right side): 1sc into each of first 2 sts or at equivalent intervals, *1SPC over next st, 1sc into each of next 4 sts; rep from * omitting 2sc at end of last rep.

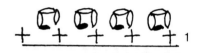

Bullion Scrolls

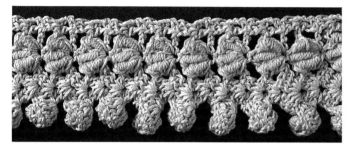

Make 12ch.

Note: For description of Bullion st see page 14. Make Bullion sts by wrapping yarn 10 times.

1st row (right side): Skip 3ch (count as 1dc), 1dc into next ch, skip 3ch, work a Bullion Group into next ch as follows: 1dc, [1 Bullion st, 1dc] 3 times, skip 3ch, work a Shell of [3dc, 2ch, 3dc] into last ch, turn.

2nd row: 7ch, 3dc into 4th ch from hook, 3dc into each of next 3ch, Shell into 2ch sp at center of next Shell, 3ch, 1sc into 2nd Bullion at center of next Group, 3ch, 1dc into next dc, 1dc into top of tch, turn.

3rd row: 3ch (count as 1dc), skip first st, 1dc into next st, skip 3ch, Bullion Group into next sc, skip 3ch, Shell into 2ch sp at center of next Shell, turn.

Rep 2nd and 3rd rows.

= Bullion st with [yo] 10 times

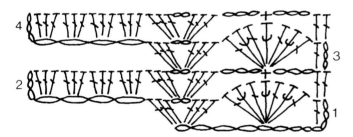

Crowsfoot Edging

Multiple of 5 sts.
Special Abbreviation
SPC (Spike cluster) = insert hook through fabric 3 times, first to right, then below, then to left of next st as required, each time pick-

Picot Edging

Multiple of 2 sts + 1.

1st row (right side): 1sc, *3ch, sl st into 3rd ch from hook, skip 1 st or equivalent interval, 1sc into next st; rep from *.

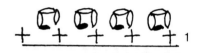

Cluster Arch Edging

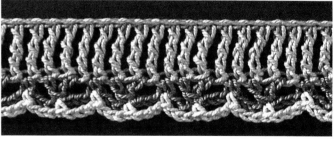

Multiple of 4 sts + 1.
Note: For description of dc2tog see page 10.

1st row (right side): Using A, 1sc, *3ch, work dc2tog inserting hook into next st or at equivalent interval for first leg, skip 1 st, then work into next st for 2nd leg, 3ch, 1sc into next st; rep from *. Do not turn.

2nd row (right side): Using B, 1sc into first sc, *3ch, skip 3ch, 1sc into next cluster, 3ch, skip 3ch, 1sc into next sc; rep from *.

2 (right side) B
1 (right side) A

Tunisian (Afghan) Crochet

Tunisian crochet requires special hooks — longer than usual and with a knob, or sometimes a second hook, at the end. These are made in the same sizes (thicknesses) as for conventional crochet. Although only one implement is used, the technique has something in common with knitting.

Tunisian crochet usually starts with a base chain with the same number of chains as there are stitches required in the first row. Odd numbered (forward) rows involve working from right to left and casting stitches onto the hook; on even numbered (reverse) rows these are bound off again as the hook travels back from left to right.

When a single ended hook is used, the work is not turned and the facing side of the fabric is regarded as the 'right side'. When there is a hook at both ends, however, the even numbered (reverse) rows may be 'bound off' from either end, if necessary, by turning the fabric and joining in another strand of yarn.

Although there are exceptions most Tunisian stitch patterns begin with the same initial forward and reverse base rows, which we call 'Standard Tunisian Base Rows', worked as follows:

Make a length of base chain with the same number of chains as stitches required.

1st row (forward): **a** Insert hook into 2nd ch from hook, yo, draw loop through and leave on hook, **b** *insert hook into next ch, yo, draw loop through and leave on hook; rep from * to end. Do not turn.

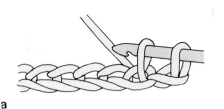

a

b

2nd row (reverse): **c** Yo, draw though 1 loop; **d** *yo, draw through 2 loops; **e** rep from * until only 1 loop remains on hook. Do not turn.

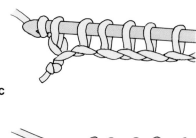

c

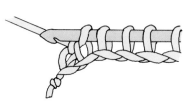

d

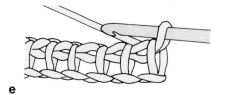

e

There are many ways of making different stitches in Tunisian crochet. Here are three basic ones.

Tunisian Simple Stitch

f Insert hook from right to left behind single vertical thread, yo, draw loop through and leave on hook.

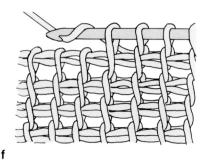

f

Tunisian Knit Stitch

g Insert hook from front to back through fabric and below chains formed by previous reverse row, to right of front vertical thread, but to left of corresponding back thread, yo, draw loop through and leave on hook.

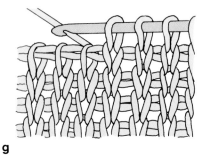

g

Tunisian Purl Stitch

h Bring yarn to front, insert hook from right to left behind single vertical thread as for Tunisian Simple Stitch, yo, draw loop through and leave on hook.

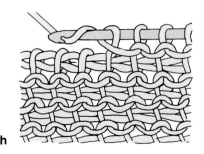

h

Generally the single loop on the hook at the end of each reverse row counts as the first stitch in the next forward row and so the first stitch is missed.

Whenever you change color, remember to make the change at the last step of the stitch before the new color is required.

Tunisian Simple Stitch I

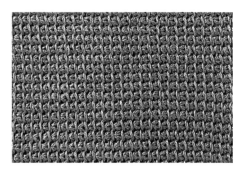

Any number of sts.
(Same for base chain)

1st and 2nd rows: Standard Tunisian Base Rows.

3rd row (forward): Skip first st, Tunisian Simple st into next and each st to end including edge st. Do not turn.

4th row (reverse): As Standard Tunisian 2nd Base Row.

Rep 3rd and 4th rows.

Tunisian Simple Stitch II

Multiple of 8 sts.
(Same for base chain)

Worked as for Tunisian Simple Stitch I, except using 2 colors, A and B, as follows:

1st and 2nd rows: Col A.

3rd and 4th rows: Col B.

5th row: *4 sts in Col B, 4 sts in Col A; rep from * to end.

6th row: *4 sts in Col A, 4 sts in Col B; rep from * to end.

Rep 5th and 6th rows 5 times.

17th and 18th rows: Col A.

19th and 20th rows: Col B.

21st row: *4 sts in Col A, 4 sts in Col B; rep from * to end.

22nd row: *4 sts in Col B, 4 sts in Col A; rep from * to end.
Rep 21st and 22nd rows 5 times.
Rep these 32 rows.
Hint: Remember to change yarn one step before new color is required each time.

Tunisian Knit Stitch

Any number of sts.
(Same for base chain)
1st and 2nd rows: Standard Tunisian Base Rows.
3rd row: Skip first st, Tunisian Knit st into next and each st to end including edge st. Do not turn.
4th row: As Standard Tunisian 2nd Base Row.
Rep 3rd and 4th rows.

Tunisian Purl Stitch

Any number of sts.
(Same for base chain)
1st row (forward): Bring yarn to front, insert hook from back to front through 2nd ch from hook, yo, draw loop through and leave on hook, *with yarn at front insert hook from back into next ch, yo, draw loop through and leave on hook; rep from * to end. Do not turn.
2nd row (reverse): As Standard Tunisian 2nd Base Row.
3rd row: Skip first st, bring yarn to front and work Tunisian Purl st into next and each st to end including edge st. Do not turn.
4th row: As Standard Tunisian 2nd Base Row.
Rep 3rd and 4th rows.

Tunisian Basketweave Stitch

Multiple of 8 sts + 4.
(Same for base chain)
1st and 2nd base rows: Standard Tunisian Base Rows.
Commence Pattern
1st row: Skip first st, work Tunisian Knit st into each of next 3 sts, *Tunisian Purl st into each of next 4 sts, Tunisian Knit st into each of next 4 sts; rep from * to end. Do not turn.
2nd row: As Standard Tunisian 2nd Base Row.
Rep 1st and 2nd rows 3 times.
9th row: Skip first st, Tunisian Purl st into each of next 3 sts, *Tunisian Knit st into each of next 4 sts, Tunisian Purl st into each of next 4 sts; rep from * to end. Do not turn.
10th row: As Standard Tunisian 2nd Base Row.
Rep 9th and 10th rows 3 times.
Rep these 16 rows.

Fan Stitch

Multiple of 14 sts + 2.
(Same for base chain)
1st and 2nd base rows: Using A, as Standard Tunisian Base Rows.
Commence Pattern
1st row: Using A skip first st, Tunisian Simple st into next and each st to end including edge st. Do not turn.
2nd row: As Standard Tunisian 2nd Base Row.
Rep 1st and 2nd rows 3 times.
9th row: Using B, skip first st, *Tunisian Simple st into each of next 7 sts, skip 3 sts, leaving last loop of each on hook and always inserting hook as for Tunisian Knit st work 7dc into next st - called Fan, skip 3 sts; rep from * ending Tunisian Simple st into edge st. Do not turn.

10th row: As Standard Tunisian 2nd Base Row.
Using A rep 1st and 2nd rows 4 times.
19th row: Using B, skip first st, *skip next 3 sts, Fan into next st, skip 3 sts, Tunisian Simple st into each of next 7 sts; rep from * ending Tunisian Simple st into edge st. Do not turn.
20th row: As Standard Tunisian 2nd Base Row.
Rep these 20 rows.

Tunisian Pebble Stitch I

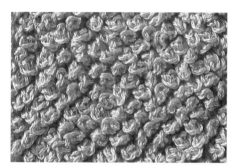

Multiple of 2 sts.
(Same for base chain)
1st and 2nd rows: As Standard Tunisian Base Rows.
3rd row: Skip first st, Tunisian Simple st into next and each st to end including edge st. Do not turn.
4th row: Yo, draw through 1 loop, yo, draw through 2 loops, *3ch, [yo, draw through 2 loops] twice; rep from * to end. Do not turn.
5th row: As 3rd row, ensuring that all 3ch loops protrude at front of fabric.
6th row: Yo, draw through 1 loop, *[yo, draw through 2 loops] twice, 3ch; rep from * ending yo, draw through last 2 loops. Do not turn.
Rep 3rd, 4th, 5th and 6th rows.

Tunisian Pebble Stitch II

Worked as Tunisian Pebble Stitch
Work 2 rows each in colors A, B and C throughout.

95

Tunisian Crochet

Tunisian Bobble Stitch

Multiple of 4 sts + 3.
(Same for base chain)

Note: For description of dc3tog see page 10.

1st and 2nd base rows: As Standard Tunisian Base Rows.

Commence Pattern

1st row: Skip first st, Tunisian Simple st into each of next 2 sts, *inserting hook as for Tunisian Knit st work a bobble of dc3tog all into next st, Tunisian Simple st into each of next 3 sts; rep from * to end. Do not turn.

2nd row: As Standard Tunisian 2nd Base Row.

3rd row: Skip first st, Tunisian Simple st into next and each st to end including edge st. Do not turn.

4th row: As Standard Tunisian 2nd Base Row.

5th row: Skip first st, *Bobble into next st, Tunisian Simple st into each of next 3 sts; rep from * until 2 sts remain, Bobble into next st, Tunisian Simple st into last st. Do not turn.

6th row: As Standard Tunisian 2nd Base Row.

7th and 8th rows: As 3rd and 4th rows.
Rep these 8 rows.

Corded Stitch

Any number of sts.
(Same for base chain)

1st and 2nd base rows: Using A, as Standard Tunisian Base Rows.

Commence Pattern

1st row: Using B, skip first st, *insert hook into next st as for Tunisian Knit st, yo, draw loop through, yo, draw through 1 loop; rep from * to end including edge st. Do not turn.

2nd row: As Standard Tunisian 2nd Base Row.

3rd and 4th rows: Using C, rep 1st and 2nd rows.
5th and 6th rows: Using A, rep 1st and 2nd rows.
Rep these 6 rows.

Pear Drop Stitch

Multiple of 16 sts + 1.
(Same for base chain)

Note: For description of dc3tog see page 10.

1st and 2nd base rows: Using A, as Standard Tunisian Base Rows.

3rd base row: Using B, skip first st, Tunisian Simple st into next and each st to end inlcuding edge st. Do not turn.

4th base row: As Standard Tunisian 2nd Base Row.

Commence Pattern

Using C, work 8 rows as 3rd and 4th base rows.

9th row: Using A, skip first st, Tunisian Simple st into each of next 5 sts, *work a Pear st of [dc3tog all into corresponding st in 4th row below and inserting hook as for Tunisian Simple st], Tunisian Simple st into each of next 3 sts, Pear st over next st as before, Tunisian Simple st into each of next 11 sts; rep from * ending last rep with Tunisian Simple st into each of last 6 sts. Do not turn.

10th row: As Standard Tunisian 2nd Base Row.

11th row: Using B, skip first st, Tunisian Simple st into each of next 7 sts, *Pear st over next st in 4th row below as before, Tunisian Simple st into each of next 15 sts; rep from * ending last rep with Tunisian Simple st into each of last 8 sts. Do not turn.

12th row: As Standard Tunisian 2nd Base Row.

Using C, work 2 rows as 3rd and 4th base rows.

15th row: Using A, skip first st, Tunisian Simple st into each of next 5 sts, *work a Long tr of [yo] twice, insert hook from right to left behind 2 vertical threads at top of cluster in 6th row below, yo, draw loop through, [yo, draw through 2 loops] twice, work Tunisian Simple st into each of next 3 sts, Long tr over next st, Tunisian Simple st into each of next 11 sts; rep from * ending last rep with Tunisian Simple st into each of last 6 sts. Do not turn.

16th row: As Standard Tunisian 2nd Base Row.

17th row: Using B, skip first st, Tunisian Simple st into each of next 7 sts, *Long tr over next st, Tunisian Simple st into each of next 15 sts; rep from * ending last rep with Tunisian Simple st into each of last 8 sts. Do not turn.

18th row: As Standard Tunisian 2nd Base Row.

Using C, rep 3rd and 4th base rows 4 times.

27th row: Using A, skip first st, Tunisian Simple st into each of next 13 sts, *Pear st over next st in 4th row below as before, Tunisian Simple st into each of next 3 sts, Pear st over next st as before, Tunisian Simple st into each of next 11 sts; rep from * ending Tunisian Simple st into each of last 3 sts. Do not turn.

28th row: As Standard Tunisian 2nd Base Row.

29th row: Using B, skip first st, Tunisian Simple st into each of next 15 sts, *Pear st over next st in 4th row below as before, Tunisian Simple st into each of next 15 sts; rep from * ending Tunisian Simple st into last st. Do not turn.

30th row: As Standard Tunisian 2nd Base Row.

Using C, work 2 rows as 3rd and 4th base rows.

33rd row: Using A, skip first st, Tunisian Simple st into each of next 13 sts, *Long tr over next st, Tunisian Simple st into each of next 3 sts, Long tr over next st, Tunisian Simple st into each of next 11 sts; rep from * ending Tunisian Simple st into each of last 3 sts. Do not turn.

34th row: As Standard Tunisian 2nd Base Row.

35th row: Using B, skip first st, Tunisian Simple st into each of next 15 sts, *Long tr over next st, Tunisian Simple st into each of next 15 sts; rep from * ending Tunisian Simple st into last st. Do not turn.

36th row: As Standard Tunisian 2nd Base Row.

Rep these 36 rows.

Open Cluster Stitch

Multiple of 4 sts + 1.
(Same for base chain)

1st row: As Standard Tunisian Base Row.

2nd row: Yo, draw through 2 loops, *3ch, yo, draw through 5 loops; rep from * until 4 loops remain, 3ch, yo, draw through last 4 loops.

3rd row: Skip first cluster, *[insert hook into next ch, yo, draw loop through] 3 times, insert hook under thread which closed next cluster, yo, draw loop through; rep from * to end. Do not turn.

4th row: As 2nd row.
Rep 3rd and 4th rows.